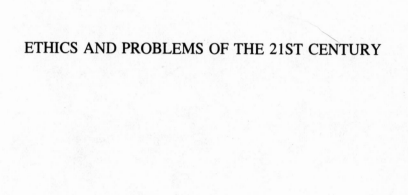

ETHICS AND PROBLEMS OF THE 21ST CENTURY

# Ethics and Problems of the 21st Century

EDITED BY

K. E. Goodpaster and K. M. Sayre

UNIVERSITY OF NOTRE DAME PRESS

NOTRE DAME                                    LONDON

**Library of Congress Cataloging in Publication Data**

Main entry under title:

Ethics and problems of the 21st century.

  Includes bibliographical references and index.
  1. Human ecology—Moral and religious aspects—Addresses
essays, lectures.   2. Social ethics—Addresses,
essays, lectures.   3. Technology and ethics—Addresses,
essays, lectures.   4. Twenty-first century—Addresses,
essays, lectures.   I. Goodpaster, Kenneth E., 1944–
II. Sayre, Kenneth M., 1928–
GF80.E84        301.31        78-51522
ISBN 0-268-00906-6

Manufactured in the United States of America

# Contents

## PART THREE

## Applications to Substantive Issues

# Introduction

THIS VOLUME IS AN INDIRECT OUTGROWTH OF AN INTERDISCIPLINARY research effort conducted at the University of Notre Dame and funded by the National Science Foundation (RANN). The title of the project was "Values in the Electric Power Industry." Its results are reported in a book of the same title edited by K. M. Sayre and published by the University of Notre Dame Press (1977).

This study aimed at analyzing the role of environmental and social values in the decision making of power companies. Early in our work it became evident that there were regrettably few discussions in the *philosophical* literature of ethical topics of this sort. Few philosophers have systematically addressed the difficult problems associated with applying ethical theory to social and environmental issues. In hopes of encouraging such a literature, we decided, with support from the National Science Foundation, to commission a group of prominent moral philosophers to write original essays exploring the interface between ethical theory and certain practical problems of an environmental and social nature. That such explorations are still only in the beginning stages is as much an embarrassment to moral philosophy as it is a liability to practical decision makers. The purposes of this volume, then, are (1) to stimulate the interest of other moral philosophers in applying their resources to issues of the sort described and (2) to serve as an illustration (for teaching and research) of the results that can be achieved when moral philosophers turn their attention to such practical themes.

The papers collected here are all original essays, with the qualified exception of R. M. Hare's contribution, which is a revised and modified version of a paper in the Royal Institute of Philosophy Lectures (*Nature and Conduct*, volume 8, 1975). The principle of division is straightforward. Moral philosophy (metaethics and normative ethics as standardly understood) can contribute to the guidance of action on several levels. First is the level of *conceptual analysis*, where central notions of normative discourse are scrutinized critically in an effort to provide clarification, to assess claims of logical connection, and to explore foundations of moral argument. Inquiries of this sort often support or call into question forms of practical argument which appeal to conceptual warrants for their validity or soundness.

Second is the level of *normative methodology* or, as Sidgwick would put it, the search for "methods of ethics." Here the focus is less on analysis than on the articulation and defense of broad rules or principles to guide substantive moral deliberation. On this level, questions arise not so much about the meanings of moral terms as about the ways in which those terms can be given systematic use and about the problems attending that use. For example, What are the most general principles of moral obligation or of virtue? and, How should we approach decisions having to do with certain broad types of issues affecting other persons and the environment?

Methodological issues, however, often remain programmatic and general. Thus we need a third level of ethical input, a level of *concrete application*, where such methods are employed in more or less specific decision-making contexts. It is on this level that questions of analysis and methodology make contact with questions of empirical fact and public policy in such domains as human rights, energy use, medical practice, and environmental protection. One might distinguish numerous sublevels here, of course, exhibiting differing degrees of concreteness, from guidelines for social policy to guidelines for individual decisions. But the unifying theme is always the same: the employment of a critical or self-conscious ethical method to contexts calling for practical moral response.

Using this brief sketch of the types of inputs which moral philosophy should be expected to provide, we can order the essays which follow in terms of their contributions to the several levels respectively. The first group of essays is unified internally around the concept of "moral considerability." Each of the authors here is concerned to probe the *breadth* of our ethical framework with attention to the sorts of beings or systems that lay claim to moral consideration. William Frankena, in a style which has come to be widely respected, sets out a number of possible interpretations for the phrase "environmental ethics" and subjects each to thoughtful scrutiny. He concludes with a carefully drawn defense of what he calls a "Type 3" ethic: "the class of moral patients must be extended to include not only human beings but all consciously sentient beings."

The following article by K. E. Goodpaster is less conservative on this issue. After an overview of the Humean and Kantian roots of modern moral reflection, it is suggested that a certain model for extending ethical concern (even to nonhuman beings) may inhibit the development of a genuine ecological ethic. Only by exploring the concept of living systems and their moral importance, it is argued, can we hope to lay the groundwork for such an ethical perspective.

Richard and Val Routley also question the legitimacy of what they take to be the modern view of morality ("human chauvinism"), albeit from a standpoint different from that of the preceding essay. Challenging the various warrants that have been offered for restricting respect for nonhuman beings to a purely instrumental or humanistic concern, they conclude that much of Western morality manifests a deep arbitrariness in its dealings with the environment.

The second group of essays enters upon the quest for general guidelines in decision making, often by way of criticizing conventional methodologies. R. M. Hare sets out two contrasting approaches to individual and social decisions affecting the environment—the "means-end" approach and the "trial-design" approach—and examines their strengths and limitations. He then elicits certain basic moral questions which lie behind a choice between differing planning strategies, questions on whose answers his own theory of universal prescriptivism sheds considerable light.

Jonathan Glover is also concerned with contrasting approaches to planning, but in a different context. The question in his title is discussed in terms of alternative ways of responding to present and future persons' wants and desires. Given that our policies can affect not only the satisfaction of wants and desires but also the very existence and nature of certain wants and desires, how are we to guide those policies "for the best"? How can we draw the line between actions which legitimately modify present and future persons' conceptions of what is good and actions which intrude upon the autonomy or even the identity of such persons in a morally indefensible way?

Richard De George is concerned, like Glover, about the effects of present policies on future persons, but he approaches the issue with future wants and needs held relatively constant. After defending his view that talk about present rights of future persons is misguided, he seeks to provide some basic principles for morally responsible conduct which avoid "assuming the burden of the future on some mistaken notion of the need to sacrifice the present to the future." Thus while Glover is concerned about interpersonal and intergenerational conceptions of the good, De George is concerned about interpersonal and intergenerational rights and obligations.

Robert Coburn examines "technology assessment" in one of its standard forms: cost-benefit analysis. He finds this procedure seriously wanting in ways which will recall the earlier discussions of Hare and Glover (as well as the discussions in Part One). Coburn then sketches his view of a more adequate approach in which human freedom and egalitarianism play central roles. Drawing upon Rawls's work on justice, he traces the implications of a principle which would assess technological changes in terms of their tendencies to maximize freedom subject to the constraint of like freedom for all present and future persons.

The final contribution to this second group exhibits a striking contrast to those which precede it, both in its idiom and in its aspiration. Alasdair MacIntyre's project is not to provide a method or set of guidelines for individual and social decision, but rather to display the roots of what he perceives to be the impossibility of such a method. Moral philosophy, in his view, is fragmented in a way which is mirrored in modern organizational structures, and this fragmentation presents serious obstacles to the very quest for a shared normative methodology.

In the third group of papers, as in the second group, there is considerable discussion of methodology. The motivation, however, is discernibly different in that the guiding theme in each case is a relatively specific moral problem: starvation, life-affecting medical technology, landmark preservation, and our behavior toward animals. Whereas the movement in Part Two is largely from theory toward practical methodologies, the movement in Part Three is from practical problems toward principles of resolution tailored to those problems.

Alan Gewirth confronts the moral conflicts raised by a basic and distressing fact about our *human* environment: hunger and starvation. "Do persons threatened with starvation have a strict right to be given food by those who have it in abundance?" In answering this question, Gewirth is sensitive to the differences between persons and nations which complicate an affirmative response, and through his Principle of Generic Consistency unites a number of methodological themes at work in the discussions of Part Two.

Kurt Baier is concerned to understand and to resolve certain moral problems which have arisen and will arise more frequently in the future as a result of advances in medical technology. The reader will therefore want to compare this discussion with the more general treatment of technology assessment offered by Coburn in Part Two. Specifically, Baier examines the compatibility of several senses of "the sanctity of life" with techniques of prolongation, prevention, and modification (through brain-manipulation) of life. His conclusions on these controversial topics derive from his conviction that "the right to life may begin later and end earlier than the individual's biological life."

Martin and Naomi Golding center their attention on the "cultural" dimension of the human environment. They seek to provide a response to the puzzles engendered by a growing awareness of the importance of *preservation,* specifically landmark preservation, for the quality of human life. What rationale can be provided in terms of traditional ethical categories, they ask, for the kinds of restraint which many persons are insisting human artifacts (as well as natural objects) should elicit from us?

Finally, Peter Singer echoes several themes from Part One in a more concrete way as he discusses the moral responsibilities which we have toward animals. Like the Routleys, he treats "speciesism" as logically indistinguishable from racism and defends a principle of "equal consideration of interests." Singer applies this principle to such issues as pest control, timber clear-cutting, and hunting, while contrasting its implications for species preservation.

It would, of course, be unrealistic to claim that these essays fit rigidly into the categories assigned. Some might well be placed in different groups, since they contribute on more than one level. Nevertheless the ordering does not represent an arbitrary separation, and the unities of emphasis within each group are substantial. The most important unity, however, should not be overlooked. These papers reflect the efforts of moral philosophers to come to grips with the implications of their discipline for the guidance of human behavior. And they do this at a time in history when that behavior is increasingly consequential for human life and for life in general. One might be excused for hoping that these discussions will be salutary in their own right as well as useful departures for others—philosophers and nonphilosophers alike—who understand that the twenty-first century will demand much more from us than goodwill and patience. Action without thought, perhaps, is blind. But ethical thought without application may be in a worse predicament.

The editors wish to thank the National Science Foundation for its support of this project, and to affirm that any opinions, findings, conclusions, or recommendations in the volume are those of the contributors and do not necessarily reflect the views of the National Science Foundation.

KENNETH E. GOODPASTER
KENNETH M. SAYRE

ETHICS AND PROBLEMS OF THE 21ST CENTURY

PART ONE

# Broadening the Concept of Morality

# Ethics and the Environment

## W. K. FRANKENA

AS HAS OFTEN BEEN POINTED OUT BY ENVIRONMENTALISTS, WE HUMANS have for the most part, at least in the West and until recently, thought of our ethics in terms of what we are or do or are disposed to be or do in relation to other people, ourselves, or God—or, in other words, to persons; we have thought of it very little in terms of our relations to other animals and still less, if at all, in terms of what we do or how we "relate" to plants, air, earth, water, or minerals. Thus, for example, Samuel Clarke wrote in the eighteenth century that "the eternal law of righteousness" has "three great and principal branches, from which all the other and smaller instances of duty do naturally flow, or may without difficulty be derived," namely, a rule of righteousness in respect of God, another in respect of our fellow-creatures, and a third with respect to ourselves; and, although in spelling out the second he says that "every rational creature *ought* . . . to do all the good it can to all its fellow-creatures," he actually equates our duties under this head with those of love and justice for other human beings or "men.'"[1] Lately, however, many people have become environment watchers, looking at what we have done, are doing, or seem about to do to the nonhuman things around us, and not liking what they see. It is not necessary for me to recount the story as they see it here; nor shall I quarrel with their judgment that much of what is going on is wrong. The question is, By what ethics is it to be judged and by what ethics should we redirect our conduct?

We have had a number of calls for a "new ethics" in recent times, and today we are again told that we need a new one for dealing with the environment. "New lamps for old" is once more the cry. Actually, however, there is another possibility that should be explored first, namely, that our old ethics, or at least its best parts, are entirely satisfactory as a basis for our lives in the world, the trouble being only that not enough of us live enough by it enough of the time—that is, that what we need is not a new ethics but a new "moral rearmament," a revival of moral dedication. One might agree that our prevailing treatment of nature is wrong, and that we need important changes in our

3

actions, laws, and practices, and yet argue that what is wrong is not due to our ethics but to our failure to live by it. After all, a lot of us do act out of thoughtlessness, self-interest, or disregard for the requirements or ideals of morality, and the present status of environmental matters may reflect an inadequacy, not in our ethics, but in our morals. I believe myself that there is much to be said for this line of thought, and that a good deal of what is needed would come about if enough people could be persuaded to be really moral by standards that are already widely accepted. However, I am not here concerned to try to show that what we need is not a new morality but only a new devotion to one we already have, especially since John Passmore has already so ably discussed the question "whether the solution of ecological problems demands a moral or metaphysical revolution."[2] What interests me now is a systematic rather than a historical question, not asking what ethical lamps are old and what new, or trading old lamps for new, but finding out what lamp is best, that is, throws the most moral light on ecological problems. Actually, though this is sometimes forgotten by recent writers in their eagerness to sell us a new "ecological ethics," every ethics that is at all complete is or includes an ethics of the environment, since every such ethics, new or old, tells us, at least indirectly, what we may or may not, should or should not do about plants, lakes, minerals, etc.; and, therefore, the main question is not which are old and which new, but which is the most satisfactory. However, while I shall be dealing with this question, I shall not try to answer it by proposing a certain specific ethics and applying it to environmental problems. Rather I shall address myself to a more general preliminary issue which is being much discussed in recent ecological literature, namely, the question which general *type* of ethics is most adequate.

<h1 style="text-align:center">I</h1>

Much of the recent discussion of this question has been too simplistic, proceeding as if there are only two contestants, our "old" type of ethics, with what it says or implies about the environment, and some "new" proposed and properly ecological ethics. Thus, for example, Holmes Rolston III, in a very helpful, perceptive, and stimulating article, talks as if the issue is between a humanistic or anthropological ethics and a planetary or ecosystemic one.[3] Actually, however, there are at least eight different types of "ethics *about* the environment," to use his phrase, that need to be distinguished, described, and compared as to their relative merits, his two falling respectively under what I shall call 2 and 5. I shall first indicate briefly what these eight types of ethics are and then proceeed by describing them more fully and commenting on them.

It is generally thought that what Clarke calls "rational creatures" are moral *agents* and they alone, and all of my types of ethics can agree about this. What they differ about is about what kinds of beings are or should be taken to be moral *patients*. Roughly the issue here is the question what kinds of beings we have duties *to*. More accurately, in G. J. Warnock's words, it is this: "What . . . is the condition of moral *relevance?* What is the condition of having a claim to be *considered* by rational agents?"[4] The point is that, in every ethics whatsoever, there are certain sorts of facts about certain sorts of things that are the ultimate considerations in determining what is morally good or bad, right or wrong, and the question now is: What sorts of things are such that certain sorts of facts about *them* are the final determinants, directly or indirectly, of moral rightness or virtue? For present purposes, this is the main issue distinguishing different types of ethics, not the usual issues between teleological and deontological ethics or between an ethics of virtue and an ethics of duty.

1. The first of my types of ethics is ethical egoism, which holds that, basically, it is certain facts about an agent himself, e.g., facts about what is in his own interest, that determine what is right or wrong, good or bad, in what he is or does. For it, an agent is or should be his own sole patient, perhaps not proximately but at least ultimately.

2. A second family of positions consists of various forms of humanism or personalism, views holding that what matters morally is finally only what happens to human beings or to persons. Clarke takes such a view, as does Kant when he maintains that "Our duties toward animals are merely indirect duties toward humanity."[5] These views are not in any proper sense egoistic, since they insist that *all* persons or *all* human beings are to be considered in morality, but they do also insist that, ultimately, only persons or only humans are to be considered.

3. The third type of ethics contends that the class of moral patients must be extended to include, not only human beings and/or persons, but all consciously sentient beings. This is Warnock's position when he answers the question, "How far down the scale, so to speak, of the brute creation should moral relevance be taken to extend?" by saying that "it extends just as far as does the capacity to suffer."[6]

4. The next type of ethics maintains that the range of moral patiency or relevance should be taken to extend even farther, namely, to include whatever is *alive,* flora as well as fauna. An example is Albert Schweitzer's well-known ethics of "reverence for life."

> A man is truly ethical only when he obeys the compulsion to help all life which he is able to assist, and shrinks from injuring anything that lives. He does not ask how far this or that life deserves one's sympathy as being valuable, not . . . whether and to what degree it is capable of feeling. Life as such is sacred to him. He tears no leaf from a tree, plucks no flower, and takes care to crush no insect.[7]

5. Another type of ethics goes even further, holding that in some sense *everything* is to be considered as morally relevant, directly and not just indirectly. What matters ultimately is everything, not just what is personal, human, conscious, or alive. Such views will be spelled out and illustrated later. They are the best candidates for being "new."

6. One might think there are no other possibilities, but, alas, there are. Of these, one is a certain kind of theistic ethics, namely, a theistic ethics in which God is conceived of as transcendent (and not just as immanent) and then is held to be, ultimately, the one and only moral patient, the only being that finally matters morally. On such a view it is, in the end, only certain sorts of facts about God that determine what is morally right or wrong, good or bad. Theists need not take such a view, but they may and, as we shall see, sometimes do.

7. It is also possible to combine two or more of the above (pure) types of ethics. For example, one might, in a way, combine a humanistic ethics of type 2 and a theistic ethics of type 6 by saying that the moral law has two basic and coordinate parts: to love the Lord thy God with all thy heart and to love thy neighbor as thyself.

8. As my final type of ethics I shall list a type of view that is sometimes suggested in recent environmental literature but may have an ancestry in the Stoic maxim, *Naturam sequere*, namely, views that tell us to let nature alone, not to interfere with it, to cooperate with it, to follow or imitate it, etc. For all such views there is such a thing as nature and its ways, and the natural is the right and the virtuous both in general and in ecological matters.[8]

## II

As I said, any ethics of any of these types is relevant to our problem, since it includes, at least by implication, certain instructions (directions, permissions, or prohibitions) about how we may or should treat the environment.

In this sense, all of them are ecological or environmental ethics; that is why I have put all eight families of them on the stage (which is not often enough done). It is, however, not possible to study them all here in any detail. I shall, therefore, not look further at such combination ethics as belong to 7, except to point out, first, that some such combination ethics may be more plausible than any pure one; second, that just because they combine two or more basic ethical norms, they may be faced by a problem of possible conflict between them, as pure forms of ethics are not; and, third, that some proponents of "new" ecological ethics seem actually to be subscribing to what I am calling a combination of it with an older one. Rolston appears to do so, for example, when he writes

> As a partial ethical source, [this eco-systemic or planetary environmental ethics] does not displace functioning social-personal codes, but brings into the scope of ethical transaction a realm once regarded as intrinsically valueless and governed largely by expediency. The new ethical parameter is not absolute but relative to classical criteria. Such extension will amplify conflicts of value, for human goods must now coexist with environmental goods. In operational detail this will require a new casuistry. Mutually supportive though the human and the ecosystemic interests may be, conflicts between individuals and parties, the rights of the component members of the ecosystem, the gap between the real and the ideal, will provide abundant quandaries.[9]

I shall also not say much about an ethics of type 8. Such literally naturalistic ethics flourished in the heyday of evolutionism and appear to be surfacing again in our present upsurge of ecologism (which is itself in considerable part a revival of evolutionism). They were acutely and interestingly dealt with by J. S. Mill and Henry Sidgwick in the nineteenth and again by Basil Willey and others in the twentieth century, and I could at best add but little to their reflections.[10] As for ethical egoism—it has been much discussed in other contexts and, to my mind, satisfactorily disposed of.[11] Even it has an environmental ethics of a sort, namely, that it is morally permissible for an individual to treat his environment, including other individuals as well as plants, animals, rocks, etc., in any manner he pleases, provided only that doing so is not contrary to his own interest. That this is the rational way for an individual to live with the rest of his world may be true, though I hope not, but that whatever is to one's own interest is morally permissible, no matter what it may be, is simply paradoxical. In any case, ethical egoism is almost universally opposed by ecological moralists, as might be expected; it is, in fact, the type of ethics that many of those who "exploit" and "violate" the environment live by and might appeal to in their own defense. Here, like the environmentalists, I shall assume that it is mistaken. It should be pointed out, however, that it is logically possible for an ethical egoist to argue that it is to an individual's own interest, carefully considered, to behave toward his environment in precisely the ways in which environmentalists desire him to. In other words, an egoist can come out exactly where the "planetary altruist" comes out. The trouble is that, given his premises, he can just as well come out at an entirely different place and claim to be equally moral.

This brings us to theistic ethics of type 6. If they conceive of God as a person, then they agree with ethical egoism and what I call *personalism* in holding that only persons are moral patients; these views differ only but, of course, importantly about which persons they regard as morally considerable. In any event, views that regard only God as ultimately morally relevant, and only certain facts about him as finally morally determinative, may take various forms. (i) A theist who believes that God can be harmed, benefited, or lied to by us may hold that, basically, all that matters morally is whether we are benefiting God, harming him, being honest or just to him, etc. (ii) One who rejects this conception of God may contend instead that all that matters morally is whether or not we are obeying his commands, doing what is dear to him, or loving what he loves (whatever it may be that he commands or cares about). This is a more common view among theologians than (i); it is held, for example, by theological voluntarists. (iii) Another possibility for theists is to maintain that what matters basically in morality is whether we are working to promote "the glory of God," if we may assume that doing this is not reducible to living by (i) or (ii). This view has sometimes been ascribed to, and apparently subscribed to, by Calvinists. (iv) A type 6 theist can insist that the whole law and the prophets, morally speaking, is to love the Lord thy God with all thy heart, and with all thy soul, and with all thy mind, and with all thy strength. And then he may put under loving God as much of what is called for by (i), (ii), and (iii) as he sees fit; he may also put under it loving one's neighbor as oneself. What he cannot say is that love of neighbor is another commandment "like unto" love of God, if this means that the former is independent of or coordinate with the latter. To affirm this is to hold a view of type 7, combining 2 and 5, as I indicated earlier.

These forms of theistic ethics can readily generate conclusions dealing with the environment, excepting possibly the first. For example, they can argue that God commands us to care for all his creatures, including plants, rocks, and lakes; that God cares for all of these creatures, and so we should too; or that respecting the heavens is a way of joining them in declaring the glory of God. They deserve more attention than they can be given here. I shall only say now that there are problems about all of them, and that, in addition, they all make ethics dependent on theology in ways that, along with other moral philosophers (as well as some theologians), I find troubling and wish to avoid.[12]

### III

We come now to the types of ethics I mainly wish to study and assess. Let us begin with those of type 2. Here we must first distinguish between personalism and humanism.[13] Personalism holds that the class of moral agents and the class of moral patients both coincide with that of persons. For us the main point about it is that it insists that all persons and only persons matter morally; nothing else matters morally unless it bears on the lives of persons in one way or another. Personalism need not hold that all human beings are persons, nor that all persons are human beings. If fetuses, neonates, and imbeciles are not persons, then, even if they are human, personalism maintains that they have no more moral status than brute animals, plants, or rocks, unless it is as potential persons. Humanism can agree that all and only persons are moral agents, but it equates the class of moral *patients* with that of human beings, not with that of persons. Thus it will hold that non-human persons, if there are any, are not moral patients and have no moral claims, and that fetuses, newborn babies, imbeciles, and idiots, if they are human, have status as moral patients, even if they are not persons. Both personalism and humanism contend, of course, that brute animals, plants, air, rocks, etc., have no moral status, except indirectly via their relations to persons or humans respectively.

Ethics of both kinds can be aretaic or deontic, as well as utilitarian or deontological. Clarke and Kant are deontologists, but personalists and humanists can also be utilitarians. On the question whether what is morally right or good is what is conducive to the greatest balance of good over evil in the community of humans or persons, humanists and personalists can take either side; also people on either side can be either deontologists or utilitarians.

We need not discuss here the relative merits of humanism and personalism. Our question is whether or not any such ethics will do as an environmental ethics. Now, such an ethics may take the line that any kind of treatment of animals, plants, or inorganic objects and substances is morally permissible, or that no way of treating them is morally either obligatory or wrong. Then it would not require, but it would permit, a ruthless and exploitative approach to the environment of the kind that has been causing so much agitation recently. More plausibly, it might maintain that some ways of treating animals, plants, etc., are morally right or wrong, though they are so only because through them persons or human beings are or will be gainers or losers, directly or indirectly, sooner or later. And then it might go on to defend the practices that have been characteristic of the industrial and technological revolutions of recent times as being necessary to or at least not inconsistent with the welfare of humans and/or persons. On the other hand, however, it might argue, depending on the evidence available, that the present and future well-being of persons and/or human beings requires all the measures of conservation, antipollution, etc., that environmentalists support. There are so many ways in which nature is important to us and our successors, economically, aesthetically, cognitively, and psychically, that the case for such measures can be made very plausible indeed, without giving up the premises of humanism or personalism. In effect this is sometimes recognized by new ecological moralists, for example, by Rolston when he says, borrowing from Réné Dubos and Paul Shepard,

> It is only as man grants an intrinsic integrity to nature that he discovers his truest interests . . . biotic-environmental complexity is integrally related to the richness of human life. . . . Without oceans, forests, and grasslands, human life would be imperiled. . . . For maximum noetic development, man requires an environmental exuberance. . . . Remove eagles from the sky and we will suffer a spiritual loss.[14]

It may even be that "when people everywhere come to view the native black bear as an indicator of environmental health, a symbol of wilderness, there will be more hope for bears and people alike."[15]

Such claims ring a bell for a birdwatcher like me, but they are compatible with a type 2 ethics. Therefore, as I said, it is possible to argue persuasively, on humanist and personalist grounds, for all of the measures and practices desiderated by environmentalists. What then is wrong with humanism and personalism? They are alleged to embody a kind of "anthropological egoism" and "human chauvinism,"[16] but I am not impressed by these charges. The ascription of egoism to an ethics of type 2 is misleading. Such an ethics is in no way a form of ethical egoism; it can take the form of the law of love, the Golden Rule, Kant's second version of the Categorical Imperative, or utilitarianism. In any case, labeling it "species egoism" or "species chauvinism" does nothing to show that it is morally inadequate; in fact, it has no moral force unless it is presupposed that such an ethics is unacceptable from the moral point of view. But since that is precisely the question at issue, using such pejorative labels is simply begging the question and hanging out red herring.

I agree, however, that humanism and personalism are not morally adequate. Like Warnock, I believe that there are right and wrong ways to treat infants, animals, imbeciles, and idiots even if or even though (as the case may be) they are not persons or human beings—just because they are capable of pleasure and suffering, and *not* just because their lives happen to have some value to or for those who clearly are persons or human beings.[17]

## IV

If what I have just said is correct, then we must prefer an ethics of type 3 to one of type 2 on simple moral grounds, independently of any findings of ecological science. Clearly an ethics of type 3 will also give us a somewhat better basis for arguing for conservation, antipollution laws, etc., than will any ethics of type 2. The really interesting question at this point, then, is whether we should move on to an ethics of type 4 or type 5. An ethics of type 4 holds, it will be recalled, that we should have respect for persons, human beings, animals, and plants just because they are alive. It is therefore reasonable to think that it will provide an even better basis for conservation, etc., than an ethics of type 3.[18] The difficulty about it, to my mind, is that I can see no reason, from the moral point of view, why we should respect something that is alive but has no conscious sentiency and so can experience no pleasure or pain, joy or suffering, unless perhaps it is potentially a consciously sentient being, as in the case of a fetus. Why, if leaves and trees have no capacity to feel pleasure or to suffer, should I tear no leaf from a tree? Why should I respect its location any more than that of a stone in my driveway, if no benefit or harm comes to any person or sentient being by my moving it?

An ethics of type 4 strikes me, consequently, as merely an implausible half-way house between one of type 3 and one of type 5, and this leads me to think that our crucial choice in a quest for an environmental ethics is between a type 3 ethics and a type 5 one, not between one of type 2 and one of type 5, as Rolston and others tend to assume. The rest of this essay will be devoted to this issue. Should we opt for an ethics of type 5 rather than one of type 3? I have my doubts. But first we must get clearer about the nature of a type 5 ethics and about the forms it may take—clearer than we can get just by reading its recent proponents.

## V

Type 5 covers a variety of views, all of them denying what those of types 1 to 4 (and 6) affirm. Now, ethics of these other types all assert that what is morally right or wrong, good or bad, is ultimately to be determined, solely and wholly, by looking to see what happens to persons, human beings, sentient creatures, or living things. Ethics of type 5 (pure ones) hold that this is not so; for them, in making moral judgments on what we do or are, we must consider what happens to other things as well, in fact, we must consider *everything;* and we must consider everything as such and not merely because of some relation it may have to what is alive, sentient, human, personal, or divine. What is alive, sentient, human, personal, or divine is not all that matters morally. Everything matters. Everything is a moral patient.

But everything may be viewed either distributively or collectively, and so two somewhat different kinds of type 5 ethics are possible. In the first, the world is viewed as made up of a number of things, and they are thought of separately and considered as moral patients in themselves, even those that are

not alive, sentient, human, personal, or divine. All of them, taken distributively, are morally relevant as such. Rolston seems to think in this way when
he describes his proposed ethics as "recognizing the intrinsic value of every
biotic component."

> Consider how slowly the circle [of "persons"] has been enlarged fully
> to include aliens, strangers, infants, children, Negroes, Jews, slaves,
> women, Indians, prisoners, the elderly, the insane, the deformed, and
> even now we ponder the status of fetuses. Ecological ethics queries
> whether we ought again to universalize, recognizing the intrinsic value
> of every ecobiotic component.[19]

The other kind of "planetary altruism" is more properly "holistic" or
"ecosystemic" and is the favorite of our new ecological moralists. It involves
thinking of everything as forming a system or Whole, and then considering
the system or Whole as what matters morally. Thus, what makes our actions
or traits morally right or good is the character of their effects on the system.
What happens to persons, sentient beings, etc., is not morally relevant as such
but only because of its bearing on the character of the Whole. As Rolston puts
it (for he seems to like this way of thinking too, without distinguishing it from
the first): "The focus does not only enlarge from man to other ecosystemic
members, but from individuals of whatever kind to the system. . . . here the
community holds values."[20]

Such a holistic ethics seems to be envisaged in T. B. Colwell's talk
about "the balance of Nature," as well as in Rolston's about "maximizing
the ecosystem." A nice example of it is Aldo Leopold's affirmation: "A thing
is right when it tends to preserve the integrity, stability, and beauty of the
biotic community. It is wrong when it tends otherwise."[21] Even better, because much clearer, is C. D. Broad's, made well before the rise of our current
environmentalism, if we take it as speaking, not just of a society of minds, but
of the whole "community" of nature.

> I think that, in the case of a community of interrelated minds, we must
> distinguish between the total goodness in the community and the total
> goodness of the community. The latter depends partly on the former,
> partly on the way in which the former is distributed among the members
> of the community, and partly on certain relations between the members.
> What we ought to try to maximize is the total goodness of the whole
> community of minds, and it is conceivable that we may sometimes have
> to put up with less total goodness in the community, than might oth-
> erwise exist, in order to accomplish this.[22]

Broad is here espousing a teleological ethics, but it is not clear that a holistic
ethics must be teleological in the sense of maximizing the intrinsic value of
the whole. It might be that other features of the system, such as its balance or

integrity, are to be considered independently of any value they promote, and a holism that so maintained might well be called deontological. It might hold, for example, that the universe constitutes a cosmos with a certain kind of order or plan, and that human beings should copy its order in their lives or fit themselves into its plan.

Holists, as far as I can see, may be atheistic or theistic. Sometimes they come close to pantheism, and I suppose that a pantheistic view in which God is not conceived as a person but is identified with the universe would be a holism of type 5, though it might perhaps be put under type 6 with equal justice for all.

## VI

What are we to think of these two sorts of type 5 ethics? Take first the nonholistic ones. These entail believing that there are, at least *ceteris paribus,* morally right or wrong ways of treating rocks, air, etc., considered simply as such, independently of any relation they may have to living, sentient, or conscious beings, human or nonhuman. I find this belief incredible when it is thus openly formulated, just as earlier I found it incredible that we should give moral consideration to beings that are alive but without any conscious experience. If possible, it is even harder to believe. If we owe no moral consideration to things that are merely alive, why should we accord it to things that are not even alive? It will be replied that both things that are merely living and those that are unliving have a variety of values—they are interesting to watch and study, they are beautiful to contemplate, it may heal us to be with them, etc.—and these values are not just instrumental or utilitarian, they are "inherent."[23] All this is true, as any good birdwatcher knows, but still the reply misfires. For even these inherent values are values that the things in question have in relation to us, for example, on being contemplated by us; they are not values those things have in and by themselves, and so it does not follow that we owe those things moral consideration as such. It may follow that it is morally wrong for me to do certain things to such beings, but this will follow only because we conscious ones will be losers if I do them. The substance of the reply is correct, but it is compatible with an ethics of type 3 or even 2.

Another possible reply involves an appeal to metaphysics. According to some metaphysicians, all things consist of minds, monads, or spirits, even plants and inorganic objects. These minds are not all conscious, and presumably those that make up plants and rocks are not, but still they are minds (for there is such a thing as unconscious mind), and consequently we owe them moral consideration, even if we need not give them equal consideration with minds of other kinds. To this reply I can only say once more that I see no reason why we should extend the range of moral relevance to minds that are unconscious; even if it makes sense to say that they have feelings or thoughts, why should we care what their feelings or thoughts are if they are unaware of them? How can I visit good or evil upon them, lie to them, etc., if they know not what they do, feel, or think? I should also point out, of course, that, while I find the type of metaphysics here appealed to attractive, it is a rather speculative foundation on which to build one's ethical house.

What about a holistic ethics of type 5? First, I wish to point out that a holist might believe that the Whole is itself a person or at least a mind (God, the Absolute, etc.). If he does this, however, then he shares with views of types 1, 2, 3, 4, and 6 the belief that finally what matters is only mind, life, or personality and has not wholly dissociated himself from such "egoism" or "chauvinism." Be this as it may, we must now review the arguments for holism. One is precisely the claim that all the other types of ethics are guilty of a kind of species-egoism or chauvinism; they all "discriminate" against something. This claim can, of course, also be used in favor of a non-holistic type 5 ethics. I have already dealt with it, however, in expounding and discussing ethics of types 2 and 3. Here I only wish to add that at least some ecological moralists of type 5 may be more justly charged with egoism than those of type 2. This comes out nicely in Rolston's essay. Like many other environmentalists he does not hesitate to pin the labels of "egoism" and "chauvinism" on humanistic ethics. But, again like many of his allies, he also makes much of the "coincidence of human and eco-systemic interests," as we have already seen. In all honesty, he recognizes that doing this is "ethically confusing," but adds that it is also "fertile." Then he writes:

> To reduce ecological concern merely to human interests does not really exhaust the moral temper here, and only as we appreciate this will we see the ethical perspective significantly altered. That alteration centers in the dissolution of any firm boundary between man and the world. Ecology does not know an encapsulated ego over against his environment. Listen, for instance, to Paul Shepard: "Ecological thinking, on the other hand, requires a kind of vision across boundaries. The epidermis of the skin is ecologically like a pond surface or a forest soil, not a shell so much as a delicate interpenetration. It reveals the self ennobled and extended, rather than threatened, as part of the landscape, because the beauty and complexity of nature are continuous with ourselves." Man's vascular system includes arteries, veins, rivers, oceans, and air currents. Cleaning a dump is not different in kind from filling a tooth. The self metabolically, if metaphorically, interpenetrates the ecosystem. The world is my body.
>
> This mood frustrates and ultimately invalidates the effort to understand all ecological ethics as disguised human self-interest, for now, with the self expanded into the system, their interests merge. One may,

from a limited perspective, maximize the systemic good to maximize human good, but one can hardly say that the former is only a means to the latter, since they both amount to the same thing differently described. We are acquainted with egoism, *égoïsme à deux, trois, quatres,* with familial and tribal egoism. But here is an *égoïsme à la système,* as the very etymology of "ecology" witnesses: the earth is one's household. In this planetary confraternity, there is a confluence of egoism and altruism.[24]

There it is, all eloquently laid out. Reading it, however, one suspects that such enthusiasm for the interests of the Whole depends on two premises: one, that one's self is at least a part of the Whole so that its interests cannot be wholly lost in those of the Whole in any case; the other, that, praises be, it turns out that one's self and the Whole are or may become one so that one cannot lose at all by being planetarily "altruistic." If this be not egoism, make the least of it! I do not mean that we are incapable of loving the system disinterestedly; I believe we can, and just for that reason am unhappy with those who insist that there is no call for such love after all.

As I said earlier, however, the real question is whether it is clear, from the moral point of view, that we must consider everything in trying to determine what moral judgments to make. Now, as I also said, I can see that we ought to consider animals that are capable of pleasure and pain, as well as human beings and/or persons. I cannot, however, see in the same way, at least not without further argument that we ought morally to consider unconscious animals, plants, rocks, etc. I also cannot see at all directly that we ought to consider the Whole as such, at least not if the Whole is not itself a conscious sentient being. But perhaps there are further arguments to lead me and others like me out of darkness into light.

Here again much may be said by holists about the balance, beauty, integrity, etc., of the Whole, but once more it may be replied that these values are or may be viewed as inherent values the Whole has as an object of contemplation or study by beings capable of contemplation and study; that is, as values it has, not in or by itself, but in relation to minds like ours. If this is so, then such considerations give us no reason for relinquishing views of types 2 or 3. Even if beauty and other such qualities of nature are not dependent on the reaction of some observer, not just in the eye of the beholder, it may still be true that there is a moral call to do something about them only if and insofar as doing this enriches the lives of such observers, present or future.

Writers like Rolston make much of the recent findings of ecological science. These show, they claim, that nature is a homeostatic system with a *nisus* (nice word!) for balance, equilibrium, and wholeness, and they conclude that we ought to protect, preserve, and cooperate, or even to affirm, admire, and love. Now, I cannot try to determine what ecological science does or does not show. There is a question, however, whether from its facts, whatever they are, one can infer any ethical conclusions. Can one infer an Ought from an Is? There has been much debate about this. I do not think such an inference can be claimed to be logical, except perhaps in certain uninteresting cases. But I do believe that, given certain Ises, some Oughts become more reasonable than others, and this may be all that "ecologically tutored" moralists would wish to claim for their ethics. In any case, Rolston for one is rather careful about this, being well aware of the problem. He argues, as I understand him, that, being ecologically informed about the Ises of nature, one just naturally frames new evaluations, new judgments of what is good or bad, and then just as naturally moves on to espouse a new holistic Ought.

> The transition from "is" to "good" and thence to "ought" occurs here . . . but is an evaluative transition which is not made under necessity. . . . What is ethically puzzling, and exciting, . . . is that here an "ought" is not so much *derived* from an "is" as discovered simultaneously with it. . . . the sharp is/ought dichotomy is gone; the values seem to be there as soon as the facts are fully in.[25]

It is hard to know what to say about this. Again, it rings a bell in me; I do believe, as Rolston does, that we shape our values in great measure by our conception of the universe we live in. I have, however, not yet heard the knell that summons me to heaven or to holism. Perhaps I am simply obdurate, but, for instance, I am more troubled than Rolston is by the fact that "ecosystems regularly eliminate species."[26] Nature wiped out the dinosaur. Yet I am supposed to draw the conclusion that I ought to help preserve endangered species. But if nature herself extinguishes them, why should not I? In fact, even if I do it, it is only nature doing it through me, since I am a part of nature. Thus viewed, the dispatch of a species "by human whim" does not seem to be of as different an order "from their elimination by natural selection" as Rolston thinks.[27] Anyway, he allows that we need not simply maintain the status quo in nature; we must promote its integrity, stability, and beauty, but we may be creative and innovative about this, even interfering with and rearranging "nature's spontaneous course."[28] But if our art may improve on nature in this way, then, even though it may learn a great deal from the science of ecology, we may still wonder whether it can learn anything that it cannot learn if it proceeds from an ethics of types 2 or 3. Even if it proceeds from such a base, it might still find that, at least among other things, it should promote the integrity, stability, and beauty of nature.

At any rate, I am not yet convinced that the findings of ecological science make a holistic ethics of type 5 more reasonable than one of type 3 or even 2. I am also not convinced that a concern, say, for the integrity, stability, and beauty of the Whole is a *moral* one if or insofar as it goes beyond a concern about the lives of the persons and consciously sentient beings that are involved. This, however, raises questions of an order we cannot take up here. Another ground for a holistic ethics, of a sort very different from the science of ecology, is mystical experience, which is supposed to witness to the fact that all being is one, and a word must be said about it. If a mystic identifies the one reality with God, then he is a pantheist of the sort described before. But he need not do this; in fact, as the example of Schopenhauer shows, he may even be an atheistic pessimist ending up with an ethics of resignation, hardly what an environmentalist is looking for. What worries me about mysticism, apart from my having doubts about its theory of knowledge, is its insistence that, ultimately at least, all the differentiation and variety of nature is mere appearance and unreal. This makes it hard to see how there can be any reason for treating it in one way rather than another, as any ethics seems to require. What, for instance, does it matter whether I appear to wipe out passenger pigeons or not, or humans for that matter, if I do not really change anything by doing so? Maybe the moral of mysticism is that one should not do anything— or even appear to do anything—except to contemplate the One, but, once more, this moral will hardly give aid and comfort to an environmentalist, not even if all he wants to do is to *watch* the *show*.

To my mind, the strongest argument for a holistic ethics of type 5 is suggested by what Broad says in the passage quoted earlier, if we apply it to a community of interrelated entities, such as "the biotic community" or "ecosystem" is supposed to be, instead of to one of interrelated minds. Then the argument will be (a) that such a community has or may have a value that is not *reducible* to the value in or of the lives or beings of the entities that make it up, though it may *depend* on the value in or of the lives or beings of those entities and on the way in which this is distributed; and (b) that we ought to try to maximize the value of the community even if this involves lessening the value in or of the lives or beings of its constituents. Both of these theses have been much debated, and it is hard to show that they are false. But it is certainly not clear that they are true. I see how a community can have an *instrumental* or even an *inherent* value (in the sense indicated earlier) that is not reducible to those of its members. Perhaps even the *moral* goodness or virtue of a state is not reducible to that of its members, as Plato thought, though this is more doubtful. I do not see, however, how anything can have *intrinsic* value except the activities, experiences, and lives of conscious sentient beings (persons, etc.). Thus I also do not see how a community can have intrinsic value over and above that contained in the lives of its members, unless it is itself a conscious sentient being or mind—something I find hard to believe. As for (b)—if what I have just said is true, then (b) simply does not make sense.

It has been held that there are intrinsically good things that do not fall within the lives of any persons or sentient beings and whose value does not rest on any relation they have or may have to the lives of such beings. Thus, G. E. Moore once held that a beautiful world would be intrinsically good even if there were no minds or sentient beings to contemplate or enjoy it, and W. D. Ross believes that a state of affairs in which happiness is distributed in proportion to merit or virtue is as such intrinsically good.[29] If there are such "impersonal" goods or values, then a holist can reply to what I have just said by contending that a certain kind of ecosystemic Whole is one of them, perhaps the greatest or most inclusive of them all, and should therefore be kept or brought into existence. If he holds that it should be our sole ultimate end, he will be a holist of an "extended ideal utilitarian" kind. I do not find this line of thought convincing. Even if a world can be beautiful apart from any beholder, I cannot see that it would be intrinsically good if it contained and occasioned no enjoyment whatsoever. It might be "inherently" good, that is, such that the contemplation of it would be intrinsically good, but that is not a point in favor of a type 5 ethics. I would say the same thing about the alleged intrinsic value of any pattern of distribution of happiness or "personal" goods or about that of any ecosystemic Whole that is not itself a conscious sentient being. As for the claim that they are nevertheless intrinsically good or good as ends, this seems to me, at this point, to be just another way of insisting that they ought to be preserved or promoted for their own sakes. I can discern no *other* sense in which they are intrinsically good; nor do I see that they are intrinsically good in *this* sense. For to say that they are intrinsically good in the sense that they ought to be taken as ends is to assert precisely what is at issue.[30]

# VII

Our review of the various possible types of ethics about the environment is now complete. Like our ecological moralists, I find ethical egoism, humanism, and personalism morally inadequate. Unlike them, however, I see no convincing reason for going beyond an ethics of type 3 unless we move to a theistic one of type 6, which I have doubts about, or to a combination ethics of type 7. Rolston asks, "After the fauna, can we add the flora, the landscape, the seascape, the ecosystem?" and votes, somewhat speculatively, to accept the challenge. I see the challenge, but my vote remains no. As he says,

> Much of the search for an ecological morality will . . . remain . . . "conservative," where the ground is better charted, and where we mix ethics, science, and human interests [I would add some animal interests] under our logical control.[31]

This does not mean that I think we should not share the environmentalist's concern for the flora, the landscape, the seascape, or the ecosystem. I believe we should, but, as I said, I also believe that a type 3 ethics provides an adequate basis for justifying and directing that concern, at least if it is informed by the facts of ecological history and science, as I agree it should be.

An ethics of type 3, like those of type 2, can be either teleological (e.g., utilitarianism) or deontological, and either aretaic or deontic; and it remains, of course, to see which form is most satisfactory from the moral point of view and to work out its environmental implications. On the first of these questions I have said something elsewhere, though, unfortunately, without any explicit reference to animals.[32] The second task must be left to others.

## NOTES

1. See D. D. Raphael, ed., *British Moralists* (Oxford: Clarendon Press, 1969), I: 207-12.
2. John Passmore, *Man's Responsibility for Nature* (New York: Charles Scribner's Sons, 1974), p. x.
3. Holmes Rolston III, "Is There an Ecological Ethic?," *Ethics* 85 (1975): 103ff. Later references to Rolston are to this article.
4. G. J. Warnock, *The Object of Morality* (London: Methuen and Co., 1971), p. 148. I take the term "moral patient" from Warnock.
5. T. Regan and P. Singer, eds., *Animal Rights and Human Obligations* (Englewood Cliffs, N.J.: Prentice-Hall, 1976), pp. 122f.
6. Ibid., 151f. Note that then "the object of morality" is not merely "the amelioration of the *human* predicament."
7. A. Schweitzer, *Civilization and Ethics,* 3d ed. (London: A. C. Black, 1949), p. 344. See also M. de Montaigne, *Essays* (New York: Modern Library, 1933), pp. 384f.
8. Such a view is suggested by T. B. Colwell, Jr., "The Balance of Nature: A Ground for Human Values," *Main Currents in Modern Thought* 26 (1969): 50.
9. 105f. See also pp. 93, 97. On the whole, however, I shall take Rolston as proposing a type 5 ethics.
10. See J. S. Mill, "Nature," *Three Essays on Religion,* 3d ed. (London: Longmans Green, 1874), pp. 1-65; H. Sidgwick, *The Methods of Ethics,* 7th ed., (London: Macmillan and Co., 1907), pp. 80-83; B. Willey, *The English Moralists* (London: Methuen, 1964), pp. 73-90. See also A. Flew, *Evolutionary Ethics* (London: Macmillan and Co., 1967).
11. For more on egoism, see W. K. Frankena, *Ethics,* 2d ed. (Englewood Cliffs, N.J.: Prentice-Hall, 1973), pp. 17-23.
12. I say something about these matters in ibid., pp. 28ff., 102.
13. There are other senses of these terms; my uses of them here are simply for present purposes.

14. Rolston, "Is There an Ecological Ethic?," p. 104. Remember, e.g., how Heidi's grandfather learned from the eagle.

15. George Laycock, *Audubon* 79, no. 3 (May 1977).

16. E.g., Rolston, "Is There an Ecological Ethic?," p. 103.

17. See Warnock, *Object of Morality*, pp. 148-51.

18. I do not mean to imply that the fact that an ethics provides a better basis for conservation, etc., is much of an argument in its favor. To do this would be like picking out a certain particular cart and then looking for a horse to put it before. One must, in a fundamental sense, have one's ethics first, before one can decide, on moral grounds, for or against conservation, etc. Even so, however, it is also true that one cannot be satisfied with one's ethics unless one is satisfied with its environmental implications.

19. Rolston, "Is There an Ecological Ethic?," p. 101. In fairness, it should be observed that proponents of type 5 ethics of this (or even of the next) kind are probably not insisting on the moral relevance or considerableness of literally everything, e.g., dirt, junk, decayed vegetation, useless cars, etc., and perhaps artifacts generally. I owe this point to a conversation with Nicholas P. White.

20. Ibid., p. 106.

21. A. Leopold, "The Land Ethic," *A Sand County Almanac* (New York: Oxford University Press, 1949), pp. 201-6. See Colwell, "The Balance of Nature."

22. C. D. Broad, *Five Types of Ethical Theory* (New York: Harcourt Brace and Co., 1930), p. 283.

23. "Let us call those values which objects have by their capacity to contribute directly to human life by their presence, *inherent* values. And let us call the mere usefulness of an object for the production of something else which is desirable, an *instrumental* value of it. An art-object... has inherent value... the painter's brushes... have a value which is instrumental only." C. I. Lewis, *The Ground and Nature of the Right* (New York: Columbia University Press, 1955), p. 69. Cf. my *Ethics*, p. 81.

24. Rolston, "Is There an Ecological Ethic?," p. 104.

25. Ibid., p. 101f. For more discussion see my *Ethics*, pp. 97-102.

26. Rolston, "Is There an Ecological Ethic?," p. 102.

27. Ibid., p. 102.

28. Ibid., p. 106.

29. See G. E. Moore, *Principia Ethica* (Cambridge at the University Press, 1903), pp. 83f.; W. D. Ross, *The Right and the Good* (Oxford: Clarendon Press, 1930), pp. 27, 138.

30. For some discussion, see R. B. Brandt, *Ethical Theory* (Englewood Cliffs, N.J.: Prentice-Hall, 1959), pp. 303f., 317, 355f., 395f.; Frankena, *Ethics*, pp. 42f. and chapter V.

31. Rolston, "Is There an Ecological Ethic?," p. 109.

32. Frankena, *Ethics*, chs. 2-3, 4. On a subject related to this one see my "The Ethics of Respect for Life," in Owsei Temkin, W. K. Frankena, and S. H. Kadish, *Respect for Life in Medicine, Philosophy, and the Law* (Baltimore: Johns Hopkins University Press, 1977), pp. 24-62.

# From Egoism to Environmentalism

## K. E. GOODPASTER*

In the alteration of our conceptual environment, philosophy has a major role to play. Whether or not philosophy plays it, the task urgently waits to be done by someone. We are on a collision course that is far more than a conflict of political and economic ideologies. It is the mad scramble by human beings, following outmoded ideas of their relationship to the earth, for control of the natural resources of the planet.

—Thomas Colwell, "Ecology and Philosophy"

The "key-log" which must be moved to release the evolutionary process for an ethic is simply this: quit thinking about decent land-use as solely an economic problem. Examine each question in terms of what is ethically and esthetically right, as well as what is economically expedient. A thing is right when it tends to preserve the integrity, stability, and beauty of the biotic community. It is wrong when it tends otherwise.

—Aldo Leopold, *A Sand County Almanac*

A GREAT DEAL OF TWENTIETH-CENTURY ETHICAL THOUGHT HAS BEEN devoted to foundational questions. By foundational questions, I mean questions about the justification of ethical claims and the explanation of ethical motivation. This is not to say that classical ethics, from Plato and Aristotle through the modern period, has not been concerned with foundational questions—perhaps even centrally. It is to say that the contemporary period

*I wish to acknowledge the O'Brien Foundation and the University of Notre Dame who together helped support this inquiry during the writer's leave in Oxford (January–July 1976).

21

has shown an unusual intensity about these sorts of questions to the point of exclusivity.

Another phenomenon characteristic of the twentieth century is the emergence, again with a new intensity, of environmental stresses hitherto unknown in human society. Together with the emergence of environmental problems (pollution, conservation, preservation, population) has gone, in the last few decades at least, an increasing puzzlement over the *roots* of the problems. Specifically, many thinkers have sought to relate the emergence of environmental crisis to the framework of ethical or evaluative presuppositions which have characterized the period in question.[1] And it has occurred to some to wonder about the rather general impotence of moral philosophy vis-à-vis the sorts of problems we are facing.

The reflections which follow are *not* an attempt to suggest a causal connection between the preoccupations of moral philosophy with foundations and the emergence of our environmental difficulties. Such a suggestion would be ludicrous and far too arrogant an assessment of the causal significance of philosophy in any age. Nevertheless, with a certain amount of fear and trembling, I do want to venture the hypothesis that ethical theory has, in its concentration on foundational issues, left itself vulnerable and relatively uncritical on certain other fronts. And this vulnerability may well be manifesting itself currently in an incapacity to deal with the needs being expressed for an "environmental ethic" and for a relevance of moral philosophy to public affairs in the environmental context. In other words, though philosophical preoccupations are probably not the cause of certain social problems, they may well be part of an explanation for our current conceptual weakness in providing ethically enlightening solutions to these problems. And as the saying goes, one who is not a part of the solution . . . is part of the problem.

I shall attempt to clarify and defend my hypothesis simultaneously, beginning with a brief sketch of the two dominant foundational views of the modern period in ethics. I shall then proceed to exhibit what I take to be the basic procedural flaw common to both approaches (classically and in their more recent versions). Then, after a short discussion of what might seem to be a potent objection to my allegations, I shall begin (but *only* begin) the task of elucidating environmentalism as a normative ethical posture.

I

Broadly speaking, the dominant foundational preoccupations of modern ethical thought can be sketched in terms of two families of views: what I shall call the H-family and the K-family.[2] The families are pitted against one another and together against moral skepticism.

The H-family is a loose association of positions on a number of topics which relate to ethics, ranging from the nature of moral knowledge through the analysis of human action to the content of moral virtue. The approach is fundamentally empiricist in spirit, inviting us to construe morality as a system of hypothetical imperatives, deliverances of a sentiment capable of explaining causally both judgment and action. Ethical predicates are understood as resting on factual criteria whose practical bearing derives not from Reason, but from Interest. Actions are events—assessments of actions, therefore, claims about the causes and effects of those events. Virtue is a characteristic of the *tendencies* of action, often but not exclusively organized around a principle of utility.

The H-family, as I am understanding it, stands against skepticism in the sense that interpersonal justification is provided for, albeit justification of a sort which would hardly satisfy the stronger demands of the K-family.

In contrast to the H-family, the K-family represents an association of positions systematically contrary to empiricist ethical theory as normally understood. It is just as pervasive and extensive as the H-family in terms of its range of views on foundational issues, but in almost every case the positions are contrary. For example, morality (according to the K-family) is a system of categorical imperatives, deliverances not of sentiment but of a critique of sentiment: practical reason. Explanation of judgment and action is crucial, as with the H-family, but explanation *not* in causal terms so much as in terms of principles of conduct. Ethical predicates are understood not as resting on factual criteria but as regulating those criteria a priori, their practical bearing deriving not from Interest but from Reason. Actions are not simply events: assessments of actions, therefore, not simply claims about the causes and effects of events. Virtue is a characteristic of the will, not of overt (or even dispositional) behavior—often but not exclusively organized around a principle of "respect for persons."

Like the H-family, the K-family stands against moral skepticism in the sense that interpersonal justification is provided for, though justification of a sort which mystifies the more empirical minds in the H-family.[3]

## II

Despite their radical differences over foundations, and aside from their common opposition to skepticism, the H- and K-families are congruent from other points of view. Most important, for my present purposes, is the fact that within both families we see a concentrated effort in the direction of vindicating "benevolence" and "justice" (both psychologically and logically) over "egoism." This effort manifests itself in the H-family primarily in an impartialist analysis of the moral sentiment or point of view and in the rejection of psychological egoism as either logically confused or empirically simplistic.[4]

In the K-family, the same animus emerges in the universalization or generalization test for moral maxims and in the rejection of self-referentiality in our understanding of reasons for action. Respect for persons, all persons, is a conceptual demand on rational action.

It is this shared antagonism for egoism and the associated affinity with what might, broadly speaking, be called "humanism" that I wish to focus on. It is on this point, I think, that the perspective of moral philosophy is most in need of critique, and it is here that the quest for an environmental ethic meets its most important procedural obstacles.

Let us return first to the H-family. In unfolding the content of the moral sentiment, the H-family of positions typically examines empirically the objects of moral esteem in an effort to organize them around one or more basic principles. In the course of this enterprise, psychological and ethical egoism are invariably portrayed as inadequate accounts of human motivation and obligation respectively. What is more, the moral object of concern is quite often described *by contrast* to the egoistic position, e.g., as including not only the interests of the self *but also the interests of other selves*. It is as if the moral sentiment is viewed as a kind of generalization of self-love or self-interest: the same sort of sentiment, but wider with respect to its class of beneficiaries (and presumably more intersubjectively accessible—and acceptable—for that reason). Hume writes in the *Enquiry:*

> Usefulness is agreeable, and engages our approbation. This is a matter of fact, confirmed by daily observation. But *useful?* For what? For somebody's interest surely. Whose interest then? Not our own only: For our approbation frequently extends farther. It must, therefore, be the interest of those, who are served by the character or action approved of; and these we may conclude, however remote, are not totally indifferent to us. By opening up this principle, we shall discover one great source of moral distinctions.[5]

and Mill in *Utilitarianism:*

> The happiness which forms the utilitarian standard of what is right in conduct is not the agent's own happiness but that of all concerned. As between his own happiness and that of others, utilitarianism requires him to be as strictly impartial as a disinterested and benevolent spectator . . . education and opinion, which have so vast a power over human character, should so use that power as to establish in the mind of every individual an indissoluble association between his own happiness and the good of the whole, especially between his own happiness and the practice of such modes of behavior, negative and positive, as regard for the universal happiness prescribes.[6]

This tendency to form morality from the rib of egoism is further emphasized in the pressure toward accounting for justice in terms of social utility or benevolence alone. The neatness of the direct generalization of egoism is disturbed if justice, for example, is admitted as a separate form of moral concern altogether.[7]

When one looks for some argument for the general approach to morality as multiplied egoism, very little is available. One has the impression that it just *goes without saying* in the H-family that there must be some unified account of our considered moral judgments and principles, and that self-interest provides the common denominator in terms of which the fractions of the virtues can be summed.

When we come to contemporary exponents of the H-family view, the same pattern manifests itself, and occasionally we even get a hint of the underlying motivation. Gilbert Harman, for example, in his recent book *The Nature of Morality* (Oxford, 1977) writes:

> Taking an interest in someone for his own sake is not difficult; we do it all the time if only to make our contacts with others more bearable. The difficulty is maintaining such an interest over time. You have to go through the motions over and over again until it becomes habitual. Then, by the same *psychological principle of generalization* that leads the miser to become habitually interested in money for its own sake rather than for what it can buy, you may find yourself habitually taking an interest in other people for their own sake and not just for your own benefit. Paradoxically, in thus casting away your egoism and becoming concerned with others, you act in your own interest and help make yourself happy.

And again: "Moral reasons are not reasons of self-interest. They derive from an intrinsic concern or respect for others *as well as yourself* [italics mine]."[9]

The suggestion, clearly, is that the only way to conceptualize and psychologically explain the moral sentiment is in terms of extending self-interest to include other bearers of the sentiment. But why should this be? Why should it be thought that our moral sentiments are best ordered by variations on self-interest? Perhaps we are supposed to believe that self-interest so clearly provides a paradigm of practical rationality that only by working off *its* persuasive power (only by tying our carts to *its* automotive wagon) can we hope to ground an adequate set of moral principles.

I am not, of course, suggesting that the moral sentiment in the H-family, is at bottom reducible to self-interest as its ground—quite the contrary. *Ex hypothesi,* self-love is *not* its ground.[10] What I am suggesting is that self-love is its guiding model—providing its "key-log," to use Leopold's term. Value is tied to the interests of persons and is moralized by being tied to the interests of all or most persons.

A consequence of this model of the moral philosophical enterprise is that normative ethical principles or ideals which are not easily reducible to some function of the interests of selves both fail to be readily intelligible and fail to be plausibly defended. Specifically, as I shall discuss more fully a bit further on, environmental ethical principles and ideals are antecedently less likely to be well-received on this model.[11]

## III

Let us turn now to the K-family. Here, despite expectations and initial appearances, things are not much different. On first glance, it might seem that a perspective on moral judgment which strenuously denies its connections with interest and inclination would be one whose tie to both self-interest and benevolence (and so to the model I have been questioning) would be sufficiently weak to escape my line of criticism. But the lack of hospitality to environmental ideals turns out not to be a function of the "interest" components of phrases like "self-interest" and "general interest." It is the "self" and the "general" that seem to be at the root of the problem, and a Kantian ethic traditionally has stood fast here. This is most evident in Kant's own discussion of the second formulation of the categorical imperative test—the supreme principle of morality. This formulation comes closest in Kant's account to providing something like substantive action-guidance in a theory otherwise charged with being too formal to be practically helpful. After insisting that the ends which a rational being proposes to himself are only relatively or subjectively valuable (giving rise, therefore, only to hypothetical imperatives), Kant writes:

> Supposing however, that there were something whose *existence* has *in itself* an absolute worth, something which, being *an end in itself,* could be a source of definite laws, then in this and this alone would lie the source of a possible categorical imperative, that is, a practical law.
> Now I say: man and generally any rational being *exists* as an end in himself, *not merely as a means* to be arbitrarily used by this or that will. . . . Beings whose existence depends not on our will but on Nature's, have . . . if they are nonrational beings, only a relative value as means, and are therefore called *things;* rational beings, on the contrary, are called *persons,* because their very nature points them out as ends in themselves, that is, as something which must not be used merely as means, and so far therefore restricts freedom of action (and is an object of respect).[12]

And this leads Kant directly to his humanistic formula: "So act as to treat humanity, whether in thine own person or in that of any other, in every case as an end withal, never as a means only."

Now, I am not claiming either that the foundational theory itself or other formulations of the supreme principle have the consequences for normative ethics which I am challenging. Indeed, I think that there is evidence that Kant's more important first formulation of the supreme principle precisely avoids many of my difficulties.[13] I do want to claim, however, that this formulation, by far the most popular and the source of the "respect for persons" ethic, is hostage to the same sort of model of morality attributed to the H-family. Kant's conception of the "end in itself," necessary and insightful as it is as part of his view of the categorical force of moral judgment, is translated for purposes of application into the (quite independent) doctrine of "persons versus things." Kant moved (in his own view, naturally) from the contention that the notion of an end-in-itself was presupposed in our moral conceptual framework, to the view that the only candidate for the status of end-in-itself is the (rational) person. Perhaps his view was that *some* entity or entities had to be the bearer(s) of this status, and that no given rational will *alone* could qualify (egoism?). This belief, together with Kant's conviction that using persons as mere means was bad, may have led him in the quoted context to his fallacious conclusion—fallacious because it equivocates on the term "end-in-itself."[14]

For a more contemporary example of the K-family's egoistically modeled humanism, we can look to Thomas Nagel's *The Possibility of Altruism* (Oxford, 1970). There is no time here for an adequate discussion of Nagel's difficult but rewarding reinterpretation of Kant. Suffice it to say that the main theme or project of the book is precisely to show how egoism can be defeated by a consideration of the nature of "objective" reasons for action. As Nagel puts it:

> My argument is intended to demonstrate that altruism (or its parent principle) depends on a full recognition of the reality of other persons. Nevertheless the central conception in my proposed interpretation will be a conception of *oneself,* and the argument will rest on self-interested action. . . .
> The precise form of altruism which derives from this argument will depend on . . . the nature of the primary reasons for action which individuals possess. If these are tied to the pursuit of their interests, in some ordinary sense of that term, then a normal requirement of altruism will be the result.[15]

In his discussion of "objective" reasons for action, then, Nagel moves naturally with the assumption that the road to altruism is the important moral road and that it is to be reached by a discipline of "objectifying" subjective or egoistic reasons for action. By making moral concern a matter of subjecting egoistic or personal reasons to impersonalizing constraints in order to vindicate (non-"solipsistic") rationality, Nagel is suggesting, in effect, that moral reasons are essentially related to a class of "persons" in the same sort of way that the H-family relates them to a class of "interests." As with Kant, the insight of objectivity, itself quite independent of humanism, is transformed into a sword with which to fight egoism and vindicate its generalization or universalization.

## IV

I have been arguing so far that the two major foundational accounts of morality share, both in their classic formulations and in their contemporary interpretations, a fixation on egoism and a consequent loyalty to a model of moral sentiment or reason which in essence generalizes or universalizes that very egoism. And I have suggested that it is this fact about modern moral philosophy that makes it particularly inhospitable to our recent felt need for an environmental ethic—an ethic which, in the words of Leopold, takes the integrity, stability and beauty of the biotic community as its central touchstone. For such an ethic does not readily admit of being reduced to "humanism"—nor does it sit well with any class or generalization model of moral concern.

As I have noted in passing, however, this last point needs more attention. Indeed, the spirit of an increasing amount of recent literature on environmental "obligations" seems to be against me here. For example, the distinction is made between "shallow" and "deep" environmentalism in order to emphasize the difference between justifications which ultimately appeal to human concerns in addressing environmental problems and justifications which focus on the interests of nonhuman beings.[16] The implication is that the former path is merely instrumentalist, utilitarian environmentalism— "human chauvinism"—while the latter path is the path of the new environmental sensitivity, avoiding arbitrariness in extending its moral concern to a far larger class of beneficiaries: birds, fish, whales, and other animals; plants, trees and forests; lakes, rivers, air and land.[17]

Does this move toward "deep" environmentalism not show that my thesis is mistaken, at least in its contention that it is the generalized egoistic model that is the problem? After all, it is exactly this model which many of the new environmentalists invoke in their defense of the "biotic community" and in their charges of human chauvinism. Peter Singer invokes it in his book *Animal Liberation*. Christopher Stone invokes it in his *Should Trees Have Standing?* Far from it being the case that generalizations of egoism are inhospitable to environmental obligations and ideals, it appears to be the case that exactly such generalizations (only more extravagant) are what we need to ground our environmental obligations and ideals. It may be true that modern ethics has been unduly human-centered, but this is a problem with the degree of its impartiality, not a problem with the structure of its thought.

Such is the objection, and a persuasive one it seems to be. Nevertheless, I think it is misguided. In fact, it is the structural tie to the generalization model in these thinkers which seems to me to be the right explanation for the (often) counterintuitive implications of their views. What I want to suggest is that the *last* thing we need is simply another "liberation movement"—for animals, trees, flora, fauna, or rivers. More importantly, the last thing we need is to cling to a model of moral judgment and justification which makes such liberation movements (with their attendant concentric reasoning) the chief or only way to deal with moral growth and social change.

What I am maintaining is *not* that the "individualistic" model cannot be pressed into service, epicycle after epicycle, to deal with our obligations in matters environmental. Rather my point is that when this is the only model available, its implausibilities will keep us from dealing ethically with environmental obligations and ideals altogether. Such a "deep" or "generalized" version of environmentalism strains our moral sensitivities and intuitions to the breaking point, inviting talk of the "rights of animals," from dolphins to mosquitos; "rights," and even duties, of natural objects like trees and rivers; "chauvinism"; and court suits brought in the names of personified species or even historical landmarks. And this not to mention conceptual problems of individuation, interspecies comparisons of utility, and justice between nonhumans.[18]

None of this is meant to suggest that extensions of the conventional class of morally significant beings are either unintelligible or undesirable. Though I have doubts about the extension of the concept of 'rights' beyond certain limits, this latter concept seems to me not to be crucial in the present context. What is at stake, rather, is a more generic notion which might be called "moral considerability." Indeed, I believe that philosophers who challenge the conventional humanistic constraints on moral considerability are performing a great service in helping to clarify the necessary and sufficient conditions involved.

Nevertheless, I am convinced that the mere enlargement of the class of morally considerable beings is an inadequate substitute for a genuine environmental ethic. Once the class of morally considerable beings is enlarged, no hint of a method for assessing or commensurating the newly recognized claims is provided. Nor does it seem likely that it *could* be provided in a nonarbitrary way, given the lack of structure in the model. In fact, I would want to argue, though I shall not attempt it here, that the very resources needed to see that moral considerability is not tied to human individuals at the same time provide the realization that such considerability is not tied to individuals at all. The place-holders for moral respect could (and I think do) range over systems of individuals as well. Once this awareness dawns, environmental ethics opens up beyond the constraints of the model I have been criticizing.

It is the inability to understand the range of the moral sentiment (or practical reason) in any but an abstract extensional mode that seems to be the problem: the single-minded mapping of morality onto "beneficiaries" and "communities of ends" whose relation to *their* environment is still left outside except instrumentally. I am suggesting that our normative ethical theorizing, when it becomes substantive, is hostage to the complex question: If not one's own interests or dignity, then whose?

The oft-repeated plea by some ecologists and environmentalists that our thinking needs to be less atomistic and more "holistic" translates in the present context into a plea for a more embracing object of moral consideration. In a sense, it represents a plea to return to the richer Greek conception of a man by nature social and not intelligibly removable from his social and political context—though it goes beyond the Greek conception in emphasizing that societies too need to be understood in a context, an ecological context, and that it is this larger whole which is the "bearer of value."

## V

Having got to this point, I am somewhat at a loss as to how to go on. If the line of argument pursued in the previous sections is plausible, then it suggests an approach to environmental ethical obligations and ideals which is *not* a simple extension of the humanist model (nor a pure humanism in its own right). This means that the criteria in terms of which actions and policies are to be assessed must be

  A. either nonrelational in character, or if relational, then not relational
     to an extended class but to something else; and
  B. not practically *empty*.

The challenge which these present to moral philosophy is substantial and significant. Can we make sense of, let alone render plausible, a normative ethical posture satisfying these conditions?

Kant, in the *first* formulation of the categorical imperative test, seems to have been hinting at something that *might* be interpreted along the lines of Leopold's ethic when he writes: "Act as if the maxim of your action were to become through your will a universal law of nature." And in his reflections on beauty and the sublime:

> For since each one pursues actions on the great stage according to his
> dominating inclinations, he is moved at the same time by a secret

impulse to take a standpoint outside himself in thought, in order to judge the outward propriety of his behavior as it seems in the eyes of the onlooker. Thus the different groups unite into a picture of splendid expression, where amidst great multiplicity unity shines forth, and the whole of moral nature exhibits beauty and dignity.[19]

And Henry Sidgwick too seems to hint at something beyond what I have called the "extended egoism" model when he talks of grounding moral obligation not only from an agent's own (relational) point of view but "from the point of view of the universe."[20]

But neither of these philosophers gives us very much to go on, failing in practice if not in principle to satisfy B above. It is interesting to speculate, however, whether their accounts would have differed had they had available to them the emerging science of ecology.

When we look to contemporary literature, many are the voices but few the answers. Thomas Colwell, in his essay "Ecology and Philosophy," quotes approvingly from ecologist Paul Sears and suggests that the "balance of Nature" provides the normative content that we seek:

> The balance of Nature really has to do with the way in which natural processes relate to their environments: namely, through the efficient recycling of energy. . . . The concept of the balance of Nature, so conceived, therefore becomes a *normative* concept for the life of natural communities. Of the many things a natural community must accomplish, it cannot fail to achieve balance in the pattern of its energy utilization. This is the first law of the morality of Nature.[21]

Colwell seems to be suggesting that Leopold's "integrity, stability, and beauty" can be cashed in in scientific terms by use of ecological notions like "homeostasis" and an abandonment of the Man/Nature dichotomy so characteristic of traditional ethical thought. And these suggestions seem to me well made.

Nevertheless, as Holmes Rolston ("Is There an Ecological Ethic?") observes, Colwell's perspective, for all its healthy emphasis on ecological wisdom, tends to remain anthropological. In Rolston's words: "All goods are human goods, with nature an accessory. There is no endorsement of natural rightness, only the acceptance of the natural given."[22] Rolston himself, on the other hand, appears to be pressing in a more radical direction, when he writes (of an environmental ethic which is not simply anthropological):

> While it is frequently held that the basic criterion of the obligatory is the nonmoral value that is produced or sustained, there is novelty in what is taken as the nonmoral good—the ecosystem. Our ethical heritage largely attaches values and rights to persons, and if nonpersonal realms enter, they enter only as tributary to the personal. What is proposed here is a broadening of value, so that nature will cease to be merely "prop-

erty" and become a commonwealth. The logic by which goodness is discovered or appreciated is notoriously evasive, and we can only reach it suggestively. "Ethics cannot be put into words," said Wittgenstein, such things "*make themselves manifest.*" We have a parallel, retrospectively, in the checkered advance of the ethical frontier recognizing intrinsic goodness, and accompanying rights, outside the self. If we now universalize "person," consider how slowly the circle has been enlarged fully to include aliens, strangers, infants, children, Negroes, Jews, slaves, women, Indians, prisoners, the elderly, the insane, the deformed, and even now we ponder the status of fetuses. Ecological ethics queries whether we ought again to universalize, recognizing the intrinsic value of every ecobiotic component.[23]

The difficulty lies in understanding whether Rolston intends, as he seems in this passage, to be embracing the individualistic model. The following remark in the same article suggests that he is aware of a difference: "The focus does not only enlarge from man to other ecosystemic members, but from individuals of whatever kind to the system."[24]

The equivocal character of Rolston's description here serves to intensify my concern about its implicit model. For what may appear to be an essentially rhetorical distinction (between "enlarging" moral concern to include all living individuals and conceiving the environmental imperative as inviting respect for something more unified than simply the set of its "members") is not, I think, only a matter of terminology. Rather, it is a distinction whose implications for the structure and plausibility of environmental ethics are central.

Let me put the matter this way. If we approach the question as to the proper object(s) of moral respect solely in terms of extending or augmenting the class of already acknowledged moral persons, we run the risk of constraining our moral sensitivity to the size of our self-wrought paradigms. Human persons may well be paradigms, of course, but paradigms provide clues and starting points—not stopping points. They may be exemplary but they need not be the most embracing integral units in our moral universe. Indeed our moral universe might contain structures *inclusive* of persons respect for which is just as incumbent upon us morally. Such, I would want to argue, is the biosystem as a whole: not as a mere collection of biotic particles, but as an integrated, self-sustaining unity which puts solar energy to work in the service of growth and maintenance. The history of evolution is the drama of the biosystem's successful self-protection. Recent industrial history may well be an episode in that drama which will lead to a destruction of the system by some of its own participants, a kind of biotic hemorrhage.

I have no wish to sound either metaphorical or apocalyptic.[25] Much less do I wish to suggest for a moment that biosystemic respect should dilute human concerns for happiness and justice. I do, however, suggest that if an "environmental ethic" is to be made both genuinely intelligible and morally persuasive, it must abandon a class-membership model of what can count as an "end-in-itself" or deserve respect. We must, I think, take literally and seriously the possibility that to be worthy of (moral) respect, a unified system need not be composed of cells and body tissue: it might be composed of human and nonhuman animals, plants, and bacteria.

To be sure, these suggestions need further working out. I hope, in fact, to be able to provide more along these lines in the near future myself. An important part of this task will be a general account of what might be called "bearers of moral value"—setting out not only sufficient but also necessary conditions for the proper application of that notion.[26] And essential to this effort, in my view, will be a careful avoidance of the pitfalls involved in demanding more of paradigm cases than they can supply. Ethical egoism is a posture which falls into the pit right off. Humanism and "extended" humanisms fall in only after circumambulation. Perhaps when it occurs to us that we may not be the measure of all things moral, we shall have taken the required giant step.

In any case, an environmental ethic must, while paying its respects to the individualistic model and to humanism, break free of them *without* breaking free of rational discourse and scientific method. The invitation, in Rolston's terms, to "get in gear with the way the universe is operating"[27] needs to be accepted and requires an understanding of that operation. The motivational force, one can hope, will take care of itself as it normally does—in the face of integrity, stability, and beauty.

## NOTES

1. Numerous examples can be found in the following: Commoner, *The Closing Circle* (New York: Random House, 1972); Hardin, *Exploring New Ethics for Survival* (London: Pelican, 1972); Schumacher, *Small Is Beautiful* (New York: Harper & Row, 1973); Barbour, ed., *Western Man and Environmental Ethics* (Reading, Ma.; Addison Wesley, 1973); Disch, ed., *The Ecological Conscience* (Englewood Cliffs, N.J.: Prentice-Hall, 1970); and Blackstone, ed., *Philosophy and Environmental Crisis* (Athens, Ga.: University of Georgia, 1974).

2. H and K for Hume and Kant, though permit me to beg off of exegetical niceties by the use of the "family" and initial letter disclaimers.

3. I shall assume that membership in the respective families is not impossible to assign on the basis of the above characterizations. For those who need names, Hume, Mill, Perry, Toulmin, Baier, Foot, Rawls, Stevenson, Warnock, Brandt, and most recently Gilbert Harman are just a few whom I would include in the H-family. Kant, Price, Moore, Prichard, Ross, Ewing, Gewirth, and most recently Thomas Nagel are examples of the K-family. Doubtless readers will wonder about the inclusions here and there on the respective lists, and probably would want to classify some on a skepticism

list instead. There are also some important philosophers (such as R. M. Hare and W. K. Frankena) who resist classification on either list. And though I am prepared to defend the lists in terms of my sketches of the families, this is really not to the point. For my main goal is to distinguish the families in order to examine what they have *in common*.

4. See, for example, James Rachels, "Egoism and Moral Skepticism," in *A New Introduction to Philosophy*, ed. Steven Cahn (New York: Harper & Row, 1971).

5. David Hume, *An Enquiry concerning the Principles of Morals*, section V, last paragraph of Part 1.

6. J. S. Mill, *Utilitarianism*, chapter 2, seventeenth paragraph.

7. This fact should not be taken to imply that those who insist on a different analysis of justice are counterexamples to my conjecture. For a distributionally sensitive account of generalized self-interest is offered in most contractarian views. Usually such accounts are offered as alternative monisms, however, not simply as *complementing* the utilitarian mode of generalization.

8. Gilbert Harman, *The Nature of Morality* (London: Oxford University Press, 1977), p. 150 (italics mine).

9. Ibid., p. 152.

10. For this reason, I acknowledge that the use of the term "egoism" might mislead. Perhaps "individualism" would be a better term.

11. I am not suggesting that the "individualistic" framework exhibited above renders an approach to environmental ethics impossible. In section IV, I will consider examples of recent attempts to ground an environmental ethic on exactly this model. My point is rather that this format is the only format possible in terms of standard moral theory, and that therefore environmental ethics tends to stand or fall with the plausibility of further "extending" the moral class of beneficiaries or contractors to include nonhumans and future humans. If one is struck, as I am, by the contrived and artificial character of the results of this effort to extend humanistic ethics, one will see it as the exception proving my point.

12. Immanuel Kant, *Fundamental Principles of the Metaphysics of Morals*, second section, paragraphs 42 and 43.

13. See below, section V.

14. "End-in-itself" may be the opposite of "End-for-someone" or the opposite of "Means (for someone)." In the argument

Moral judgment requires that there exist an End-in-itself;

All and only rational beings exist as ends-in-themselves, not as mere means;

Therefore, all and only rational beings deserve respect in terms of the requirements of moral judgment,

this ambiguity appears to be a source of invalidity.

15. Thomas Nagel, *The Possibility of Altruism* (London: Oxford University Press, 1970), p. 89.

16. I first heard this distinction from Richard Routley.

17. See Peter Singer, *Animal Liberation* (New York: Random House, 1975); Christopher Stone, *Should Trees Have Standing?* (Los Altos, Ca.: Kaufmann, 1974); and John Passmore's discussion of the trend in *Man's Responsibility for Nature* (New York: Charles Scribner's Sons, 1974), ch. 5. Also see the essays by Peter Singer and R. and V. Routley in this volume.

18. Stone, *Should Trees Have Standing?*, notes 26, 49, and 73; Passmore, *Man's Responsibility for Nature*, ch. 5; and parts 3 and 4 in Regan and Singer, eds.,

*Animal Rights and Human Obligations* (Englewood Cliffs, N.J.: Prentice-Hall, 1976). I should hasten to add that none of this should be taken to imply that we do not have moral obligations—and many more than we sometimes recognize—where animals are concerned. It is the model of reasoning to these views which worries me. So the implication is not that we must remain with "human chauvinism" or "shallowness"—God forbid—even though philosophers who would defend these latter views will probably share many of my difficulties with the "deep" model.

19. See T. C. Williams, *The Concept of the Categorical Imperative* (London: Oxford University Press, 1968), pp. 22, 121.

20. Henry Sidgwick, *The Methods of Ethics,* 7th ed. (New York: Dover, 1966) p. 420.

21. Thomas Colwell, "Ecology and Philosophy," reprinted in Rachels and Tillman, eds., *Philosophical Issues* (New York: Harper & Row, 1972), p. 360.

22. Holmes Rolston, "Is There an Ecological Ethic?" *Ethics* 85 (Spring 1975): 98.

23. Ibid., p. 101.

24. Ibid., p. 106.

25. That the biosystem is appropriately viewed as an "organism" in a firmly empirical, nonmetaphorical sense is becoming clearer to at least *some* respected scientists. See "The Quest for Gaia," by J. Lovelock and S. Epton, *The New Scientist* 65, no. 935 (1975): 304-9.

26. If the biosphere is such a "bearer of value," then "respect for life" may involve seeing its various forms as manifestations of value without seeing them as simply ends in themselves. But this need not be interpreted to mean that they are to be seen as "mere means." The ends-means distinction is not the contrast being evoked here. What is being evoked is the conception of a system whose integrity, stability, and beauty can be cashed in ecological (v. mystical) terms, and whose relationship to its specific "forms of life" is not simply that of class inclusion. It may be the persistence of life itself, of which the forms of life (including man) are multiple investments, which provides the environmental imperative (if there be one).

27. Rolston, "Is There an Ecological Ethic?," p. 108.

# Against the Inevitability
# of Human Chauvinism

## R. and V. ROUTLEY

## I

IN OUR ENLIGHTENED TIMES, WHEN MOST FORMS OF CHAUVINISM HAVE BEEN
abandoned, at least in theory, by those who consider themselves progressive,
Western ethics still appears to retain, at its very heart, a fundamental form of
chauvinism, namely, human chauvinism. For both popular Western thought
and most Western ethical theories assume that both value and morality can
ultimately be reduced to matters of interest or concern to the class of humans.

Class chauvinism, in the relevant sense, is substantially differential,
discriminatory, and inferior treatment (characteristically, but not necessarily,
by members of the privileged class) of items outside the class, for which there
is not sufficient justification. Human chauvinism, like other varieties of
chauvinism, can take stronger and weaker forms; an example of the weaker
form is the Greater Value Thesis, the invariable allocation of greater value or
preference, on the basis of species, to humans, while not however entirely
excluding nonhumans from moral consideration and claims.[1] We will be
concerned primarily with strong forms of human chauvinism, which see value
and morality as ultimately concerned entirely with humans, and nonhuman
items as having value or creating constraints on human action only insofar as
these items serve human interests or purposes.

In recent years, since the rise of the "environmental consciousness,"
there has been increasing, if still tentative, questioning of this exclusive
concern with, or at least heavy bias toward, human interests; and indeed, at a
time when human beings are rapidly accelerating their impact on the natural
world, the question as to the validity of this basic assumption is not merely an
abstract one, but is of immediate and practical concern in its implications for
human action. In reply to this questioning (which appears to originate largely
from people with environmental interests), modern moral philosophers—

36

fulfilling their now established function of providing a theoretical superstructure to explain and justify contemporary moral sensibilities rather than questioning fundamental assumptions—tend to argue that the bias toward human interests, which is an integral part of going ethical theories, is not just another form of class chauvinism which it is both possible and desirable to eliminate, but is rather a restriction dictated by the logic of evaluative and moral concepts, and that there is no coherent, possible, or viable alternative to the "human chauvinism" of standard ethical theories. In this paper, we want to consider and reject a series of arguments in the theory of value designed to show that this is so and thereby to advance the cause of an alternative, nonchauvinistic, environmental ethic.

The orthodox defense of human chauvinism argues that it is inevitable that humans should be taken as the exclusive subjects of value and morality. Humans are uniquely and exclusively qualified for moral consideration and attributions of value, according to this defense either because the human species alone does, as a matter of fact, possess properties which are a precondition for such ascriptions or because, as a matter of the definition or the logic or the significance of moral concepts in natural language, such considerations are restricted as a matter of logic to the human species. In the first case the restriction of morality and value to the human species will be taken as contingent, in the second necessary. In either case, if the argument is correct, the bias in favor of humans in current theories is inescapable so that, depending on one's definition of chauvinism, either human chauvinism itself is inevitable, or human bias is, because justifiable, not a real chauvinism at all. We shall consider the logical or definitional approach first.

According to the definitional approach, moral and evaluative terms are, as a matter of their *definitions*, restricted in their application to members of the human species; only in a secondary way at best do such terms find a wider application, according as evaluated items are instrumental to human interests. The thesis is often backed up by the production of definitions which are so restricted, for example, "the value of a thing is its capacity to confer a benefit on someone, to make a favorable difference to his life,"[2] where in the intended context "someone" is obviously restricted to humans.

The attempt to preserve human chauvinism in an unchallengeable form through definitions involves the fallacy of taking definitions to be self-validating and unchallengeable, and appears to be based on the confusion of abbreviative definitions with those involving or presupposing substantive claims, such as creative definitions, which may be accepted or rejected. Such definitions as those above cannot be merely abbreviative because they attempt to characterize or explicate already understood terms, such as 'moral' or 'value'. Worse still, they do so in a way which is not dictated by prevailing usage—which does not require that moral and value terms be restricted in range to humans in order that they continue to apply to humans in the ordinary way. Alternative definitions which do not so restrict the range of application may be supplied; they can in fact be found by looking up dictionaries, and these alternatives quite properly do not close off genuine issues which natural language itself leaves open.

The fallacy of the definitional move is that of believing that by converting the substantive evaluative theses of human chauvinism to matters of definition they become somehow exempt from challenge or need for justification. This is comparable to justifying discriminatory membership for a club by referring to the rules, similarly conceived as self-validating and exempt from question or need of justification. Since a similar move could obviously be employed to limit membership of the Moral Club to, say, white male humans in place of humans generally, it is plain that such a definitional argument does far too much and is capable of use to produce completely unacceptable conclusions.

But of course substantive theses involved in definitions, like club rules, are not exempt from challenge and may be arbitrary, undesirable, restrictive, and in need of justification. Once this is grasped the definitional move can be seen as entirely question begging, since the question of the acceptability and inevitability of human chauvinism is simply transformed into the question of the acceptability and inevitability of the definition. The production of such human chauvinist definitions has done nothing to advance the case of human chauvinism other than to throw a spurious air of unchallengeability and necessity over the highly challengeable and arbitrary substantive theses they embody.

The attempt to settle substantive issues "by definition" is both philosophically facile and methodologically unsound and is especially so when there are clearly alternative definitions which would not settle the issue in the same way. What, however, of the substantive claim presupposed by the definitional move, namely, that as a matter of natural language usage, or the logic of moral and evaluative concepts, the meaning of moral and value terms, it is logically necessary that direct, noninstrumental application of such terms be restricted to the human (a claim made at least in the case of rights by Ritchie,[3] and subsequently by Passmore,[4] and by others). But usually, when it is asserted that nonhumans cannot have rights, obligations and such like, what sort of "cannot" is involved is not specified—whether it is a "cannot" of logical impossibility, or of non-significance or absurdity, or something else again (the point is nicely illustrated by Feinberg's discussion of McCloskey,[5] and by McCloskey himself.[6] In any case, however, the thesis appears to be mistaken, for it rules out as logically impossible or absurd a number of positions and theses which are very plainly neither and which it may even, in some circumstances, be important to consider. For example, it is surely neither impossible nor absurd to consider moral questions concerning conduct of humans toward other species, for example, to a race of sensitive and intelligent extraterrestrial beings, and similarly moral questions arising from their conduct toward or concerning humans; indeed science fiction writers do this commonly without producing nonsense or contradicting themselves. Not only does the proposed restriction appear quite mistaken given current usage, but there seems indeed to be something logically unsound about the attempt to place a logical restriction to a particular species on such terms, just as there would be in restricting membership of the Moral Club to people with blue eyes and blond hair who are over six feet tall. The accident of being a zoological human, defined in terms of various physical characteristics, cannot be morally relevant. It is impossible to restrict moral terms to particular species, when species distinctions are defined in terms of physical characteristics which are not morally relevant.

More generally, any attempt to derive a logically necessary connection between humanity itself and the applicability of morality is bound to fail. For creatures anatomically and zoologically distinct from humans which are identical with humans in terms of all morally relevant features are logically possible, upsetting any logical linkage. But attempts to establish a logical tie between humanity and morality through features which all and only humans possess and which are themselves linked logically to morality would, of course, involve a modal fallacy, namely, that of substituting a contingent equivalence within an opaque modal context of logical necessity. In order for such an argument to be valid, it would have to be logically necessary that nonhumans do not possess such features, not merely a contingent fact that they do not; but this assumption must be incorrect for morally relevant characteristics.

The only proposal which has a chance of succeeding, then, is the factual one which makes the selection of just humans for the Moral Club a contingent matter, the claim being that as a matter of contingent fact all and only humans possess a certain set of characteristics, which characteristics themselves are logically tied with qualification for moral consideration and for direct attribution of value to the possessor.

What this contingent form of human chauvinism has to produce then, in order to establish its case, is a set of characteristics which satisfy the following conditions of adequacy:

1. The set of characteristics must be possessed by at least all properly functioning humans, since to omit any significant group usually considered subject to moral consideration, such as infants, young children, primitive tribesmen, etc., and to allow that it was permissible to treat these groups in the way it is considered permissible to

treat non-humans, that is, as mere instruments, would certainly be repugnant to modern moral sensibilities and would offend common intuitions as to the brotherhood of man, the view that all humans are possessors of inalienable rights. Thus human chauvinism, if it is to produce a coherent theory which does not unacceptably rule out some groups of humans, must find some set of features common to the most diverse members of humankind, from Rio Tinto executives to hunter-gatherer tribes of Amazonian Indians, from those who engage in highly abstract activities such as logic and mathematics to those who cannot, from the literate and cultured to the illiterate and uncouth, from the poet and professor to the infant. This alone will be no easy task.

2. In order for human chauvinism to be justified, this set of characteristics must not be possessed by any non-human.

3. The set of characteristics must be not merely morally relevant but sufficient to justify, in a non-circular way, the cut-off of moral consideration at exactly the right point. If human chauvinism is to avoid the charge of arbitrariness and unjustifiability and to demonstrate its inevitability and the impossibility of alternatives, it must emerge from the characteristics why items not having them may be used as mere instruments to serve the interests of those which do possess them. There must be some explanatory logical connection between the set of characteristics and membership of the Moral Club.

Chauvinists are always anxious to stress distinguishing points between the privileged class and those outside it—and there is no lack of characteristics which distinguish humans from nonhumans, at least functioning healthy adult ones. The point is that these distinctions usually do not warrant the sort of radically inferior treatment for which they are proposed as a rationale. On the basis of the characteristics, then, the proposed radical difference in treatment between the privileged and nonprivileged class and the purely instrumental treatment of the nonprivileged class, must be *warranted,* that is, the distinguishing characteristics must be able to carry the moral superstructure placed upon them.

A large and exceedingly disparate collection of features has been suggested as distinguishing humans from nonhumans and justifying human chauvinism. But it turns out that every one of these, on examination, either fails to pick out the desired privileged class of humans in an unequivocal fashion, that is, it applies to some nonhumans or excludes some humans who should not be excluded, or, when it does select the desired class, fails on condition 3 and does not warrant the exclusive claim to moral consideration of the privileged class. Many suggested criteria in fact fail on more than one count.

The traditional distinction between humans and the rest in terms of rationality illustrates the point. Once the theological doctrines of the exclusively human soul on which the distinction once rested are abandoned, it is not so easy to see what is meant by this term. Indeed it often appears to function as little more than a self-congratulatory predicate applied exclusively to humans, with no other clear function at all. However various clarifications are sometimes offered. For example rationality may be said to be the ability to reason, this being tested by such basically linguistic performances as the ability to do logic, to prove theorems, to draw conclusions from arguments and to engage in inductive and deductive linguistic behavior. But such stringent and linguistically loaded criteria will eliminate far too many members of the human species who cannot perform these tasks. If, however, behavioral criteria for rationality are adopted, or the ability to solve problems and to fit action to individual goals becomes the test—that is, practical reasoning is the test—it is obvious that many nonhuman animals will qualify for rationality, perhaps more easily than many humans. But in either case the distinction fails on condition 3, for why must the ability to perform such tasks be *the* criterion for admission to the Moral Club rather than the ability to perform some other tasks or meet some other set of standards, such as orienteering ability, or the ability to mix concrete (the use of concrete being, after all, a far more conspicuous feature of modern human society than the use of reason)? One senses also in the appeal to such criteria (and especially to linguistic criteria) the overvaluation of the things in which the privileged class typically excels and the under-valuation of the skills—not obviously, in any noncircular way, inferior—of the nonprivileged class, which is such a typical feature of chauvinism.

We list some of the suggested characteristics supposedly justifying human chauvinism and indicate in brackets after each some of the conditions they fail: using tools (fails 1, 2, 3); altering the environment (1, 2, 3); possessing intelligence (2, 3); the ability to communicate (1, 2, 3); the ability to use and learn language (1, 2, 3); the ability to use and learn English (1, 3); possession of consciousness (2, 3); self-consciousness or self-awareness (1, 2?, 3); having a conscience (1, 2?, 3); having a sense of shame (1, 2?, 3); being aware of oneself as an agent or initiator (1, 2, 3); having awareness (2, 3); being aware of one's existence (1, 2?, 3); being aware of the inevitability of one's own death (1, 2?, 3); being capable of self-deception (1, 3); being able to ask questions about moral issues such as human chauvinism (1, 3); having a mental life (2, 3); being able to play games (1, 2, 3); being able to laugh (1, 3); to laugh at oneself (1, 3); being able to make jokes (1, 3); having interests (2, 3); having projects (1, 2, 3); being able to assess some of one's performances as successful or not (1, 2, 3); enjoying freedom of action (2, 3); being able to vary one's behavior outside a narrow range of instinctual behavior (1, 2, 3); belonging to a social community (1, 2, 3); being morally responsible for one's actions (1); being able to love (1, 2); being capable of altruism (1, 2); being capable of being a Christian, or capable of religious faith (1, 3); being able to produce the items of (human) civilization and culture (1, 3).[7]

It appears that none of these criteria meets the conditions of adequacy; furthermore it seems most unlikely that any other characteristics or any combination of these characteristics does so. Thus we conclude that these contingent direct arguments for human chauvinism do not establish its inevitability and that indeed the position rests on a shaky base and so far lacks a coherent theoretical justification.

Human chauvinism cannot be restored by a detour through the concept of a person, that is, by linking personhood with membership of the Moral Club and identifying the class of persons contingently with the class of humans. For then the same problem as above arises with different terminology since, even if the notion of person can be specified in such a way as to justify the restriction of moral privileges to persons, the class of persons will then not coincide (even approximately) with the way human chauvinism requires with the class of humans, but will either include a great many nonhumans or exclude a good many humans normally morally considered.

Attempts to enlarge the privileged class—for example, to persons (broadly specified)—or to sentient or preference-having creatures may avoid many of the problems of arbitrariness and justification which face the strong form of human chauvinism, but, as we shall argue, it will face a set of problems of coherence and consistency common to all instrumentalist theories of value and morality.

## II

There are a number of indirect arguments for human chauvinism based on features of value and morality. We turn now to consider these. One abstract argument which is supposed to establish that values are, or must be, determined through the interests of humans or persons—a central argument underlying chauvinism—takes the following form:

A. Values are determined through the preference rankings of valuers (the *no detachable values assumption*).

B. Valuers' preference rankings are determined through valuers' interests (the *preference reduction thesis*).

C. Valuers are humans [persons] (the *species assumption*).

D. Therefore, values are determined through human interests [through the interests of persons].

Hence, it is sometimes concluded, not only is it perfectly acceptable for humans to reduce matters of value and morality to matters of human interest, but moreover there is no rational or possible alternative to doing so; any alternative is simply incoherent.

Although this argument does not, so far as we are aware, appear anywhere with its premises explicitly stated, it does seem to reflect the sorts of consideration those who claim that there is no rational or coherent alternative to organizing everything in human interests usually have in mind. Of course once the premises are exposed, it is easier to see that this initially persuasive argument, like others in the area, rests on fallacious assumptions. We shall claim that although the argument to conclusion D is formally valid—given only some quite conventional assumptions such as that the relation of determination or functionality is appropriately transitive and the principle of replacement of necessary identicals—not all the premises should be accepted.

The argument can be treated as the major representative of a family of similar arguments. For there are many variations that can be made on the argument with a view to amending it, tightening it, varying or strengthening its conclusion, and so on. Our criticisms of the argument will, for the most part, transfer to the variations. A first group of variations replaces or qualifies the determining relation; for example, "determined through" or "determined by" may be replaced by "answer back to," "reflect," "are a matter of," "can be reduced to," or "are a function of." (The latter functional form makes it plain that "determined" has to mean "exactly determined," which ensures that no extraneous factors enter into the chauvinistic determination; mere partial determination would be quite compatible with the rejection of human chauvinism.) Alternatively, "determined" may be modally upgraded to "have to be determined," in order to reveal the sheer necessity of conclusion D. (In this case, it is essential that premise C be of modal strength and not merely contingent, as it would be if the original form were retained; otherwise the argument would contain a modal fallacy.)

Another familiar, and appealing, variation we have already bracketed into the form of the argument given; namely the replacement of humans as base class by persons. This straightaway increases the cogency of premise C, which otherwise—while better than, say, "Valuers are white (North American) humans"—would at best be *contingently* true (which is not good enough for the argument and in fact appears false, since some valuers may not be human; and certainly not all humans are valuers), while at worst it is simply a circular way of reintroducing the logical version of human chauvinism by restricting the class of valuers a priori to humans. That *all* valuers are persons *may* be made analytic on the sense of "person"—given a redefinition of "person" away from its normal English usage, which philosophical English appears almost to tolerate—thus shielding premise C from criticism. Other base classes than persons can replace humans in premise C—for example animals—thus leading to the conclusion, of animal chauvinism, that values are determined through the interests (considerations and concerns) of animals, sentient creatures, or whatever. In the end, of course, premise C could be absorbed (as, for example, valuers are valuers or valuing creatures) and accordingly omitted, leaving the conclusion: Values are determined in the interests of valuers. However even the analytic form of premise C does not, as we shall see, save the argument.

Much the same applies in the case of premise A. The premise is certainly not unobjectionable in the usual sense of 'determined'; but there are ways of repairing it so that the argument still works in a sufficiently damaging form, and one way goes as follows: What is true, analytically, if sufficiently many valuers are taken into account, is that values are determined through the *value* rankings of valuers. Value rankings cannot however be cashed in for preference rankings since, as is well-known, preference rankings and value rankings can diverge; a valuer can prefer what has less value and can value what is not preferred.[8] Let us amend the argument then—so that we can locate the real cause of damage—by replacing premise A by the following premise:

A₁. Values are determined through the value rankings of (appropriate) valuers. Correspondingly, B will be adjusted to B₁ in which "value" replaces "preference."

The really objectionable premise in the central argument is neither premise A nor premise C, but premise B—or, more exactly, where A is repaired, premise B₁. Suspicion of premise B may be aroused by noticing that it plays an exactly parallel role in the class chauvinism argument to that the critical premise

BE. One's preferences or choices are always determined through self-interest,

plays in familiar arguments for egoism, that whatever course of action one adopts, it is always really adopted in one's own selfish interest. The argument for egoism runs along the following, parallel, lines:

AE. Individual persons [agents] always act (in freely chosen cases) in the way they prefer or choose, i.e. in accordance with their preference rankings.

BE. Individual preference rankings are always determined through [reflect] self-interest.

Therefore:

>DE. Individual persons [agents] always act in ways determined by self-interest [that reflect their own interests].

Thereafter follows the slide from *in their own interests* to *to their own advantage* or for their own uses or purposes. The final conclusion of egoism, again paralleling the class chauvinism case, is not only that the egoistic position is perfectly in order and thoroughly rational but that there are no alternatives, that there is, or at least ought to be, no other way of acting, "that men can only choose to do what is in their own interests or that it is only rational to do this."[9]

Thus human chauvinism, as based on the central argument, stands revealed as a form of group selfishness, group egoism one might almost say. Likewise, the criticisms of the Group Selfishness argument, as we shall now call the central argument, parallel those of egoism; in particular premise B ($B_1$) succumbs to similar objections to those that defeat premise BE ($BE_1$). Group selfishness is no more acceptable than egoism, since it depends on exactly the same set of confusions between values and advantages, and slides on such terms as 'interests', as the arguments on which egoism rests. Nowell-Smith's very appealing critique of egoism[10] may, by simple paraphrase, be converted into a critique of group selfishness. This is obvious once we recast $B_1$ and $BE_1$ and set them side by side:

>$BE_1$. Individual value rankings are determined through [individual] self-interest.
>
>$B_1$. Valuers' [groups'] value rankings are determined through valuers' [group] interests [joint interests of groups].

Because, however, one sets up or selects one's own preference or value rankings, it does not follow that they are set up or selected in one's own interests; similarly in group cases, because a group determines its own rankings, it does not follow that it determines them in its own interests. Just as $BE_1$ is, prima facie at least, refuted by a range of examples where value, and also preference, rankings run counter to self-interest, e.g., cases of altruism, so prima facie at least, $B_1$ is refuted by examples where value, and also overall preference rankings, vary from group interests, e.g., cases of group altruism. In the case of limited groups, examples are easy to locate, e.g., resistance movements, environmental action groups, and so on; in the case, however, of the larger human group, examples are bound to be more controversial (since $B_1$ unlike $BE_1$ is a live thesis), but are still easy to find, especially if future humans are discounted; e.g., it is in humans' selfish interests to have plentiful supplies of this and that, electricity from uranium, oil, whalemeat, fish, etc., right now rather than the more limited supplies which would result from restraint, but altruistic value rankings would rank the latter above the former. It is often in selfish human interests (no less selfish because pertaining to a group) to open up and develop the wilderness, strip mine the earth, exploit animals, and so on, but environmentalists who advocate not doing so, in many cases not merely because of future humans, are apparently acting not just out of their own or human group interests.

But, just as $BE_1$ is not demolished by such counterexamples of apparently altruistic action, neither is $B_1$: in each case it can be made out that further selfish interests are involved; e.g., in the case of $B_1$, that an agent did what he did, an altruistic action, because he *liked* doing it. As Nowell-Smith explains in the egoism case, interest is written in as an internal accusative, thereby rendering such theses as $BE_1$ true at the cost, however, of trivializing them. More generally, valuing something gets written in as a further sort of "interest"; whatever valuers value that does not seem to be in their interests is said to provide a further interest, either the value itself or an invented value surrogate; for example, the environmentalist who works to retain a wilderness he never expects to see may be said to be so acting only because he has an interest in or derives benefit or advantage from just knowing it exists, just as he would be said to be acting in the egoist case. By such strategies the theses can be retained; for then a valued item really is in valuers' interests, in the extended sense, even if they are in obvious ways seriously inconvenienced by it, that is, even if it is *not* in their interests in the customary sense.[11] Thus, $B_1$, like $BE_1$, is preserved by stretching the elastic term "interests," in a way that it too readily admits, to include values, or value surrogates, among interests. Then however the conclusion of the Group Selfishness argument loses its intended force and becomes the platitude that values are determined through valuers' values, just as egoism, under the extension which makes us all covert egoists, loses its sting and becomes a platitude. It can be seen that human chauvinism in this form, like egoism, derives its plausibility from vacillation in the sense of "interests," with a resulting fluctuation between a strong false thesis—the face of human chauvinism usually presented—and a trivial analytic thesis, between paradox and platitude.

To sum up the dilemma for the argument then: when "interest" is used in its weaker sense premise B may be accepted but the argument does not establish its intended conclusion or in any way support human chauvinism. For the intended effect of the argument in the crude form is this: in determining values it is enough to look at human advantage; nothing else counts. If the argument were correct, then one could assess values by checking out the local (selfish) advantage of humans, or, more generally, the advantage of the base class somehow assembled. If, on the other hand, "interest" is used in its strong sense, the conclusion would license a form of human chauvinism, but premise B now fails.

Most philosohers think they know how to discredit the egoist arguments. It is curious indeed then, that an argument which is regarded as so
unsatisfactory in the individual case—that for egoism—remains unchallenged
and is still considered so convincing in a precisely parallel group case—that
for human chauvinism.

## III

The Group Selfishness argument is often employed in another way, as
the presentation for a choice between the conclusion D, that value is determined by or reducible to a matter of human interests, and the denial of
premise A, which denial is seen as entailing a commitment to a detached,
intrinsic, or naturalistic theory of value. Thus, it may be said either one
accepts the conclusion, with its consequent instrumentalist account of value,
or one is committed to an intrinsic or detached value theory which takes
values to be completely independent of valuers, and no way determined by
them. But, it is assumed, the latter theory is well known as untenable, and
may even be seen as involving mysticism or as being irrational.[12] Thus, it may
be concluded, there is no real coherent alternative to such an instrumental
account of value, and hence no real alternative to human chauvinism.

The form of the argument then, is essentially: $\sim A \lor D$, but A, therefore D—or, if a stronger connection, of intensional disjunction, is intended:
$\sim D \to \sim A$, but A, therefore D. It can be seen that the main premise, $\sim A \lor D$,
has resulted from the exportation and suppression of premises B and C of the
Group Selfishness argument. This suppression does nothing to improve the
standing of the premises although it does have the (possibly advantageous)
effect of making it more difficult to see the fallacious assumptions on which it
is based. For of course the choice presented, $\sim A \lor D$, is a false one, and
for precisely the same reasons that led us to say that premise B was false. To
reject the instrumentalist conclusion D is by no means to be committed to A,
or to the view that the valuers and their preference rankings play *no* role in
determining values, and that values are a further set of mysterious independent items in the world somehow perceived by valuers through a special (even
mystical and nonrational) moral sense. Valuers' preference rankings may be
admitted to play an important role in evaluations;[13] we are still not committed
to D unless we assume—what amounts to premise B—that these preference
rankings reflect, or can be reduced to, valuers' interests.

The dichotomy frequently presented between instrumentalist accounts
of value, on the one hand, and detached theories (or what are mistakenly taken
to be the *same*, intrinsic theories) is, for the same reason, a false one. Instrumental theories are those which attempt to reduce value to what is instrumen-

tal to or contributes to a stated goal. Typically such theories take the goal to be the furtherance of the interest of a privileged class; for example, the goal may be taken to be determined in terms of the interests, concerns, advantage, or welfare of the class of humans, or of persons, or of sentient creatures, depending on the type of chauvinism. In particular, human chauvinist theories are, characteristically, instrumentalist theories. In contrast, an item is valued intrinsically where it is valued for its own sake, and not merely as a means to something further; and an intrinsic-value theory allows that some items are intrinsically valuable. Intrinsic theories then, contrast with instrumental theories, and what ''intrinsic'' tells us is no more than that the item taken as intrinsically valuable is not valued merely as a means to some goal, i.e., is not merely instrumentally valued. Accordingly detached value theories, since disjoint from instrumental theories, are a subclass of intrinsic value theories; and they are a proper subclass since intrinsic values need not be detached. Something may be valuable in itself without its value being detached from all valuing experience. It is evident, furthermore, that the identification of intrinsic and detached value theories presupposed in the argument is no more than a restatement of the false dichotomy $\sim A \lor D$, or $\sim D \rightarrow \sim A$, i.e., noninstrumental, therefore detached. The assumption that if preference or value rankings are involved at all the resulting assignments must be instrumental is either false or is a variation of the fallacious premise B which plays a crucial role in the Group Selfishness and Egoist arguments. The variation is that if value or preference rankings are involved they must reflect valuers' interests; therefore such values are instrumental because the items valued are valued according as they reflect valuers' interests; and therefore according as they are a means to the end of satisfying the valuers' interests. It follows that intrinsic value theories may allow for a third way between instrumental and detached theories because of the possibility of value rankings (and also preference rankings) which are not themselves set up in a purely instrumentalist way, that is, attributing value to an item only according as it is a means to some goal.

The argument that there is no coherent alternative to instrumentalism does not, however, rely just on misrepresenting alternative intrinsic accounts as logically incoherent by assimilating them to detached accounts. It also trades on a contemporary insensitivity to the serious logical and epistemological problems of instrumental accounts of value, problems which were well known to classical philosophers (see e.g., Aristotle, *Metaphysics* 994b9–16). It does not appear to be widely realized that the classical arguments apply not just to a few especially shaky instrumentalist theories which adopt questionable goals but to instrumentalism in general, since they assume only quite general features of the instrumentalist position.

Instrumentalist positions take as valuable (or in the moral case, as creating moral constraints) just what contributes to a stated end. An obvious example which comes to mind is utilitarianism. However, in the more general case we are concerned with, of instrumentalist forms of human chauvinism, there may be a *set* of goals, not just a single goal such as that of maximizing net happiness of humans; the human-chauvinist assumption is that the values (indeed constraints) are goal reducible, and that all goals reduce in some way to human goals, or at least can be assessed in terms of human concerns and interests. Human chauvinist positions are not necessarily instrumental, but those that are not (e.g., the position that just humans and nothing else are intrinsically valuable) tend to make the arbitrary chauvinistic nature of their assumptions unwisely explicit—most successful contemporary chauvinisms being covert ones.

Problems for instrumentalism arise (as Aristotle observed) when questions are asked about the status of the goal itself. Instrumentalism relies entirely for its plausibility upon selecting a set of goals which are widely accepted and are, in the theory, implicitly treated as valuable. It relies at bottom on an implicit valuation which cannot itself be explained in purely instrumental terms. Of course, a value assumption is not eliminated in this fashion; it is merely hidden under the general consensus that such a goal is appropriate, that such an end is valuable. But the strategy of successful instrumentalism is to avoid recognition of the fact that the goal is, and indeed *must be,* implicitly treated as valuable, by selecting a set of goals so much part of the framework of contemporary thought, so entrenched and habitual as a valued item by humans, that the value attached to the goal becomes virtually invisible, at least to those within the framework. Thus it is with the assumption of human chauvinist instrumentalism that goals are exclusively determinable in terms of human interest. The basic, convincing and self-evident character of this assumption rests on nothing more than the shared beliefs of the privileged class of humans concerning the paramount and exclusive importance of regarding their own interests and concerns, on a valuational assumption or goal which is "self-evident" because it is advantageous and is habitual. The consensus features, of which instrumentalists make so much, are nothing more than the consensus of the privileged class about the goal of maintaining their own privilege, that is, a consensus of interests. This sort of agreement of course shows very little about the well groundedness of the position.

Unless the goals set are widely accepted as valuable, the account will be unconvincing to those who do not share the goal and even to those who appreciate that it is possible to reject the goal. In order for instrumentalism to work logically however, the goal must be implicitly treated within the theory as valuable, for otherwise the proposed analysis loses explanatory and justificatory power and lacks compulsion. For how can the value of an item be explained and justified in terms of its contribution to an end not itself consid-

ered valuable? Serious problems also arise about the nature of value statements under the instrumentalist analysis unless the goal is treated as valuable.
For if the goals themselves are not so treated within the theory, but are taken
simply as unevaluated facts, then a valuational statement "x is valuable"
becomes, under the proposed analysis, simply the statement that x tends to
produce a certain result, to contribute to certain human states, a statement
whose logical status, openness to verification, allowance for disagreement,
and so on, does not substantially differ from the statement that x tends to
produce ferric oxide, to contribute to the rusting of human products. Such an
account of value statements is open to the same sort of objections as other
naturalistic reductions of value, for example, Mill's account of the desirable
in terms of the desired. The special logical and epistemological character of
value statements then, especially with respect to verification and disagreement, must be supplied in instrumentalism, if it is to be supplied at all, by the
implicit treatment of the goal itself as valuable.

The fact that the goal of an instrumental account must be taken as itself
valuable gives rise to two choices. In the first, the goal is taken as itself
instrumentally valuable, which creates an infinite regress. For if the end,
reason, or assignment for which other items are instrumentally valuable is
itself only instrumentally valuable, then there must in turn be some other end,
reason, or assignment in terms of which it is valuable (by definition of instrumental). A regress is thus begun, and if this regress is not to be viciously
infinite, it must terminate in some end or feature which is taken as valuable
just in itself, that is, with intrinsic values.

On the alternative option, the goal is not taken to be instrumentally
valuable but is admitted to be valuable in some other way. Unless an "except" clause is added to the original instrumentalist account so that all values
are held to be instrumental with the exception of the goal, the account will of
course be contextually inconsistent, since it is inconsistent when contextually
supplied assumptions are added. For these include the assumption that the
goal itself is valuable, but not in the way that the instrumentalist thesis claims
is the only way possible. Thus the goal is taken to be both valuable and not
valuable.

If, on the other hand, an "except" clause is added, this amounts to an
admission that the goal is taken to be noninstrumentally valuable. Thus the
account may be able to retain consistency, but does so at the expense of
explicitly admitting a value, that of the goal, which cannot be accounted for in
purely instrumental terms; in short, the goal is taken as intrinsically
valuable.

To sum up, the dilemma for the instrumentalist can be put as follows:
Consider the desirability of the goal of the instrumental theory; it must implicitly be judged to be desirable, for otherwise nothing could be justified by

reduction to it. Ask: Is this goal also instrumentally desirable (valuable) or not? If it is, i.e., it is only desirable as a means to a further goal, then either a regress is initiated or the same issue arises with respect to the new goal. But if it is not, then the instrumental theory is again refuted, since the goal is desirable though not desirable according to the test of the theory because it is not instrumental to the goal.

Whichever horn of the dilemma is taken, then, the outcome is the same: The instrumentalist must rely on treating the goal itself as implicitly valuable in a way not purely instrumental, that is, as intrinsically valuable. Thus the instrumentalist is, at bottom, guilty of precisely the same crime of which he accuses the adherent of an intrinsic account, with the added delinquency of failing to admit and face up to his basic assumptions. The logical and epistemological position of such an instrumental account is certainly no better than that of an intrinsic account, since there is logically no difference between the recognition of one intrinsic value (or one set in the case where goals are multiple) and the recognition of many of them, and the logical and epistemological status of the instrumentalist's account is no better than that of the goal to which his values are taken as instrumental. Since the instrumentalist has implicitly admitted the legitimacy of an intrinsic value assignment in setting up his account, he cannot claim any superiority over a more general intrinsic theory which allows for many intrinsic values, since what is legitimate in the case of one value assignment must be equally legitimate in the multiple case.

This abstract dilemma for human-chauvinist instrumentalism is illustrated in a concrete case by Passmore's procedure in *Man's Responsibility for Nature*; for Passmore (1) wishes to say that there is no coherent alternative to instrumental values, that an item is valuable insofar as it serves human interest, and (2) wants to explain the unique value attributed to humans in terms of their production of valuable civilized and cultural items. But (2) involves the admission of values, that of civilized items, which cannot be valuable in the way (1) states, and indeed (2) amounts to the admission of noninstrumental values. The proposed account is inconsistent because if intrinsic values are admissible in the case of civilized items, they cannot be logically incoherent in the way (1) claims.

The sort of problem faced by Passmore is however not a readily avoidable one for the instrumentalist; for if the charge of arbitrary and unjustifiable human chauvinism is to be avoided by those who opt for (1), and humans are not themselves to be awarded intrinsic values—thus conceding the logical legitimacy of intrinsic values generally, and hence the avoidability of human chauvinist accounts of value—some explanation must be provided for the exclusive value attributed to humans. But any explanation capable of justifying this valuation in a nonarbitrary and nonchauvinistic way would have to refer to properties of humans and would have to say something like: "Humans are uniquely valuable because they alone have valuable properties x, y, z, . . . or produce valuable items A, B, C. . . . " The list of proposed distinguishing features already considered above is usually what will be employed here. But this is to admit intrinsic value for the properties which explain the exclusive value of humans. The dilemma for the human chauvinist is that he must either take the exclusive human-value assumption (the goal) as ultimate—laying him open to the charge of arbitrary chauvinism and of attributing intrinsic values to humans—or attempt to explain it—in which case he will again end by conceding noninstrumental values.

Thus the case for the inevitability of human chauvinism, that alternatives to it must be based on an incoherent and logically and epistemically defective account of values, namely a noninstrumental account, has not been established by these arguments.

# IV

Egoism, not group selfishness, is one of the assumptions underlying the next series of abstract defenses of chauvinism. The leading ideas of the representative argument we first consider are essentially those of social contract theories. This argument takes the following form (the bracketed parameters X and Z are filled out in the representative argument respectively by: "justification of moral principles," and: "enter into contracts"):

J. The only justification of moral principles [only X] is a contractual one, i.e., the entry into contracts of agents [Zry].

K. Agents only enter into contracts [only Z] if it serves their own interests. (The *egoist assumption*)

L. Humans [persons] are the only agents that enter into contracts [that Z].

Therefore, by K and L: M. Humans [persons] only enter into contracts [only Z] if it serves their own interest.

Therefore, from J and M: N. The only justification for moral principles [only X] is the (selfish) interests of humans [persons].[14]

The argument can be varied by different choices of parameters, X and Z. For example, X could be filled out by "determination of value judgments," and "contractual" replaced by "community-based" (i.e., Z is filled out by "are community-based" or some such) yielding in place of J the familiar premise that the only justification of value judgments is a community-based one, and leading to a conclusion, analytically linked to D above, that all value judgments are determined by human self-interest. Alternatively, just one of X or Z may be so replaced, leaving the other as in the original example. Another variation of the argument that has figured prominently in the discussion of animal rights fills out X and Z respectively by "determination of rights" and "belong to human society." Under this assignment, the parametric premise J becomes essentially that commonly adopted statement[15] (already criticized above) that rights are determined solely by reference to human society.

As the arguments are in each case valid, the issue of the correctness of the conclusions devolves on that of the correctness of the premises. In each case too, the arguments could be made rather more plausible by replacing "humans" by "persons" (and correspondingly "human society" by "society of persons", etc.); for otherwise premises such as L and its variations are suspect, since there is nothing, legally or morally, to prevent consortia, organizations, and other nonhumans from entering into contracts (and these items are appropriately counted as persons in the larger legal sense). Given that amendment to premise L, the correctness of the arguments turns on the correctness of premises J and K. But both these premises are false and premise J imports the very chauvinism that is at issue in the conclusion.

Though the representative contract argument is only one of several important variations that can be made on the general parametric argument, it is often regarded as having special appeal, because the contract model appears to explain the origin of obligation, and offer a justification for it, in a way that no other model does, and appears thus to provide a bulwark against moral, and political, scepticism. That the appearance is illusory, because the obligation to honor contracts is assumed at bottom, is well enough known and not our concern here. What is of concern is the correctness of representative premises J and K.

The egoist assumption K is faulted on the same grounds as egoism itself. For agents sometimes enter into contracts that are not in their own interests but are in the interests of other persons or creatures, or are undertaken on behalf of, for instance to protect, other items that do not have interests at all, e.g., rivers, buildings, forests. The attempt to represent all these undertakings as in human interests, because done in the "selfish interests" of the agents, is the same as in the egoist arguments, and the resolution of the problem is the same, namely, to distinguish acting, valuing, and so on, clearly from acting in one's own selfish (or in-group) interests. However even if premise K were amended to admit that agents may enter into contracts on behalf of nonhuman items, it would still result in a form of human chauvinism given familiar assumptions, since nonhuman items will still be unable to create moral obligations except through a human sponsor or patron, who will presumably be able to choose whether or not to protect them. Natural items will generate no more constraints unless humans freely choose to allow them to do so; since the obligatory features of moral obligation thus disappear, no genuine moral obligations can be created by natural items under such an amended account. Thus the amended premise assumes the question at issue.

Premise J, the view that moral obligations are generated solely by contracts undertaken by moral agents, is then the crucial assumption for this argument for human chauvinism. J, however, has serious difficulties, for there are many recognized moral principles which apparently cannot be explained as contractually based, at least if "contract" is to be taken seriously. There is no actual contract underlying the principle that one ought not to be cruel to animals, children, and others not in a position to contract. Adherents of a social contract view of moral obligation are of course inclined to withhold recognition of those moral principles that cannot be contractually based so that the contract thesis becomes not so much explanatory as prescriptive. But even allowing for this, the thesis has many unacceptable consequences just concerning humans, and if the notion of contract plays a serious role, it is difficult to reconcile with the view of all humans as possessing rights.

A crucial feature of contracts is that they are freely undertaken by responsible parties. If they can be freely undertaken there must be a choice with respect to them—the choice of not so contracting. But then we are left with the conclusion that it is permissible to treat those who do choose not to contract as mere instruments of those who do, in the way that the nonhuman world is presently treated; these contractual dropouts, like those outside society, can have no rights and there can be no moral constraints on behavior concerning them, whatever their capacity for suffering. A similar conclusion emerges if humans who are not morally responsible are considered, for although we are normally thought to have quite substantial obligations to such humans, e.g., babies, young children, those who are considered mentally ill or as having diminished responsibility, they cannot themselves be free and responsible parties to a contract and will, on the social contract view, presumably have to depend for their rights on others freely choosing to contract on their behalf. If, for some reason, this does not occur we will be left with a similarly unacceptable conclusion as in the case of the contractual dropouts. Obviously then, moral obligations do not require morally equal, free, and responsible contracting parties, in the way the social contract account presupposes. Worse, the argument would appear, with but little adaptation, to justify the practices of such groups as death squads, multinational corporations, and the Mafia, or any other group that contracts to protect the interests of its own members.

If these unacceptable conclusions are to be avoided, all humans will have to be somehow, in virtue of simply being human, subject to some mysterious, fictional, social contract which they did not freely choose to enter into, cannot get out of, and which can never exclude any member of the human species. So the unacceptable consequences are avoided only if crucial features of the notion of contract such as freedom and responsibility are dropped, and the notion of contract and premise J so seriously weakened as to become virtually without conditions. For the argument to work the residue has to be mere common humanity, and the "contract" little more than the convention of morally considering just other members of the human species. Such a convention differs little however from a restatement of human chauvinism; the preferred explanation is really no explanation, for such a convention can neither justify human chauvinism nor, since different conventions could be arranged, explain why it is inevitable.

The social contract account of moral obligation is defective because it implies that moral obligations can really only hold between responsible moral agents and attempts to account for *all* moral obligation as based on contract. But of course the account is correct as an account of the origin of some types of moral obligation; there are moral obligations of a type that can only hold between free and responsible agents and others which only apply within a social and political context. Yet other types of obligation, such as the obligation not to cause suffering, can arise only with respect to sentient or preference-having creatures—who are not necessarily morally responsible—and could not significantly arise with respect to a nonsentient such as a tree or a rock. What emerges is a picture of types of moral obligation as associated with a nest of rings or annular boundary classes, with the innermost class, consisting of highly intelligent, social, sentient creatures, having the full range of moral obligations applicable to them, and outer classes of such nonsentient items as trees and rocks having only a much more restricted range of moral obligations significantly applicable to them. In some cases there is no sharp division between the rings. But there is no single uniform privileged class of items, no one base class, to which all and only moral principles directly apply, and moreover the zoological class of humans is not one of the really significant boundary classes. The recognition that some types of moral obligation only apply within the context of a particular sort of society, or through contract, does nothing to support the case of human chauvinism.

The failure of the contract theory nevertheless leaves the issue as to whether there is some logical or categorial restriction on what can be the object of moral obligations, which would reinstate human chauvinism or animal chauvinism. There is, however, no such restriction on the object place of the obligation relation to humans or sentient creatures. Even if the special locution "Y has an obligation toward X" requires that X is at least a preference-having creature, there are other locutions which are not so restricted, and one can perfectly well speak of having duties toward land and of having obligations concerning or with respect to such items as mountains and rivers, and without necessarily implying that such moral constraints arise only in an indirect fashion. Thus neither natural language nor the logic of moral concepts rules out the possibility of nonsentient items creating direct moral constraints.

There is then, given this point and the annular model, no need to opt for the position of Leopold[16] as the only alternative to human (or animal) chauvinism, that is, for a position which simply transfers to natural items the full set of rights and obligations applicable to humans, leading to such nonsignificance as that rocks have obligations to mountains. Distinctions between the moral constraints appropriate to different types of items can be recognized without leading back to human chauvinism. The point is an important one since many objections to allowing moral obligations to extend beyond the sphere of humans, or in some cases the sphere of sentient creatures, depend on ignoring such distinctions, on assuming that it is a question of transferring the full set of rights and obligations appropriate to intelligent social creatures to such items as trees and rivers—that the alternative to chauvinism is therefore an irrational and mystical animism concerning nature.[17]

## V

The ecological restatement of the strong version of human chauvinism, according to which items outside the privileged human class have zero intrinsic value, is the Dominion thesis,[18] the view that the earth and all its nonhuman contents exist or are available for man's benefit and to serve his interests and, hence, that man is entitled to manipulate the world and its systems as he wants, that is, in his interests. The thesis indeed follows, given fairly uncontroversial, analytic assumptions, from the conclusions of the main chauvinistic arguments examined, notably D, that values are determined through human interests. The earth and all its nonhuman contents thus have no intrinsic value, but at best have instrumental value and so can create no direct moral constraints on human action. For what has only instrumental value is already written down, in this framework as serving human interests. And since what has no instrumental value cannot be abused or have its value diminished, it is permissible for humans to treat it as they will in accord with their interests. Therefore, the Dominion thesis. Conversely, if nonhuman items are available for man's use, interests and benefits, they can have no value except insofar as they answer his interests. Otherwise there would be restrictions on his behavior with respect to them, since not any sort of behavior is permissible as regards independently valuable items. Accordingly value is determined through man's interests, that is, D holds. Thus the Dominion thesis is strictly equivalent to D. It follows that the Dominion thesis, like D, strictly implies human chauvinism. Conversely, the strong version of human chauvinism strictly implies D, and so the Dominion thesis, completing the sketch of the equivalence argument. Since the positions are equivalent, what counts against one also counts against the others. In particular, then, the Dominion thesis is no more inevitable than, and just as unsatisfactory, as strong human chauvinism.

The upshot is that the dominant ethical systems of our times, those clustered as the Western ethic and other kindred human chauvinistic systems, are far less defensible, and less satisfactory, than has been commonly assumed, and lack an adequate and nonarbitrary basis. Furthermore, alternative theories are far less incoherent than is commonly claimed, especially by philosophers. Yet although there are viable alternatives to the Dominion thesis, the natural world is rapidly being preempted in favor of human chauvinism—and of what it ideologically underwrites, the modern economic-industrial superstructure—by the elimination or overexploitation of those things that are not considered of sufficient instrumental value for human beings. Witness the impoverishment of the nonhuman world, the assaults being made on tropical rainforests, surviving temperate wildernesses, wild animals, the oceans, to list only a few of the victims of man's assault on the natural world. Observe also the associated measures to bring primitive or recalcitrant peoples into the Western consumer society and the spread of human-chauvinist value systems. The time is fast approaching when questions raised by an environmental ethic will cease to involve live options. As things stand at present, however, the ethical issues generated by the preemptions—especially given the weakness and inadequacy of the ideological and value-theoretical basis on which the damaging chauvinistic transformation of the world is premised and the viability of alternative environmental ethics—are not merely of theoretical interest but are among the most important and urgent questions of our times, and perhaps the most important questions that human beings, whose individual or group self-interest is the source of most environmental problems, have ever asked themselves.

## NOTES

1. This thesis has, among other unacceptable outcomes, the consequence that, if there is only room in one's boat for one and one must choose between saving Adolf Hitler and a wombat which has lived a decent and kindly life and never harmed a living creature, one is morally obligated to choose the former. That would not be the choice of the authors.

2. Baier, in *Values and the Future,* K. Baier and N. Rescher, eds. (New York: The Free Press, 1969), p. 40.

3. D. G. Ritchie, *Natural Rights* (London: Allen and Unwin, 1894), p. 107.

4. J. Passmore, "The Treatment of Animals," *Journal of the History of Ideas* 36 (1975): 212; and *Man's Responsibility for Nature* (London: Puckworth, 1974), pp. 116, 189.

5. *In Animal Rights and Human Obligations*, T. Regan and P. Singer eds. (Englewood Cliffs: Prentice-Hall, 1976), p. 195.

6. H. J. McCloskey, "Rights," *Philosophical Quarterly* 15 (1965): 115-27.

7. This feature typifies a number of rather circular distinguishing characteristics, or at least ones which raise serious theoretical problems for human chauvinism because they attempt to explain the unique value of humans in terms of their ability to produce items which are taken to be independently valuable, thus contradicting human chauvinism. (See the discussion in V. Routley, "Critical Notice of Passmore, *Man's Responsibility for Nature*," *Australasian Journal of Philosophy* 53 [1975]: 177.)

8. There is nonetheless an esoteric, semantical, sense of "determined" in which premise A is demonstrably true, and so a sense in which it is analytically true that value rankings are semantically determined by the *preference* rankings of situations by a class of valuers. The details of these semantical foundations for values are set out in R. and V. Routley, "Semantical Foundations for Value Theory," *Nous* (forthcoming). But while premise A can be corrected by replacing "determined" by "semantically determined" and giving this an appropriate construal, such a move would do nothing to restore the intended argument; for it would either invalidate the argument, through change in the key middle term "determined," or, alternatively, if "determined" is systematically replaced throughout the argument, drastically alter the intended conclusion D—so that looking at the interests that humans in fact have would no longer provide a guide to values (instead the interests of hypothetical valuers with respect to worlds that never exist would have to be gathered).

9. P. H. Nowell-Smith, *Ethics* (London: Penguin, 1954), p. 140.

10. Ibid., pp. 140-44.

11. The technique of rescuing philosophical theses by natural extensions and accompanying redefinitions of terms, including the thesis "We're all selfish really," is delightfully explained in J. Wisdom, *Other Minds* (Oxford: Blackwell, 1952), ch. 1.

12. J. Passmore, *Man's Responsibility for Nature*, ch. 7.

13. Value rankings can be semantically analyzed in terms of preference or interest rankings, as in R. and V. Routley, "Semantical Metamorphosis of Metaphysics," *Australasian Journal of Philosophy* 54 (1976) explains. The semantical foundations, while conceding nothing to subjectivism or instrumentalism, make it easy to concede main points of the case (attributed to Dewey) against detached values, against the view that there are values somehow out there (in Meinong's *assersein*), purely naturalistic values completely detached from all valuers, or from all preference rankings of valuers. Put differently, there are no values that do not somehow answer back to preference rankings of valuers, and so no values that are entirely detached from valuers and valuational activity such as preference-ranking of situation. But the answering back is made explicit and precise by the semantical analysis, *not* by any syntactical reduction or translation of value statements into statements about valuers' preference or interest rankings; and the valuers of the analysis are, like the situations introduced, ideal and need in no way exist. As a result then, valuations may be independent of the aggregated preference rankings of all actual humans or, for that matter, of all persons over all time. Thus too the semantical analysis makes it easy to navigate a course between the alternatives of two influential false dichotomies, to the effect that values are either instrumental or else detached, or that values are either subjective or else detached. For though a semantical analysis can be given, upsetting

the detached value thesis, no translation or syntactical reduction of the sort subjectivism assumes is thereby effected.

14. The logical transitions in the argument take on more evidently valid form upon analytic transformation of the premises, to those now illustrated:

J'. All justifications of moral principles are cases of (justified by) the entry into contracts of agents.

K'. All cases of the entry into contracts are cases of self-interests of agents. And so on for L' through M'.

15. See notes 3 and 4 above.

16. A. Leopold, *A Sand County Almanac* (New York: Ballantine, 1966).

17. See Passmore, *Man's Responsibility for Nature,* pp. 187ff.

18. This view encompasses what Passmore has isolated as the Western environmental ideologies, both the dominant view and the lesser traditions; see V. Routley, ''Critical Notice of Passmore, *Man's Responsibility for Nature.*''

PART TWO

# Methods of Moral Reflection

# Contrasting Methods
# of Environmental Planning

## R. M. HARE

IN PLANNING THE CONDUCT OF HIS AFFAIRS IN RELATION TO NATURE, man is faced with many problems which are so complex and so intermeshed that it is hard to say at first even what kind of problems they are. We are all familiar with the distinction between factual and evaluative questions, and I do not doubt that there is this distinction; but the actual problems with which we are faced are always an amalgam of these two kinds of questions. The various methods used by environmental planners are all attempts to separate out this amalgam, as we have to do if we are ever to understand the problems—let alone solve them. I wish in this essay to give examples of, and appraise, two such methods. I shall draw from this appraisal not only theoretical lessons which may interest the moral philosopher but also practical lessons which, I am sure, those who try to plan our environment ought to absorb. Though my examples come mostly from urban planning because that is the kind of planning with whose problems (although only an amateur) I am most familiar, what I have to say will apply also to problems about the countryside and the environment in general.

Suppose that I am a single person living by myself in a flat and have decided to remodel my kitchen. I can please myself—questions about other people's interests are unlikely to arise, and in any case let us ignore them. Even in this simple situation it is possible to illustrate some of the pitfalls that practical thinking can fall into. What I have to do, according to the first method that I am going to consider, is to decide upon certain ends or goals, and then look for means to them. I shall call this way of doing things the *means-end* model. I think you can see its disadvantages. What are the ends that I am setting myself in remodeling the kitchen? It is not difficult to make a list of them: convenience, economy, beauty, hygiene, and so on. But this is going to be of not much use for my purposes for several reasons. The first is that even if we confine ourselves to one of these ends it may be difficult to say *how much* of the quality in question is required or even to find a way of

63

measuring how much of it has been provided. This is obviously true of beauty; but even if we take economy, which looks more promising, because we can at least measure how much gas and at what price, it takes to boil a pint of water, we are still in difficulties because we do not know how small a gas consumption would satisfy us. Similarly with convenience; it is possible to do ergonomic studies—and very useful ones have been done—to determine how many steps or arm-movements are required on a certain layout in order to wash a given collection of dishes. But how many is too many?

However, it is when we come to comparisons and trade-offs between the various desiderata that we are in real trouble. We should need to know how much convenience we are prepared to sacrifice for how much economy, or how much beauty for how much hygiene. For example, if the old copper pans which we keep on the shelf just for show collect the dust and harbour flies, are we going to put up with this because they look so good? Economists discuss this sort of problem and help with it up to a point; but the philosophical problems about method remain, and I can illustrate them without doing more than the simplest economics, if any.

One of the things that tend to happen if we use the means-end model is that the goals whose attainment is in some degree measurable and which can therefore easily be put into cost-benefit calculations, tend to get taken care of, whereas the ones that are not measurable, like beauty, tend to get left out. It may help us to understand the problem if we contrast the means-end model with another model which I am going to call the *trial-design* model. It is the one in fact used by nearly all architects in dealing with their clients because it is so much more helpful than the means-end model. In this way of doing things, the designer just produces more or less detailed particular designs for the client to look at, all of which he certifies as at least feasible, and attaches perhaps a rough costing to them; and the client then chooses the one that he prefers. The process of choice is then in its logical aspects very similar to that which I go through when I go to a shop and choose a pair of shoes, except that I cannot actually try on the shoes, but have to choose them from drawings.

This difference is, however, of very great practical consequence. For clients are often not very good at understanding from the drawings what the finished product is going to be like to live with (in our example, what it is going to be like cooking in this kitchen); and some designers are not very good at explaining it to them. However, the system can work and is not in principle different from choosing goods from a mail-order catalog when you are not allowed to have them on approval.

It is important not to exaggerate the difference between the two models. No doubt even in the trial-design model the designer will have had some idea, obtained by preliminary questioning, of what the client's goals and preferences are; so the alternative designs he produces for the client to choose from are not churned out at random. Knowing the client's preference, he gives him a short list of designs, or in the first instance just one, which he thinks the client will like. A certain amount of means-end reasoning has gone into this process. And even in a means-end system there may be trial-designs produced in the later stages. It may be that in a complete and adequate procedure both models would play a part. But it is still important to distinguish between them, and above all not to think that the means-end model by itself is enough.

I want now to illustrate the important difference between these two models or methods by contrasting two studies in which they are employed, each in a fairly pure form. These are, first, the book *Urban Transportation Planning,* by Roger Creighton,[1] an American transportation engineer, which advocates a certain method in transport planning and illustrates its use in two important studies which his team did for Chicago and Buffalo; and secondly, Sir Colin Buchanan's Edinburgh study published in two books *Alternatives for Edinburgh* and *Edinburgh: The Recommended Plan.*[2]

The first of these studies uses the means-end model. Before I go into detail, I must repeat that one of the chief things that all planning procedures have to do, if the thinking is going to be clear and unconfused, is to distinguish questions of fact from questions of value. I am not going in this lecture to try to justify this remark; anybody who spends much time reading about planning problems cannot help noticing the terrible confusions which result when people think, either that they can answer factual questions by making value-judgments (which we call ''wishful thinking'') or that they can answer evaluative questions by elaborate observation of the facts. It is neither the case that you will make a certain proposed road network lead to a certain reduction in traffic in some environmentally sensitive area just by thinking how nice it would be if it did have this result; nor that you can by traffic statistics prove that it is the *best* solution to the problem. You can prove, perhaps, within certain limits of error, that *this* is what the traffic will do when you have built the network; but the public still has to decide what kind of city it prefers to have.

The two methods that I am discussing are essentially two rival ways of separating factual from evaluative judgments. The means-end model used in Creighton's book strikes many people at first as an obvious way of achieving this separation. We incorporate all our value-judgments at the beginning of the planning process into statements of what are called ''goals.'' Having thus, as it were, put all our values into the machine once for all, we cause the machine to turn out various plans and to evaluate them with reference to these goals, and the best plan will automatically be chosen. This process is represented schematically on p. 136 of the book:

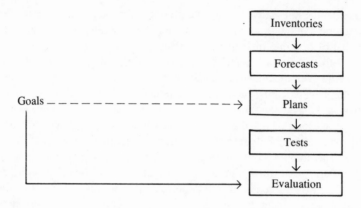

We first make our factual enquiry into the inventories, that is to say, into the actual statistics of the present situation: existing road networks, traffic counts on them, the same for rail and other public transport networks, distribution of population and of places of work, and so on. We also check one of these groups of statistics against the other; there are certain reasonably reliable models which allow one to predict the distribution of travel over a network given the distribution, as to places of residence and of work, of the people who are going to use it. So we can test these models for their predictive accuracy by seeing whether, by using them, the existing population- and work-distribution can be made to generate the observed existing traffic flows. All this is common to both the methods I am considering, so I shall not have to repeat it.

So is the step called "forecasts." This consists in making predictions, on sociological, economic, and other grounds, of the *future* distribution of population and places of work, and thus of the "desire for travel," in the future, along various lines within the area to be covered by the plan. A date is normally set for which the plan is being made; twenty years is thought to be about the limit of human prescience by existing methods.

The two methods now start to diverge. The Creighton method, having made its inventories and forecasts, requires the determining at this point, once and for all, of a number of "goals." The approach of the author is well illustrated by this excerpt:

> *Scientific Method: Objectivity.* In great part due to the influence of Carroll, the transportation studies adopted the scientific method as the standard for their work. The features of observation, advancement of hypotheses, and replicability of calculations were considered to be the proper guidelines for all the analysis and development of theory which

were done by transportation studies. Although the preparation of plans necessarily included the subjective element of human goals, even this part of the planning operation was treated with extreme objectivity once the list of goals was adopted. And even in selecting goals, attempts were made to deduce goals from an observation of what people actually choose to do. In short, judgement was out and the rules of evidence and demonstration were in as the standards by which decisions were made. (p. 146)

In order to fit into this method, the goals have also to be stated in very simple terms, and such that the extent to which they are realized is not only quantifiable but quantifiable in a way that enables us to compare the realization of one goal with that of another on a common scale (which in practice has to be that of money). For example, if one goal is saving of time and another saving of lives, we have to find a way of measuring both these benefits in money terms. The same applies to even more difficult items like the enhancement of the quality of life in cities or the preservation or improvements of their visual quality.

When we come to look at the actual goals listed in Creighton's book, we see how difficult the task is going to be. Eleven are listed (overlapping with one another to some extent): safety; saving time in travel; reducing operating costs; increasing efficiency; mobility; beauty; comfort and absence of strain, noise or nuisance; reducing air pollution; minimizing disruption; increasing productivity of the economy; and ability to move about without an automobile (pp. 199 ff.). In the Chicago study in which the author was involved, says Creighton,

> One of the tasks the staff set for itself was to build a formal bridge between goals and plan. *We wanted to be able to prove that the plan we recommended for the Chicago area would be the best.* If the Policy Committee to whom we reported approved our statement of goals and objectives, and our reasoning processes were correct, then they would almost automatically approve the plan, because the one had to follow from the other. The ultimate extension of this idea, of course, would be one in which a computer would be given a statement of goals for a given metropolitan area, together with the facts describing that metropolitan area, and then it would be programmed to produce the best plan for the area automatically. We later achieved this, though only at very small scale. (p. 201)

The restrictions which I mentioned earlier on the kinds of goal that the machine can cope with lead in practice to the simple omission of goals the extent of whose realization is not measurable in terms of money. Thus in the two studies taken as examples by Creighton, concerned with Chicago and the environs of Buffalo, only the first four goals which occur in the list I quoted were used in evaluating the alternative plans: safety, reduction of travel time, operating costs, and capital costs. The last three of these are easily expressible in money terms; safety is so expressible if we apply to the accident statistics (actual and predicted) the values set upon loss of life, injury, and damage to property by the courts, though the basis of such valuations is quite unclear.

The other goals simply get omitted. Economists have tried to find theoretical ways around this difficulty;[3] but in practice a means-end model which insists on prior statement of goals and a mechanical operation of the evaluation process thereafter is almost bound to have this result; and the outcome of such thinking is to be seen in typical American cities. It was also to be seen in the majority report on the third London airport,[4] in which the cost-benefit analyses were expressed in money terms, and everything that was going to be considered had to have a money value set on it—the commission was in difficulties as to whether the value of an irreplaceable Norman church was to be taken as the sum it was insured for.

Is there an alternative? I think there is, and that planners are beginning to use it, although I doubt whether they really yet understand how different the new method is from the old. Perhaps I am exaggerating; perhaps traces of the new kind of thinking are to be found in Creighton's book. On p. 318 we have a trial-design method used: "The 'modal model' described in the preceding chapter was used in 1966 to test eleven different combinations of transit and highway systems for the Niagara Frontier. These tests were released to the public in December that year, but without recommendation." And on p. 343 there is another diagram, which ends:

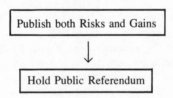

And perhaps traces of the means-end model are to be found in the Buchanan study which I am going to consider in a moment. But I have somewhat schematized the methods in order to make the contrast clearer.

Buchanan's team was called in to report on Edinburgh after a plan proposed by the corporation had aroused a lot of opposition because of the very obtrusive character of the new roads proposed in it and the destruction of the environment, especially its visual qualities, that would be entailed. What the team did, after doing the factual analyses and forecasts which, as I said, are common to both the methods, was to prepare in skeleton form a number of different plans (including an adaptation of the one which had caused the fuss), involving different degrees of reliance on public transport, different scales of road expenditure, and different amounts of restriction of access for private cars to the center). I will not say that goals were not considered at all before the plans were made (as I said, I do not want to exaggerate the break between the two methods or to represent the transition between them as having occurred suddenly). Obviously, in selecting just *these* plans for elaboration and evaluation the team had some idea in mind of what they and the public were after (just as, even in Sir Karl Popper's theory of scientific method,[5] the scientist, though he may adopt a hypothesis for testing on a mere hunch, normally has more to go on than that). But Buchanan's study is, so far as I can see, altogether free of the doctrine that goals or ends have to be stated once and for all at the beginning, the rest of the evaluation being done mechanically by application of these goals to the facts.

Instead, what the study does is to predict the factual consequences of building each of the schemes in turn, describe these in some detail and in as clear and quantified a way as the nature of the facts allows, and then ask the public (that is, the inhabitants of Edinburgh and their elected representatives) to discuss the various alternatives in the light of these facts, and, ultimately, say which they prefer. The crucial evaluation comes at the end of the process, not at the beginning. After it had received the comments of the public, the team then produced a recommended plan in the light of them which was also to be the subject of public evaluation.

This method at one blow avoids all the disadvantages of the previous one. Goals do not have to be tied up in advance. Nothing is in principle presupposed about goals until the time comes to opt for one or another of the plans. The public can just look at the plans and say which it prefers. The point of all the analysis of consequences of the plans is not to *prove* an evaluative conclusion, namely, that one of them is the best, as Creighton's method tries to do; it is, rather, to make the ultimate choice as well informed as possible, in that the public will have a clear idea of what it is choosing between. Therefore, it is not necessary to express all the goals in terms which allow of a financial comparison; they do not have to be commensurable at all, any more than the fit of shoes has to be commensurable with their cost. Thus, Buchanan's team estimated the enivronmental effects of the various proposals quite independently of the economic cost-benefit analysis. These environmental effects were predicted by working out what volumes of traffic would be present in the various streets. Then these volumes were compared with what is called the "environmental capacity" of the streets—that is, the amount of traffic that there can be in the streets without disrupting the environment to more than a certain degree. This degree is measured in terms of the amount of noise, the amount of visual intrusion of vehicles and road structures, and so on. Where precisely the "environmental capacity" is fixed is of course an evaluative matter. However, the method employed does (for me at any rate) considerably clarify the evaluative process so that when I come to choose between the plans, I feel that I know much more clearly what I am choosing between. In principle the choice is left to me; nobody is trying to prove anything to me, except that those would be the consequences of the adoption of a certain plan.

The two methods lead to two very different sorts of plans. Buchanan, unlike Creighton, is led, after the public discussion, to propose a plan which requires quite a high degree of restriction of private cars for commuting, with closure of streets in the center, restriction of some existing and new streets to buses, fairly low road expenditure, and large reliance on public transport. He does not, indeed, go as far as some people would like, and the debate in Edinburgh continues. It is also alleged that the terms of reference which he was given compelled him to concentrate too much on the scheme's effects in the central area of the city and not enough on those in the suburbs. But at least he has displayed a method which enables the debate to be conducted rationally. Those of us who on the whole share his preferences have a right to insist that those who do not work out the factual consequences of *their* preferred schemes as conscientiously and try to convince the public that these consequences would prove in practice more acceptable.

The difference between the outcomes of the two methods is not entirely due to the difference between the methods themselves; but it partly is. Another factor is a greater readiness of the British public than of the American to contemplate restrictions on private cars (due perhaps to our lower degree of motorization). The second of the two methods, if followed in America, might lead to a choice by the public of solutions involving higher road expenditure and less restriction on private cars than is likely to be acceptable in Edinburgh. And, of course, Edinburgh is an outstandingly beautiful city. Nor do I want to suggest that all Americans adhere to the means-end model in their thinking— even all professional planners.

The means-end model is naturally congenial to the engineer; the trial-design model to the architect. Buchanan is both. Engineers usually get, when they are designing a bridge, a fairly cut-and-dried statement of goals (e.g., that it should have a certain traffic capacity, take a certain maximum load, and cost as little as possible); and they then exercise their science and prove that the design which they recommend is superior in these respects to others. The architect, on the other hand, normally produces sketches and then more worked-out plans of alternative layouts, and the client has to say which he wants. Though I am convinced that the engineer is an indispensable member of the planning team, I am equally convinced that the "architectural" overall method is the better one.

I have been speaking mainly about urban problems; but what I have said is obviously applicable to all decisions about environmental planning, including those that affect nature in the narrow sense. But these latter problems are likely to bring out, even more than those of city planning, a distinction which I have not yet mentioned. This is the distinction between the work of the architect or the engineer on the one hand and that of the planner on the other. The architect and the engineer are likely to have just one client who is going to choose the final design and pay for its execution. I have been speaking as if this were so in city planning; but it is not. The planner has to satisfy great numbers of "clients" whose interests are often in conflict.

The difference is not merely a difference in complexity. I started by considering a problem about planning a kitchen. Architectural problems like this could become extremely complex without becoming a battlefield for conflicting interests. Suppose, for example, that some rich landowner is redesigning his entire mansion and perhaps a vast estate too; the problems may then be as complex as a great many planning problems. But provided that the landowner is concerned solely with his own interest, and not at all with the interests of the others affected (he is quite ready, say, to shift a whole village to improve his view, as Lord Harcourt did at Nuneham[6]), he will be able to proceed just as in the "kitchen" case. He will, that is to say, if he follows the trial-design model, get Vanbrugh or Capability Brown to give him some alternative designs, and choose between them. He will not have to consult anybody else.

In planning decisions, however, almost by definition, other people are involved and will have, in any democratic system, to be consulted. There are first of all the many different people who are going to live or work in or visit frequently the piece of land whose use is being decided; then there are the neighbors who will live where they are affected by that use; then there are other members of the public who will see it; and those who, though they will not see it, will use, or be affected by the use of, whatever is produced there (gravel for example); and so on.

There are two questions—both of them moral questions—which at once arise when many people are concerned like this. The first is about procedure. What is the most just way of arranging for the decision to be made so that the interests of all these people get their due consideration and they have some say in the decision proportionate to their interests? The second is about the substance of the decision arrived at. What makes a decision a just or a right one in such cases?

On the first question: it is obvious that whatever procedure we adopt will be some kind of *political* process. In this it is different from the "kitchen" case or even the "mansion" case; the addition of all these different people whose interests have to be considered has made politics inescapable, as it is not for our bachelor who is consulting with his architect. Even in the extreme case of a dictator who just says "Pull down the old quarter in front of St. Peter's and build the Via della Conciliazione instead," this is a political act, and it is only because the *polity* is like that (namely a dictatorship) that he can make the decision and get it executed without taking anybody else's views into consideration. If anybody objects that this is true of the landowner too, I shall not argue the point. At any rate, in normal polities, even some quite undemocratic ones, there has to be some process whereby the interests of different people are taken into account, and the question is (a moral question): Which of these arrangements is most just in the circumstances of a particular society?

The second question would arise even if the first did not. Suppose, again, that there is a dictator; or suppose, less extremely, that a particular person (say the secretary for the environment) has the sole decision about some particular issue (for example whether, or on what route, to build the extension of the expressway from Oxford to Birmingham). Suppose that *that* is the political procedure which has in fact been adopted. The first question has then been answered, but the second question still has to be answered by this dictator or minister, if he is a moral man and is trying to do the fair or the just thing.

I will only indicate my own view, without arguing for it, about how the second question is to be answered. As it happens, an answer to it is implicit in the theory about the nature and logical properties of the moral concepts which I have worked out in my books. To be prepared to say "That is the solution which ought to be adopted" is to be prepared to prescribe it for universal adoption in cases just like this. I have argued elsewhere[7] that this way of putting the matter comes to the same thing as two other theories which have had a wide currency: the so-called ideal observer theory and the so-called rational contractor theory—but only in certain of their forms, and in the latter case *not* in the form preferred by its best-known advocate, Professor Rawls. Certain forms of utilitarianism lead to the same conclusions, as do certain interpretations of the Kantian doctrine and of the Christian injunction to do unto others as we want them to do to us. So the method which I am advocating ought to have the support of a fairly wide spectrum of philosophers.

What it comes to is this. If I am prescribing universally for all situations just like this one, I shall be prescribing for situations in which I myself occupy the roles of all the persons affected by the decision. If you like to dramatize the method, you can adopt C. I. Lewis's device of imagining that I am going to occupy, seriatim, the positions of all these people in identical corresponding situations.[8] If I do this, I am bound to accord equal weight to the equal interests of each individual affected (and of course the weight will vary according to the degree to which they are affected).

So then, the first thing that the person making the decision has to do is to find out, by factual enquiry, how various alternative decisions *will* affect the interests of the various parties. And this question is divisible into two elements. He has first to find out (as precisely as needs be) what will happen if one decision or the other is taken. This includes questions like: how many aircraft will use the proposed airport; how much noise they will make and over what areas; how many passengers will travel by them, and how far they will travel, and by what means, to reach the airport; how much land and how many buildings of what sorts will be taken over or destroyed; how much the whole thing will cost; how much the passengers will have to pay in transport costs; and so on. And secondly he has to find out how all these facts will affect people's interests: the people whose homes will be destroyed or disturbed; the people who travel by air; the people who send or receive freight by air; the people who pay taxes which are used to finance the construction; and so on. The facts here are facts about the desires and likes or dislikes of these people, how much they mind what is being done to them, or how much they appreciate what is done for them. It must be emphasized that facts about people's likes and dislikes are still facts, although to have a certain like or dislike is not to state any fact. From these facts, we can get conclusions about what the people's interests are.

One of the arguments for "participation" and for democratic ways of deciding questions about planning is that they automatically give those concerned a certain voice so that they can make known how they think their interests are affected. But a procedure may be procedurally just, or be accepted as being so, but still not achieve a just solution to the substantial problem. This is because people (usually because they lack foresight) do not always use the procedure wisely in even their own interests. Shopkeepers have in the past often opposed the creation of pedestrian precincts or the building of bypasses to their towns, in the mistaken belief that this would result in loss of trade. Actually, when this is done, it seems usually to improve trade because people like shopping where they are not disturbed by traffic. So if you had tried to follow procedural justice by giving traders a big voice commensurate with the extent to which their interests are affected, they would have actually used this voice to bring about a decision (the maintenance of the status quo) which was against their interest. The same applies to members of the general public, who may object to certain features of planning schemes as against their interest simply because they are unable to foresee or visualize the actual effects of the schemes.

Another objection is that it is extraordinarily difficult by democratic procedures to ensure that people get a say in proportion to the degree to which their interests are affected. In theory, the people who are going to suffer most will howl the loudest, so if we had an instrument for measuring in decibels the loudness of howls *and* people were always the best judges of their own interests, and if posterity could howl, we could use this instrument as a just procedural means of ensuring justice in the result. But in fact it may be the people who are best organized, or who have most money, who succeed in making the most noise, and the resulting political pressures may be an extremely imperfect reflection of the degree to which people's interests are actually going to be affected. For these two reasons (ignorance and the imperfection of the participatory process), there is almost bound to have to be a certain amount of paternalism in these decisions if they are going to be just ones; one can do one's best to bring the facts before the public and to get those whose corns will be trodden on the hardest to make the most noise and the rest to pipe down a bit; but probably someone in the machine will have always to be looking after the interests of those who lack the knowledge, or the power, to stand up for their own real interests.

It is at this point that both the uses and the limitations of cost-benefit analysis are most clearly revealed.[9] In the cases considered previously, in which one person only was concerned in the choice of a design (the "kitchen" case, for example) there was no need for cost-benefit analysis at all; when the client was fully apprised of the factual consequences of adopting each of the different designs, he could just choose. There was no need to express the alternatives in terms of costs or benefits measured by some common scale (for example, money). We compared the choice with that of shoes at a shoe shop; in order to choose rationally between pairs of shoes at different prices one does not have to *price* the value to oneself of good fit, smart appearance, etc., although one may show *by one's choice* what monetary value one attaches to these qualities. The monetary value thus derived is a *deduction from* the choice made, not an *aid to making* the choice rationally.

But where many people are affected, as in most planning decisions, there is the problem of balancing their interests fairly against one another. So it looks as if it might help to work out the costs and benefits to all the parties on some comon scale and thus make the adjudication fairly. One would then not be imposing a cost on one person unless a greater benefit was thereby secured to another; and thus one would be maximizing utility. Alternatively, if one were an adherent of some nonutilitarian system of distributive justice, one would seek to distribute costs and benefits in some other way considered just. Any of these processes, however, depends on knowing what value, on a common scale, each of the individuals affected attaches to the "costs" and "benefits" in question. And this, as before, can only be a deduction from the choices which are made,[10] or which it is predicted would be made, by these individuals. Cost-benefit analysis can therefore not be a substitute for making these choices. It can never altogether take the place of voting and other political procedures or of selective purchase and other economic procedures. We can observe how people do vote, what they do buy, whether they go by car or bus when traveling from A to B, and so on, and thus make inductive inferences about what choices they and people like them *would* make in relevantly similar circumstances. But they have to do the initial choosing.

The element of paternalism, therefore, which I said is inevitably involved in planning if the ill-informed are to be protected from making choices which they will regret, is of a very limited sort. It consists in predicting what choices the ill-informed would make if they were more fully informed. For example, it might be legitimate, if the planner could get away with it politically and if he were sure of his facts, for him to make the traffic-free shopping precinct referred to in my earlier example;.if in the end the shopkeepers and the public liked it, he would have been proved right even if he went against their wishes at the time. But it is not open to the planner to dictate to them what they *shall* like or dislike or choose or reject; he can only make more or less hazardous predictions about what they *will* like or *would* choose, and an item can appear as a ''cost'' or a ''benefit'' in his calculations only on the basis of these predictions. And, if the public were much better informed than it is about the consequences of different planning policies, participation and democratic voting would be a better means of choosing policies than bureaucratic direction. If, therefore, the public wants not to be paternalized, it has to some extent to learn (or at least learn from) the planner's predictive skills. Even so, however, there are difficulties, familiar to political theorists, but beyond the scope of this essay, about whether distributively just solutions are likely to be arrived at by democratic processes however well oiled.

Behind these again lurk further difficulties, familiar to philosophers and economists, of how to determine the interests of the parties given information about their desires and likings and choices in actual and hypothetical situations, and of how to make desires and likings interpersonally commensurable. Without wishing to make light of these difficulties, I may perhaps say two things. The first is that these are not difficulties peculiar to utilitarians. They affect anybody whose moral thinking contains any element or principle of benevolence; for we cannot tell how much good on the whole we have done unless we are able to compare the good we have done to one person with that which we have done to another. Philosophers, therefore, who wish to avoid this difficulty will have to abjure all reasons for action which have to do with the welfare of others, even if, like the pluralist Sir David Ross, they make benevolence or beneficence only one of their principles. The second is that such difficulties are solved in practice, all the time, in simple cases; we are able to judge which of our children wants a certain toy most. Cost-benefit analysis is an attempt, on the basis of data about people's actual choices and predictions about hypothetical ones, to do this sort of thing on a bigger scale—an exercise which we cannot avoid if we are to do the best we can, in sum, for competing claimants.

Let us, however, suppose that the two kinds of facts that I mentioned (about the consequences of planning decisions and about how these will affect people's interests) have been ascertained. We have then a number of trial designs, each of them accompanied by an array of these two kinds of facts. The decision has, however, still to be taken. It does not follow logically from these facts. If a dictator were interested only in the glory of his national airline or, more commendably, in the preservation of the countryside just as it is, and so made his decision regardless of all the other factors, we should not be able to fault his logic. However, if he, or if the people who are making the decision, ask what they can prescribe universally for situations just like this, they are bound, as I said, to give equal weight to the equal interests of all those affected and so will choose a solution that does the best for those interests taken as a whole. And this is what planners should do.

I wish to contrast this essentially utilitarian solution, which is that adopted by the best planners, with the sort of solution that is likely to get adopted if we follow some less adequate methods. They are nearly all less adequate for the same reason, which is that they have taken a highly selective view of the facts. But this can be for a number of different reasons. First we have those who, obsessed with the need to be scientific, take into account only those facts which can be measured. I have said enough about them already. On the other hand, we have those who take a selective view of the facts for entirely nonscientific (e.g., for political) reasons, and ignore, for example, economic factors. I know people whose views on planning all stem from a pathological hatred of the automobile (sometimes because it is anachronistically taken to represent middle-class values), and others who are led to the opposite extreme by an insane love of this useful but dangerous machine. It is the one-sided character of most of what most people say about planning and conservation that makes me despair of our getting many wise decisions.

What is the philosophical interest in all this? First of all, it is an excellent illustration of the necessity for understanding ethical theory if we are going to think rationally about our practical moral problems. I have mentioned, and I hope exemplified, the usefulness of carefully distinguishing factual from evaluative questions. The most harmful theorists of all are those who say (without producing any good arguments) that this cannot be done and that therefore we are condemned to argue endlessly in terms which bend as we use them, reducing the discussion of these issues to a contest between rhetoricians. If we can separate out the questions of fact from the others, we can at least obtain reliable answers to *them*. But when we have done this, we then have to resist the seductions of the second most dangerous set of theorists— those who say that since only facts are "objective," and values are merely "subjective," there can still be no rational process for deciding questions of value, which all questions of planning to some extent are.

I have tried to explain how, having separated out the two kinds of questions, it is possible to use our knowledge of the facts in order to present ourselves with an informed choice between possible solutions. If only one party is affected by the choice, then that is all there is to be said, and his choice, if fully informed, is as rational as it could be. But if many people are affected, as in planning decisions they are, we need also a rational means of adjudicating between their interests; and this, I have claimed, ethical theory can supply. The difficulty remains of finding a political procedure which will make this rational adjudication possible; but since this difficulty takes us into the heart of all the as yet unsolved problems of political philosophy, I will not now embark on a discussion of it. I have perhaps done enough to show that moral philosophers can both profit from, and contribute to, thought about concrete environmental problems.

## NOTES

1. R. L. Creighton, *Urban Transportation Planning* (Urbana, Il.: University of Illinois Press, 1970).
2. Colin Buchanan and Partners, Freeman Fox, Wilbur Smith and Associates (Edinburgh: Edinburgh Corporation, 1971, 1972).
3. See, e.g., D. L. Munby, "Faith and Facts: Quantity and Quality," in *Human Gesellschaft,* ed. T. Rendtorff and A. Rich (Zurich, 1970).
4. *Commission on the Third London Airport* (The Roskill Commission) (London: Her Majesty's Stationer's Office, 1971).
5. K. R. Popper, *The Logic of Scientific Discovery* (Vienna, 1934; London: Hutchinson, 1959); *Conjectures and Refutations* (London, 1963), ch. 1.
6. It has been suggested that Oliver Goldsmith's *Deserted Village* is about this eviction; but the text presents obvious difficulties for such a claim.
7. *Philosophy and Public Affairs* 1 (1972), reprinted in *War and Moral Responsibility,* ed. M. Cohen, et al. (Princeton: Princeton University Press, 1974), pp. 47ff.; *Aristotelian Society* 72 (1972/3); *Philosophical Quarterly* 23 (1973).
8. C. I. Lewis, *Analysis of Knowledge and Valuation* (LaSalle, Il.: Open Court, 1946), p. 547.
9. See P. Self, "Techniques and Values in Policy Decisions," *Nature and Conduct,* ed. R. S. Peters (New York: St. Martin's Press, 1975), p. 298.
10. Cf. p. 146 of Creighton, *Urban Transportation.* On the general question see Amartya Sen, *Collective Choice and Human Welfare* (London, 1972); P. Self, "Techniques and Values"; and D. L. Munby, "Faith and Facts." Obviously, much more needs to be said than I have been able to say about the uses and pitfalls of cost-benefit analysis. In this essay I wish merely to claim that the trial-design method is less dependent on it than the means-end method, and not that the former can dispense with it altogether when more than one person's interest is involved. However, the inevitable crudities in practice of cost-benefit analysis make it a virtue of the

trial-design method that it at least allows the preference-ordering of solutions by an individual to be made without recourse to it. When it comes to converting these individual preference-orderings into a collective choice, some kind of cost-benefit analysis may be the only way of balancing them fairly against one another. But this is too big a topic for the present essay. We have at least disentangled from each other the two different problems of interpersonal commensurability and intervalue commensurability, and shown that, where the first does not arise, the second can be solved.

# How Should We Decide
# What Sort of World Is Best?

## JONATHAN GLOVER

I am speaking like an intellectual, but the intellectual, to my mind, is more in touch with humanity than is the confident scientist, who patronizes the past, over-simplifies the present and envisages a future where his leadership will be accepted.... It is high time he came out of his ivory laboratory. We want him to plan for our bodies. We do not want him to plan for our minds, and we cannot accept, so far, his assurance that he will not.

—E. M. Forster, *The Challenge of Our Time*

The problem is to design a world which will be liked not by people as they now are but by those who live in it. "I wouldn't like it" is the complaint of the individualist who puts forth his own susceptibilities to reinforcement as established values. A world that would be liked by contemporary people would perpetuate the status quo. It would be liked because people have been taught to like it, and for reasons which do not always bear scrutiny. A better world will be liked by those who live in it because it has been designed with an eye to what is, or can be, most reinforcing.

—B. F. Skinner, *Beyond Freedom and Dignity*

HOW SHOULD WE DECIDE WHAT SORT OF WORLD IS BEST? THIS PAPER will focus on, but not solve, *one* of the theoretical problems underlying discussions of social and political ends. This is the problem raised by worlds which we would not now choose for ourselves, but which would be satisfying to their inhabitants. To what extent does it count in favor of a certain kind of life that those who live it would not choose any alternative?

79

To ask this at all may seem to need some defense. There are good reasons for suspicion about questions so general and abstract. It may be said that the human race has problems enough in avoiding disasters such as nuclear war, famine, or other ecological catastrophes. And there are familiar objections to blueprints for a better world: to their narrowness, insensitivity, and tidiness, as well as to the small chance of plans being acted on.

But our preferences between kinds of life, and our thoughts about different kinds of society, are of more practical relevance than mere abstract utopias would be. Some of the pattern of our future life will emerge from the accumulated decisions of individuals and small groups. The future of the family is likely to be decided in this way. And what kind of people there will be depends a lot on our relationships with our children and our choices between different kinds of education. In the light of preferences between different kinds of life, usually not made explicit, we each make our contribution, and the result is one kind of world rather than another.

Other features of the future world depend on collective social decision or lack of it. Should we aim for an entirely industrialized world, hoping to overcome the apparent limits to our resources and to deal with pollution and other ecological problems? Or should we aim for a less industrial way of life and hope to adjust to lower material consumption? And, within any economic system, how should we decide between the claims of increased wealth and of more leisure? What advantages, if any, can outweigh an additional health hazard or the destruction of a river valley?

Anyone's thinking on these issues is bound to be incomplete. This is not only because of factual ignorance—because, say, we know so little about the effects of different kinds of child rearing or about the potential of solar energy. It is also because of the way such problems are interwoven. Industrial systems influence patterns of family life, and different kinds of family life produce different kinds of people to mold the social and economic system. Our view of these interlocking problems is bound to be inadequate, partly through ignorance and intellectual limitations and partly through limitations of sensitivity and imagination.

Debates over political or social policy are partly technological or economic, and partly about the kind of world we want. The economic and technological questions are about possibilities and hazards. Does a planned or a market economy produce more wealth? How far is economic planning compatible with workers' control of industry? What are the dangers of dumping radioactive waste into the sea? What untapped sources of food or energy are there? These questions are often difficult, but they can be discussed, and sometimes even solved, by familiar intellectual procedures. Partly for this reason, these debates often draw attention away from the underlying question, apparently less discussable, of what sort of world we want.

One way of discussing what sort of world we should aim for is to draw up detailed plans for a utopian society. The familiar objections should make us have doubts about the usefulness of this. Another way of discussing the question is to try to make clearer the kinds of values we have in mind when assessing a society. There is obviously no general consensus about these values, but to focus on these rather abstract questions of ultimate value can have other uses than that of leading to universal agreement. It can help to make clear what alternative sets of values there are, and so make people more conscious of the choices they are making. And discussion of these questions may also bring to light previously unnoticed problems.

## 1. The Aim of Satisfying People's Desires

A widely held view is that a society is better or worse to the extent that the desires of its members are satisfied or frustrated. Poverty is bad because people want the things money can buy. Freedom of speech is good because, among other reasons, people like to be able to speak their minds. To some people (supporters of one form of utilitariansim) the only adequate justification for any sort of policy decision is one which can be traced back ultimately to the satisfaction of desires. Others dissent, saying that there are other independent values, such as justice or the existence of certain admirable character traits. I do not want to discuss here the merits of having one ultimate value, or of having five, or thousands. I shall assume, without argument, that the utilitarian value of satisfying desires covers at least part of what we should aim for. (If you think that a tendency to let people have or do more of what they want is *in no way* a point in favor of a policy, I am not writing to you.)

A central problem arises from the fact that people's desires are to some extent alterable and that what makes a person happy depends partly on his history. Suppose we are wondering whether or not to support a policy of industrialization in a country lived in mainly by primitive tribal farmers. We may form the opinion that most of the people who live the tribal life would not choose to live in towns and work in factories. This may incline us to say that utilitarian considerations, as well as respect for their autonomy, count against the industrializing policy. But it may be argued on the other side that industrialization will provide resources for modern education and medicine, whose benefits the tribal people cannot now understand. It may be said that, when they have fully experienced the benefits, they will be glad of the change. Or, it may be claimed that, even if those whose outlook has been molded by tribal life will always hanker after it, their children will feel no regrets. The problem is this: Should we take the present pattern of people's desires and satisfactions as a datum and do our best to make the world fit that pattern? Or should we allow for the possibility that a different kind of world may prove even more satisfying to the different kind of person it produces?

Arguments of this sort, over the choice between peasant and urban life are, or should be, a serious problem for policymakers in many countries which are still mainly nonindustrial. But similar arguments can be found, for example, in Marxist discussions of "false consciousness." If most workers in some country do not want socialism, some theorists say that, all the same, they will be glad of it when they have it. If true, this parallels the case for industrializing the peasants. Or again, perhaps most of us now alive would not like Brave New World. But most of those living in Brave New World would not want to move to our present society. If people in Brave New World feel more satisfied with their lives than we do with ours, is this a case for aiming to produce such a society, however uncongenial we may think it? If we are choosing between policies which will lead to different kinds of world, this theoretical problem can sometimes be ignored. Where we have no means of estimating which world will be more satisfying to its inhabitants, or where any difference is too slight for our inevitably rough and ready estimates, we may as well choose the world we would prefer.

But suppose we have reason to think that, of all the worlds we could devise, one which we find unattractive (perhaps Brave New World) would contain people on the whole most satisfied with their lives? To this question there are both radical and conservative answers. The radical answer (not confined to those on the left of the conventional political spectrum) is that we ought to aim for the society in which people will be most satisfied. On this view, it is no more justifiable for our own preferences to set limits to this than it would be for our pattern of life to be limited by the outlook of people living in the Middle Ages. The conservative answer (not confined to people on the right of the conventional spectrum) is that society must be fitted to people as they are. This is held to be better than molding people to like a certain kind of society, even if such molding would lead to more satisfaction. Conservatives of this variety may quote with approval Kant's remark that out of the crooked timber of humanity no straight thing was ever made.

## 2. Problems of Method

To discuss the issue at all, certain debatable assumptions must be made. We must assume the possibility of a single person making rough estimates of the relative intensity of his different desires and satisfactions. We must also assume, contrary to the official view of many economic theorists, the possibility of making at least rough comparisons of intensity between the desires and satisfactions of different people. There are obviously real problems about these assumptions, but how crippling they are will depend on the extent to which we insist on certainty rather than plausibility. The severe skeptic who demands conclusive tests is debarred from choosing between any policies on grounds of their effects on people's welfare: He is unable to claim either that a policy makes people worse off, or that it is unjust. So, in making these admittedly debatable assumptions, we are in the company of nearly everyone who has social or political preferences.

There is, however, a special form of difficulty which arises when we are choosing between forms of society rather than between small-scale policies. The problems of making interpersonal comparisons, real enough within a single society, are magnified when we try to compare levels of satisfaction in different societies. When a happy family lives next door to a miserable one, doubts about interpersonal comparisons can seem a bit academic. But doubts about some supposed comparison between a Cambodian farmer and a German surgeon seem more real. I shall make the debatable assumption that, while this is a serious problem, it need not reduce us to complete skepticism about comparisons between life in one society and in another. Those not prepared to concede this will reject the terms of the discussion.

## 3. A Blurring of the Issue in Practice

The apparently clear-cut opposition between the radical and conservative views at the level of principle can become blurred at the level of practice. This is because, even for those who hold the radical view, the difficulties of comparing the satisfactions involved in different ways of life are a strong argument for caution about rapid social change. The insensitivity of much "social engineering" is apparent within a single community and is heightened when the "engineers" do not belong to the community being altered. Because of this insensitivity to present needs and preferences, we have good grounds for skepticism when some organizing person tries to persuade us to accept something we do not now want, on the basis that we will later be glad of it. Resistance to such a proposal may often stem from suspicion of the prediction rather than from the conservative view.

The fact that radicals and conservatives on the theoretical issue can often find themselves on the same side in practice does not eliminate their difference of principle, nor does it show that the difference is unimportant.

In thinking about the theoretical difference, it is helpful to distinguish between two ways in which the question can arise. The choice may be one within a single generation: How will the sudden introduction of tractors, medicines, television, and Coca Cola affect a certain island community now? Or the problem can be one between generations: How will our great-grandchildren like the crowded world resulting from our present breeding policies? There is some artificiality in this separation, as generations overlap with each other. But despite blurred boundaries, there are some differences in the values which might be flouted in the two cases.

## 4. The Problem within a Generation

What is the radical policy within a single generation? Sometimes the difficulties just mentioned will weigh so heavily that it will not differ from the conservative policy. But it is possible that these difficulties will be out-weighed by other considerations. Then the aim may be to create a society or kind of life which, although not one which we now find attractive, will so change our way of seeing things that we come to prefer it. Or the policy may be stated, more disturbingly, in terms not of "we" and "our way of seeing things," but of "they" and "their way of seeing things."

The idea that there could be such a policy may at first seem so far-fetched as to be not worth discussing. But it is not really. Consider first a parallel dilemma for a single person. Some people suffer from uncontrollable aggressive tendencies, which in extreme cases may mean spending most of life in institutions. Suppose such a person is offered brain surgery, which is likely to eliminate his aggressiveness but is also likely to cause much larger changes of personality. Perhaps he meets people who have had the same operation and does not much like the atmosphere they have in common. But they all say they are glad to have had the operation. The radical-conservative opposition in the individual case can be real. If it is objected that this case is too extreme because it involves mental disorder as the alternative to personal-ity change, consider the more moderate case of emigration. An unemployed Sicilian villager wonders whether to go to Germany as a factory worker to earn money. He does not like what he hears of life in Germany, but friends there say that they disliked the idea at first, but now they would never return to unemployment in Sicily. The radical-conservative tension is again a real one.

The problem as it faces a whole society can be like the emigration problem on a larger scale. The peasant community which goes through the industrialization process will have experienced a change a bit like that of the Sicilian who goes to Germany. There will be differences. They will experi-ence it together as a community. There will not be the loneliness of living abroad and the breaking up of families. But, for all the differences, the structure of the problem is the same.

The radical policy within a generation can be argued against by appeal-ing to considerations of autonomy and identity.

*Autonomy*

This objection does not apply when we opt for the radical policy applied to ourselves but can apply when "we" opt for a radical policy for "them." We, the urban politicians, opt for an industrial society where the peasants will become factory workers in towns. Or we, the colonial administration, decide to allow missionaries to propagate a new religion. Whether the radical policy involves an objectionable denial of autonomy depends on how much chance the community in question has of making an informed choice between the different ways of life, free from pressures. There may be nothing wrong with allowing in the missionaries so long as they only try to persuade by discussion as equals. But if they gain converts by emotional pressure, or because they are identified with the colonial power, we should feel doubts about how far autonomy has been respected. And this applies even if, as should happen with a successful radical policy, the converts are afterwards delighted to be brought to the true religion.

Since the radical policy involves opting for a way of life which does not now seem attractive to the people concerned, it seems likely that it will more often than not be imposed against their will—and so be open to criticism for failing to respect their autonomy.

Respecting people's autonomy is sometimes thought of as something good in itself. Or, alternatively, reasons are given in support of it. Sometimes these are utilitarian reasons, appealing to the depth and strength of the desire to be in control of one's own life and to the feelings of resentment and frustration caused by overriding someone's autonomy. Or the reasons may appeal to a belief in equality between people, which is flouted if I take the decisions about your life. (It may be this belief in equality which explains why we object more when the pattern of a person's life is determined by someone else's decisions than when it is equally determined by genetics or by "natural" environmental factors.)

*Identity*

A change in the pattern of someone's life drastic enough to alter his values can threaten his sense of identity. To many of us it is important to have some picture of our lives as a whole, to identify with the person we were, and to feel that the future pattern of our lives will be shaped partly by our present values and choices. The special horror of some kinds of brain damage is linked with the destruction of these continuities.

Where social changes also involve loss of autonomy, this is an additional threat to the sense of identity. Erving Goffman has put the matter well:

> Without something to belong to, we have no stable self, and yet total commitment and attachment to any social unit implies a kind of self-lessness. Our sense of being a person can come from being drawn into a wider social unit; our sense of selfhood can arise through the little ways in which we resist the pull. Our status is backed by the solid buildings of the world, while our sense of personal identity often resides in the cracks.[1]

This identity objection, like the one about autonomy, can be thought of as irreducible, with our sense of identity being seen as something of value in itself, regardless of our desires. Or the objection can be a utilitarian one, with our feelings of identity being important because we mind so much about them.

These objections, about autonomy and identity, will vary in theoretical importance, according to their status. Perhaps they are given weight for utilitarian reasons, or else are seen as independent values having trade-off relations with utilitarianism. On either of these interpretations, there will always be the *possibility* of these objections being outweighed by a sufficiently great gain in satisfaction. But it may be that some lexical ordering is introduced, such that no amount of satisfaction is allowed to compensate for the flouting of autonomy or for damage to the sense of identity. On this alternative interpretation, the objections are sufficient to destroy the radical policy whenever they arise.

## 5. The Problem between Generations

When we consider the radical and conservative views for different generations, the issue looks at first very similar to that within a single generation. Insofar as it is within our control, should we aim for our great-grandchildren having whatever kind of world would seem to its inhabitants most satisfying, or should we be guided by our own preferences?

But between generations there are some complications which should be mentioned first. One is the additional difficulty of making interpersonal comparisons on top of that which exists anyway between different societies. Comparing the life of the German surgeon with that of the Cambodian farmer's possible great-grandchild is obviously still further removed from the kind of comparison we feel happy with. I mention this very serious difficulty only to ignore it for the rest of the present discussion.

Another complication is our own desire to identify with our descendants, together with our desire that they should think well of us. For these reasons, we may feel great reluctance to aim for a society with radically different preferences and values from our own. (Though, if our descendants are pleased with the world we have left them, they may think well of us for having overcome our own prejudices in order to create it.) But even if the conservative policy would in general better satisfy these desires of ours, it is not obvious that we ought to count this as a very powerful reason in its favor.

It is striking that, in many intergenerational cases, the radical policy may not be open to the autonomy or identity objections. For there is no reason in the normal case why the policy should cause members of the future generation to experience any unwanted upheavals in their lives. The radical aim is likely to be for a world which the future generation will like from the start. The purest cases are provided by genetic engineering. If we use genetic engineering to produce a future population very different from us, but, as in Brave New World, very satisfied, this does not involve them experiencing any abrupt or unwanted changes. There seems no reason why the way they were produced should threaten their sense of identity. The only way either of the objections may apply is that perhaps *our* choosing *their* natures is in itself a violation of their autonomy. But one may question this view. Why does leaving people's natures to the genetic lottery leave autonomy intact, yet deliberate improvement violate it? What is the case for supporting interventionism in economics and politics but for having a policy of genetic laissez-faire?

The conservative at this point may wish to support his position by giving some account of autonomy that may answer this question. But the difficulties in such a program may make him reluctant to rest his whole position on the autonomy objection. And he is surely right that, for many people, there are other sources of unease about the radical policy. One source is a resistance to major alterations in human nature.

## 6. Conservatism and Human Nature

For many it is an assumption, so basic that it is hardly ever made explicit, that human nature has conditions in which it flourishes, and that these conditions should be created instead of human nature being adapted to fit those which now prevail. This is a pure form of conservatism about human nature, which makes no appeal to further values such as autonomy.

To evaluate a principle telling us always to mold the world to fit people in preference to molding people to fit the world, it is necessary to eliminate some related issues. For molding people to the world has traditionally been associated with exploitation. *We* mold *them* to fit into the sort of world we find convenient. Here "we" can be rulers, social classes, countries, or individuals. The history of groups exploiting each other gives rise to a justified suspicion of manipulators, and it may be that what looks like the pure conservative principle often turns out to be, at least in part, an objection to exploitation. So, to assess the pure conservative principle, it is necessary to consider changes in people's natures that are not brought about by some other group for their own advantage.

Equally, the pure conservative principle should be distinguished from the important practical considerations mentioned before, of the fallibility of predictions of the consequences of a policy, or of predictions of what people will find satisfying. (From a report a few years ago in *The Guardian:* ''Houses without windows were visualized yesterday as the trend of the future by Mr. Harry Hewitt, lighting development manager of British Lighting Industries. He told the British Electrical Power Convention, at Eastbourne: 'As people become used to higher levels of artificial lighting, they will the sooner be dissatisfied with natural light.' Mr. Hewitt added: 'Life would be simpler for lighting and heating engineers if there were no windows. Many people want windows and are not prepared to do without them. But it is not clear why they want them.' '') When this kind of thing raises doubts about some versions of the radical policy, the doubts are as likely to be based on a properly skeptical view of the predictions as on the pure conservative principle.

It is not clear how attractive is any residual conservatism, once distinguished from objections to exploitation and from doubts about whether people will really like a proposed future. We know that some features of our nature are modified by living in different kinds of society, or by having different kinds of education or job, or by marrying different kinds of people. And, on the whole, we are not very worried by these changes. The supporter of the pure conservative principle has to explain which parts of a person's nature are modifiable and which are to be left unchanged, and to give some reason for drawing the boundary where he does.

Among many possible boundaries the conservative might want to defend, two stand out as highly plausible candidates. One has to do with bodily integrity. Suppose an essential industrial process emits an unbearably disgusting smell and that eliminating this would involve enormous expense. The conservative might say that his principle would require that the smell be eliminated rather than the workers be paid to undergo an operation to destroy their sense of smell. When a person and his environment are maladapted, this form of conservatism calls for social or technological change rather than for physiological adjustments. Such a view harmonizes with the importance attached to the frontiers of the body in other contexts. (We tax people's income but not their blood. In civilized countries we cause criminals great suffering by prison sentences, but will not punish them by even the least bodily mutilation).

The other plausible boundary is that between altering a person's experience and altering his tastes and preferences. A defender of this boundary will say that we can alter a person's environment in order to make it more suited to his preferences, say, by having music played in a factory. He may even ignore the bodily boundary and say that we can use drugs which give people more interesting experiences while they work. But he will reject the use of drugs, hypnosis, or conditioning whose function is to make people take pleasure in the factory job they now find boring.

I have no way of refuting defenders of either of these boundaries, but each of them has difficulties which may make us reluctant to make their defense a matter of principle. The bodily boundary seems hard to defend, at least in cases where its breach is voluntarily accepted and where the results are prefered by the person in question. Cases of cosmetic surgery come to mind here. And, apart from any dangers involved, why is an eye operation, voluntarily undertaken, more open to objection than contact lenses? It may be replied that these are all cases of bringing someone up to normal functioning rather than of adapting normal people to a new or special environment. But this reply presupposes both that we can recognize normal functioning and that a different set of principles applies to cases of bringing people up to par from that which applies to cases of going above the norm. The first assumption works well enough in some cases: We are clear enough about the difference between normal vision and short sight. But is "normality" equally obvious when we are dealing with intellectual deficiencies or emotional disorders? And the second assumption seems in need of a lot of argument. If we can use drugs to make a depressed person normally cheerful, why can we not use drugs to make normal people more cheerful still?

The boundary between altering someone's experience and altering his tastes and preferences also involves difficulties. In the natural order of things, without any deliberate intervention by others, people's preferences change. This is true both of individuals and of societies. We do not think that anything has gone wrong if someone moves to a town he hates at first but then comes to like the place. So there is nothing sacrosanct about the particular preferences people have at a particular time. Why then should deliberate intervention to change people's preferences be wrong? If the intervention is voluntarily accepted, and cases of exploitation are excluded, it is hard to see what reasons could be produced here.

If the pure conservative principle is difficult to defend, does this mean that we have to accept the view that Brave New World is acceptable provided its inhabitants like it enough? The unease we feel here about having no criterion, other than amounts of pleasure or satisfaction, is the same unease that prompted Mill to put forward his much derided account of higher and lower pleasures. We may not like the snobbish associations of his terminology, and his criterion has defects. But it can be argued that his account, despite its weaknesses, makes a start toward giving us one of the additional criteria we need.

## 7. Mill's Test

Mill said that quality of pleasure could be distinguished from amount and proposed the following test:

> Of two pleasures, if there be one to which all or almost all who have experience of both give a decided preference, irrespective of any feeling of moral obligation to prefer it, that is the more desirable pleasure. If one of the two is, by those who are competently acquainted with both, placed so far above the other that they prefer it, even though knowing it to be attended with a greater amount of discontent, and would not resign it for any quantity of the other pleasure which their nature is capable of, we are justified in ascribing to the preferred enjoyment a superiority in quality, so far outweighing quantity as to render it, in comparison, of small account.[2]

There are obvious difficulties for this as an account of quality of pleasure. What are we to say if those who know the pleasures of reading both *The Critique of Pure Reason* and detective stories all agree that the pleasures of Kant are of superior quality but all often choose to read a detective story where both are available?

But let us forget the question of quality of pleasures and consider Mill's test as a method of choosing between ways of life or different kinds of world. In deciding between policies favoring the preservation of a traditional tribal life and policies favoring industrialization and urbanization, can we use Mill's test? Complete dismissal of Mill's test involves saying that the opinions of those who have made the transition from tribal to city life are irrelevant to the issue, which is scarcely plausible. Their preferences are surely evidence of a relevant kind, although along a different dimension from that having to do with the degree of contentment of those who have not made the transition.

But the preferences of those who have experienced both ways of life have to be interpreted with great caution. For there are irrelevant biases which may operate. Mill was aware of one when he excluded "any feeling of moral obligation to prefer it." But there can be more subtle biases, having to do with snobbery, not wanting to be old-fashioned, and other pressures toward conformity which may equally bias a person's claim about his preferences, and even bias his preferences themselves. There are also different kinds of time bias—a tendency to prefer what is now being experienced or else nostalgia.

The idealized form of Mill's test would be one where all such biases were eliminated. In practice this is scarcely likely to be possible. There are ways of detecting biases of conformity and these can be allowed for, although disagreements about the degree of bias to allow for may be hard to resolve. And the time biases could in principle be eliminated by requiring the preference between societies to be constant regardless of which society the person was in at the time, and regardless of which society he had experienced first. But again in practice the difficulties of ensuring that these conditions were met, without the introduction of yet other biases, would be very great. There is the further question of what degree of consensus would be required to justify calling one society better than the other. It seems too stringent to require complete unanimity, but far too weak to require only a bare majority.

The consensus problem shows the implausibility of supposing that Mill's test will or should generate an all-or-none answer. It is quite arbitrary to stipulate some required percentage of those who have experienced both societies, say 82 percent, who must prefer one for it to be superior. On a more flexible interpretation, the case of opting for one society rather than another is stronger to the extent that more of those who have experienced both prefer one of them, and to the extent that irrelevant biases seem to have been satisfactorily discounted. There will be few all-or-none answers to be had in applying Mill's test. But in judging human societies, it may not be surprising that evidence has to be given the kind of informal assessment characteristic of the historian rather than the yes-no decisions required by the opinion pollster.

## 8. Some Suggested Conclusions

The slightly grand question of this paper was how we should decide what sort of world is best. This was narrowed down to one of its aspects: How far does it count in favor of a certain kind of life that those who live it would not choose any alternative? Even this narrower question is of such complexity that the outlines of an answer can only be gestured at in a brief paper.

The thought of Brave New World may make us reluctant to allow that the fact that the inhabitants of a society would not opt for anything else is an adequate test of whether it is a good society or one we should aim for. The requirement of a reasonable degree of satisfaction seems only one among a number of relevant considerations.

One line of thought which has plausibility is to adopt a kind of conservatism setting limits to the ways in which states of satisfaction are brought about. This approach has not been discredited here, but some difficulties in *some* versions of it have been suggested. If these difficulties cannot be surmounted, and if they apply more generally, we should perhaps look for alternative principles to the conservative ones.

The suggestion made here is that one reason (apart from inequalities and possible lack of autonomy) why we are reluctant to regard the testimony of the inhabitants of Brave New World as conclusive is that they have not experienced alternatives. A tightened-up version of Mill's test may show the sort of question that is relevant here. There is no suggestion that this is the only further question to be considered—trying to answer even this one leaves us with problems enough.

## NOTES

1. Erving Goffman, *Asylums* (Chicago: Aldine, 1961), p. 320.
2. J. S. Mill, *Utilitarianism,* ch. 2.

# The Environment, Rights, and Future Generations

## RICHARD T. De GEORGE

THE RAPID GROWTH OF TECHNOLOGY HAS OUTSTRIPPED OUR MORAL intuitions, which are consequently unclear and contradictory on many environmental issues. As we try to handle new moral problems we stretch and strain traditional moral concepts and theories. We do not always do so successfully. The difficulties, I believe, become apparent as we attempt to deal with the moral dimension of the depletion of nonrenewable resources.

Consider the use of oil, presently our chief source of energy. The supply of oil is limited. Prudence demands that we not waste it. But who has a right to the oil or to its use? From one point of view the owners of the oil have a right to it. And we each have a right to the amount we are able to buy and use. From another point of view everyone has a right to oil, since it is a natural resource which should be used for the good of all. Americans, as we know, use a great deal more oil than most other people in the world. Is it moral of us to do so? Will our use preclude people in other parts of the world from having it available to them when they will need it for uses we presently take for granted? Will some unborn generations not have the oil they will probably need to live as we presently do?

These questions trouble many people. They have a vague sense of moral uneasiness, but their intuitions concerning the proper answers are not clear. They feel that they should not waste oil or fuel or energy. They feel that they should not keep their houses as cool in summer and as warm in winter as they used to. They feel that they should impose these conditions on their children. Yet they are not, simply on moral grounds, ready to give up too much in the way of comfort. Once forced to do so by economics, they will. But they are somewhat uneasy about their own attitude. Is it morally proper that affluent individuals or nations are able to live in greater comfort and will have to make fewer sacrifices than the less well-to-do, simply because they have more money?

93

My intuitions on the issue of energy and oil are in no way privileged. I do not know how much oil or energy I have a right to; nor can I say with any certainty how much those in underdeveloped countries presently have a right to, or how much should be saved for them, or how much should be saved for generations yet to come. Nor do I know clearly how to weigh the claims to oil of the people in underdeveloped countries vis-à-vis the future claims to oil of generations yet unborn. If all presently existing members of the human race used energy at the rate that the average American does, there would obviously be much less left for future generations. Does this mean that others in the world should not use as much oil as Americans; or that Americans should use less, so that those in other countries will be able to use more; or that people in less developed countries should not use more in order that future generations of Americans will be able to use as much as present-day Americans?

Though our intuitions are not very clear on these issues, there is some consensus that present people have moral obligations vis-à-vis future generations. Yet stating the grounds for even these obligations is not an easy task and it is one that I do not think has been adequately accomplished. The attempt to state them in terms of rights has not been fruitful. And the utilitarian or consequentialist approach has fared no better. Lack of clarity about collective responsibility further magnifies the complexity of the problem.

In this paper I shall not be able to solve the question either of the proper use of oil or of the basis of our obligations to future generations. I shall attempt only to test the ability of some moral theories and language to express them adequately. I shall negatively show why some approaches are not fruitful lines to pursue. And positively I shall argue for some considerations which I think are applicable, though by themselves they are not adequate to solve the moral problems at issue.

Talk about rights has proliferated in recent years.[1] Moral feelings and concerns have been put in terms of rights in a great many areas. It does not fit in some of them. Thus for instance some people concerned with the environment have come to speak of the rights of nature, or the rights of trees, or the rights of a landscape.[2] The intent of people who use such language is easy enough to grasp. They are concerned about man's abuse of the environment, his wanton cutting of trees, or his despoiling the countryside. But those who wish to attribute rights to nature or trees or landscapes must come up with some way of interpreting the meaning of rights which makes their assertions plausible. The usual ways of unpacking rights in terms of justifiable moral claims, or in terms of interests, or in terms of freedom do not apply to nature or trees.[3] Yet failure to provide an interpretation which both grounds the purported rights of trees and relates them to the rights of humans, while accounting for the obvious differences between them, leads to confusion and precludes arriving at a satisfactory solution to the moral problems posed.

These attempts are nonetheless instructive. For rights can be ascribed and rights-talk can be used with respect to almost anything,[4] even if the claims involved cannot always be adequately defended. When we restrict our use of rights-talk to human beings, therefore, it should be clear that the question of whether people have rights is not a factual one comparable to the question of whether they have brains, or whether they usually have two arms or two legs. The question of whether future generations have rights is similarly not one simply of fact; and the answer is compounded because there is no consensus and little precedent. Thus simply looking at ordinary language, or simply unpacking the concepts of person or rights, will not yield a definitive answer. Since the question is not a factual one, it is to be solved in part by making a decision. It is possible to say that future generations have rights. But I shall argue that we avoid more problems if we maintain that, properly speaking, future generations do not presently have rights, than if we say they do.

Future generations by definition do not now exist. They cannot now, therefore, be the present bearer or subject of anything, including rights. Hence they cannot be said to have rights in the same sense that presently existing entities can be said to have them. This follows from the briefest analysis of the present tense form of the verb 'to have'. To claim that what does not now exist cannot now have rights in any strong sense does not deny that persons who previously existed had rights when they existed, or that persons who will exist can properly be said to have rights when they do exist, or that classes with at least one presently existing member can correctly be said to have rights now. Nor does it deny that presently existing persons can and sometimes do make rights claims for past or future persons. It emphasizes, however, that in ascribing rights to persons who do not exist it is the existing person who is expressing his interests or concerns.

Those who claim that present existence is not necessary for the proper ascription of present rights sometimes cite the legal treatment of wills as a counterexample. In this instance, they argue, the courts act as if the deceased continued to have rights, despite the fact that he no longer exists. But this is not the only way of construing wills or the actions of courts. If we consider those countries in which inheritance laws were suddenly changed so that all the property of a deceased went to the state rather than to the heirs named in a will, it would be more plausible to argue that the rights of a particular heir were violated rather than the rights of the deceased. Equally plausible construals can, I believe, be made for each of the other standard supposed counterexamples.[5]

Consider next the supposed present rights of some future individual. Before conception potential parents can and should take into account the obligations they will have in connection with caring for the children they might produce. They can and should consider the rights their children will have if they come into being. But since the children do not yet exist, we should properly say they do not now have rights. Among the rights they do not have (since they have none) is the right to come into existence. By not bringing them into existence we do not violate *that* right, and we can obviously prevent their having any other rights. Now if we attempt to speak otherwise, I suggest, we invite confusion. What sense would it make to say that some entity which was not conceived had a right to be conceived? We cannot sensibly or intelligibly answer the question of whose right was infringed when there is no bearer of the right.

A similar difficulty, and therefore a similar reason for not using rights-talk, arises in speaking of the rights of future generations, providing we mean by that term some generation no members of which have presently been conceived and so in no sense presently exist. Such future generations could at least in theory be prevented from coming into existence. If they were never produced it would be odd to say that their rights had been violated. For since they do not now exist they can have no right to exist or to be produced. Now, they have no present rights at all.

Nonetheless possible future entities can be said to have possible future rights. And future generations when they exist will have rights at that time. But the temptation to consider all rights as temporally on a par should be resisted. Moreover, the weight which should now be given to the rights claims which future individuals or future generations will have should be proportional to the likelihood that such individuals will exist, and by analogy with the case of parents the obligations should be borne by those individuals (and collectively by those groups) most responsible for bringing the individuals into existence.

Future persons do not, individually or as a class, presently have the right to existing resources. They differ from presently existing persons who in general have the right to the judicious use of the goods necessary for them to continue in existence. And if some of these goods, because of present rational demands, are used up, then it is a mistake to say that future persons or future generations have or will have a right to *those* goods and that we violate their rights by using them up. Future generations or future individuals or groups should correctly be said to have a right only to what is available when they come into existence, and hence when their possible future rights become actual and present.

Many people feel that this is incorrect and that future persons and generations have as much right as presently existing persons to what presently exists, for example, in the way of resources. A few considerations, however, should suffice to show that such a view is mistaken. The first consideration is conceptual. Only once a being exists does *it* have needs or wants or interests. It has a right only to the kind of treatment or to the goods available to it at the time of its conception. It cannot have a reasonable claim to what is not available. Consider this on an individual level. Suppose a couple are so constituted that if they have a child, the child will have some disease, for example, sickle-cell anemia. Suppose the woman conceives. Does the fetus or baby have a right not to have sickle-cell anemia? Before it was conceived there was no entity to have any rights. Once it is conceived, its genetic make-up is such as it is. It makes no sense to speak of *its* having the right not to have the genetic make-up it has, since the alternative is its not being. This does not mean that it does not have the right to treatment, that if genetic engineering is able to remedy its defect it does not have the right to such remedy, and so on. But it does mean that there is no *it* to have rights before conception, and that once conceived it is the way it is. There is therefore no sense in speaking of the antecedent right for it not to be the way it is, though it may have a subsequent right to treatment. Similarly, prehistoric cave men had no right to electric lights or artificial lungs since they were not available in their times, and we have no right to enjoy the sight of extinct animals. To claim a right to what is not available and cannot be made available is to speak vacuously. Some future people, therefore, will have no right to the use of gas, or oil, or coal, if, when they come into existence, such goods no longer exist. If the goods in question are not available, *they* could not be produced with a right to them.

Second, suppose we attempt to speak otherwise. Suppose we assume that all future generations have the same right to oil as we do; and suppose that since it is a nonrenewable resource, it is used up—as it is likely to be—by some future generation. What of the next generation that follows it? Should we say that since that generation cannot be produced without violating its right to oil it has a right not to be produced? Surely not. Or should we say that if it is produced one of its rights is necessarily infringed, and that the right of all succeeding generations will similarly necessarily be infringed? It is possible to speak that way; but to do so is at least confusing and at worst undermines the whole concept of rights by making rights claims vacuous.

The third reason for not speaking of the rights of future generations as if their rights were present rights is that it leads to impossible demands on us. Suppose we consider oil once again. It is a nonrenewable resource and is limited in quantity. How many generations in the future are we to allow to have present claim to it? Obviously if we push the generations into the unlimited future and divide the oil deposits by the number of people, we each end up with the right to a gallon or a quart or a teaspoon or a thimble full. So we must reconstrue the claim to refer to the practical use of oil. But this means that we inevitably preclude some future generation from having oil. And if all future generations have equal claim, then we necessarily violate the rights of some future generations. It is clear, then, that we do not wish to let unending future claims have equal weight with present claims. The alternative, if we do not consistently treat future rights differently from the rights of presently existing persons, is arbitrarily to treat some rights, those of sufficiently distant generations, as less deserving of consideration than the same claims of generations closer to us. What I have been arguing is that our approach turns out to be less arbitrary and more consistent if we refuse to take even the first step in considering future rights as anything other than future, and if we do not confuse them or equate them with the rights of presently existing people.

To ascribe present rights to future generations is to fall into the trap of being improperly motivated to sacrifice the present to the future, on the grounds that there will possibly (or probably) be so innumerably many future generations, each of which has a presently equal right to what is now available, as to dwarf the rights of present people to existing goods. The trap can be avoided by maintaining that present existence is a necessary condition for the possession of a present right. To the extent that rights-talk tends to be non-temporal and future generations are considered to have present rights, such talk tends to confuse rather than clarify our obligations for the future, and the ground for such obligations. For this and similar reasons future generations should not be said to have present rights.

If the argument so far is correct, however, we have not solved a problem, but merely seen how not to approach it if we want a solution. That future generations do not have present rights does not mean that present people, individually and collectively, have no obligations to try to provide certain kinds of environment and to leave open as many possibilities as feasible for those who will probably come after them, consistent with satisfying their own rational needs and wants. How are we to describe this felt moral imperative?

If the language of rights will not do, a theory such as utilitarianism does not fare much better. Consider once again the problem of how much oil we can legitimately use and how much we are morally obliged to save for future generations. Let every person count for one and let us decide on the basis of what produces the greatest good for the greatest number of people. The task is difficult enough in dealing with micro-moral problems, though we have the history of human experience to help us solve with at least a certain amount of assurance many ordinary moral questions. We can be fairly sure that lying in general is wrong, as is murder, and theft, and perjury, and so on.

When we try to carry out the analysis with respect to nonrenewable resources, the question of how many future generations we are to count is one problem. We have already seen the difficulties it leads to. Second, we cannot know how long people will actually need oil. We cannot know when a substitute will be found. We therefore do not know how many generations to count and how many to discount. Third, generations of people lived long before oil was discovered and put to its present uses. As oil becomes less available, if no substitute is found people may have to go back to doing things the way they did before the discovery of oil. Will such a world be morally poorer than ours? On a utilitarian calculation the answer may well be negative. But we can plausibly argue that good is not maximized if we waste our resources, and that more good will probably be done for more people if we stretch out our resources while providing for our own rational needs. The difficulty of course, consists in specifying our rational and justifiable needs. Utilitarianism does not help us do this, nor does it help us decide between the somewhat greater good (however defined) or presently existing people versus the lesser good of more people in the future when the totals are equal. Therefore this approach, too, does not provide the key for determining the proper use of our nonrenewable resources.

There is another dimension to the problem, however, which I have ignored thus far and which it would be well to consider at least briefly. With respect to the use of oil and future generations I have spoken of "we" and "they" and have traded on our common understanding of the terms. Moral obligation and responsibility, however, have for the most part been discussed in individual terms. The notion of collective responsibility and collective obligation and other collectively applied moral terms are in need of clarification. The concept of collective responsibility, for instance, despite some of the work that has been done on it,[6] remains in many cases obscure.

One difficulty arises in attempting to allocate individual responsibility under conditions in which individual effort has no real effect by itself. Who is responsible for preserving the environment for our children and grandchildren? The answer may be all of us. But what is required of each of us individually is far from clear. How responsible for strip mining is a carpenter in New York City? How responsible for oil depletion is someone who drives to work in a car? Is he morally obliged to drive less or not at all or to buy and use a smaller car? What if smaller cars are not available or if he cannot afford to buy one or if none of his neighbors drive less or buy smaller cars? Is the collective responsibility to fall primarily on collective agencies—on corporations and government? But this collective responsibility must also be allocated to individuals. Does each person have a responsibility to preserve resources no matter what others do? Or is it a prima facie obligation which becomes a real obligation only when our action and the action of others will effect the results desired? Are we therefore individually freed of our responsibility when others do not do their share? Does collective failure to fulfill a collective moral obligation absolve an individual of his individual obligation to do what he should under the collective obligation on the grounds that his sacrifice without that of the others is inefficacious? My claim is not that these questions do not have answers but that they have not been sufficiently discussed and that until we get clear about the answers we are unlikely to feel the pressure of the moral obligations we may have or to be able to weigh them against the individual moral pressures we feel with respect, for instance, to supplying our children or our fellow citizens with as high a quality of life as we can.

Consider further the questions of resources in the light of populations. If the population of one country grows unchecked to the detriment of the people of that country and to the exhaustion of that country's resources, do the people of other countries have the obligation to keep alive the individuals produced by parents who had no regard for whether the children could be supported? Who is the "we" who should preserve resources, and for whom should they be preserved? If the people of one nation sacrifice, should it be the heirs of that nation's people who reap the rewards of such sacrifice, or should it be all people wherever they might be and whoever they are? On the one hand our intuitions tell us that no country can do everything for the whole world, that people have to help themselves, and that each country's primary responsibility is to its own people and their descendents. On the other hand we have the unrelieved plight of human misery and death, some of which could be al- leviated if some peoples would share more of what they have. By what right do some use many times more in the way of natural resources than others, especially when it is not by merit but partially by luck that they have natural riches available to them that are not available in their own countries to other people?

I mentioned earlier that our moral intuitions were still inadequate to some of the moral problems which seem to be looming before us. Part of the reason is that we have no precedent on which to build. Another is that we have no adequate institutions and practices on a global scale with which to relate global moral problems. Morality is a social institution and moral obligations are often closely tied to particular social practices. The moral obligations of parents with respect to their children, for instance, are different in a society with a nuclear family in which parents have almost exclusive responsibility for the support and care of their children, and in a society in which all children are raised by the state, cared for in communal nurseries, state schools, and so on. Moral problems about the use of resources and the preservation of the environment transcend national boundaries. Yet we have no world institutions or practices adequate to help ground pertinent moral judgments.

National sovereignty may be an anachronism in an age of such inter- dependence. But while it remains it sets a real limit to certain kinds of moral obligations richer nations have to poorer ones. Within the boundaries of a given country transfer payments can be effected in a variety of ways and are justified within the system because they achieve their goals. Within the sys- tem one practice fits together with others. But on the global scale there is no system, there is little in the way of enforceable law, there is great diversity of political systems, and there is disagreement about moral claims. Transfer payments from rich to poor within a nation can be handled, as in the United States, through taxes agreed to by the legislature representing the people. Internationally there is no such system. The extrapolation from individual moral cases to parallel national or collective cases consequently frequently falters.

If my analysis so far is correct the new large moral questions which are impinging upon us cannot be solved all at once. It may be that the most we can do individually—and where possible collectively—is to work on clarifying the problems, to suggest solutions, to impel others to work toward them, to be willing to cooperate in transcending national boundaries, to give up national sovereignty, and so on.

I have been arguing that environmental problems have developed faster than our intuitions, theories, practices, and institutions, and that some attempts to stretch our theories to fit our vague intuitions have not been successful. Yet I do not wish to imply that we are at a total loss from a moral point of view with respect to environmental problems or that they are ultimately unsolvable. I shall briefly argue three points, the first of which, I believe, is relatively uncontroversial and requires little defense.

Consider a couple planning to have a baby. Before they conceive him they have an obligation to be reasonably sure that they can raise him properly, that he will have enough to eat, and that he will under ordinary circumstances have the opportunity to grow and develop. Parents who knowingly and willingly have children whom they know they and their society cannot care for, who they know will soon die of starvation or disease, do not, if my earlier analysis is correct, violate any purported antecedent rights of the child. But they certainly seem to produce suffering and misery which they could have avoided producing. We can plausibly argue that we individually have an obligation to provide the minimum goods of life necessary for those for whom we have a rather close responsibility. And collectively we have a similar responsibility for preserving the environment in such a way that it can provide the goods necessary for those who come after us—or for roughly fifty or a hundred years. To be uncontroversial, however, the claim must be restricted to those for whom we have a rather close responsibility. For the obligation of care is tied to the causal chain of reproduction. If the population of one country goes unchecked to the detriment of the people of that country, it is not clear that other countries have the obligation to keep alive the individuals so produced. It may be that richer countries have some obligations in this regard. But it is clear that the obligation of the members of a society to care for their own people is greater than the obligation to care for people of other societies.

My two other claims are more controversial and may seem to some mistaken; hence they deserve more comment. The first is that we do not owe to others, either outside our society or to those who will come after us, what we need to maintain a reasonable quality of life and dignity for the present members of our society; the second is that we do not owe others, either in other societies or those who will come after us, a better life than we ourselves are able to attain and enjoy. Present sacrifice for a better future for others may be a noble, altruistic goal. But it is not morally demanded and cannot be legitimately forced on those who do not wish to be noble, altruistic, or heroic.

Moral theorists have long argued that each human being, if the resources are available, deserves enough of the goods of life so that he can enjoy at least a minimal standard of living required for human dignity. My claim is consistent with that view. It allows room for the moral obligation of those who are well off to help bring those below the minimal standard of dignity up to that standard. How that is to be done within our own society is easier to determine than how that is to be effectively achieved on a global scale. But my claim denies that any generation or people have to fall below that level in order to help others rise above it. The argument for that is fairly straightforward.

Starting from the equality of all persons qua persons my good for me is as valuable as your good for you. Other things being equal your good is not better or more important than mine. Hence, again other things being equal, there is no reason why, given a choice, I should be morally obliged to choose your good over mine. Otherwise, by like reasoning you would have to choose my good over yours. Secondly, my claim is that other things being equal those who, where it is possible to avoid it, bring misery on themselves or on those close to them, are the ones who should bear the brunt of consequences of their actions. This is part of what it means to accept the moral responsibility for one's actions. Hence there are limits to the sacrifice which can be morally required of one people to help those less well off than they. One limit is that equality is not required; what is required is simply helping those below the minimal standard to rise up to it. Another limit is that those who are aided can legitimately be expected, as a condition of such aid, to take the means available to them to help themselves.

My second more controversial claim was that there is no moral imperative that requires each generation to sacrifice so that the next generation may be better off than it is. Parents do not owe their children better lives than they had. They may wish their children to have better lives; but they do not owe it to them. If there is to be a peak followed by a decline in the standard of living, and if such a peak is tied to the use of natural resources, then providing there is no profligate waste, there is no reason why the present rather than a future generation should enjoy that peak. For no greater good is served by any future group enjoying the peak, since when its turn comes, if enjoying the peak is improper for us, it will be improper for them also.

We do not owe future generations a better life than we enjoy nor do we owe them resources we need for ourselves. When dealing with renewable resources, other things being equal, they should not be used up faster than they can be replaced. When they are needed at a greater rate than they can be replaced, they raise the same problem raised by nonrenewable resources. We should use what we *need*, but we should keep our needs rational, avoid waste, and preserve the environment as best we can. How this is to be translated into the specific allocation of goods and resources is not to be determined a priori or by the fiat of government but by as many members of the society at large who are interested and aware and informed enough to help in the decision-making process. Part of that process must involve clarifying the moral dimensions of the use of resources and developing the moral theory to help us state consistently and evaluate our moral intuitions.

Up until relatively recent times it may have seemed that each generation was better off than the previous one, and that just as each successive generation had received a better lot than its predecessor, it had an obligation to continue the process. But we are now at the stage where our own efforts are frequently counterproductive. Our progress in transportation has led to pollution; our progress in pest control has led to new strains of insects resistant to our chemicals or has resulted in pollution of our food; our expansion of industry has taken its toll in our rivers and in the ocean; and so on. We are now faced with shortages of the type we used to experience only during war times. So we can argue that in some ways we are already over the peak and will all be forced to cut down on certain kinds of consumption. That our children have to bear our fate is no reason for reproach. What would be reprehensible on the individual level is if we lived in luxury and allowed our children to exist at a subsistence level. It is appropriate that we help them to live as well as we, where that is possible. But we have no responsibility for helping them live better at great expense to ourselves. Nor does it make much sense to speak in those terms where overlapping generations are concerned.

What I have been maintaining is that we should be careful not to assume the burden of the future on some mistaken notion of the need to sacrifice the present to the future. The past appeal of the call to sacrifice the present to the future depended on the foreseeable future being increasingly better, and each generation both being better off than the previous one and worse off than the following in an unending chain. The realization that the goods of the earth are limited should mitigate somewhat that appeal. The earth will not in the foreseeable future be able to support limitless numbers of human beings at a high standard of living.

There is one last caveat that I should like to add, however. I have been arguing that we do not owe the future more than we have in the way of goods of the earth or in terms of standard of living. This does not mean that we do not owe them the benefit of what we have learned, that we should not preserve and pass on culture, knowledge, moral values—all increased to the extent possible. For standard of living is not the only good in life and quality of life should not be confused with quantity of goods. In fact, if we do soon suffer a decline in our standard of living either voluntarily by freely sacrificing for others or simply because we use up our resources before we find adequate substitutes, then what we should pass on to our children are the qualities of mind and spirit which will help them to cope with what they have, to live as fully as possible with what is available, and to value the quality of life rather than the quantity of goods they have.

My three claims are not a solution to the problems of limited resources or a full analysis of what we owe to future generations. They are a start which needs a fuller theory to ground it and a set of institutions to work within. But they do not constitute a call to selfishness. Enlightened self-interest may well benefit mankind as a whole more than unenlightened self-sacrifice, even if the latter could be sold to large segments of the world's population. For we have come to a point where, if we limit our use and abuse of the environment, it is in our self-interest to do so. The needs of the present and of already existing generations should take precedence over consideration of the needs of those who may exist at some far distant time. Perhaps all we can expect is that each generation look that far ahead.

The moral issues raised by environmental questions are in some ways truly new and test both our moral intuitions and concepts. Not all our moral values and intuitions are inapplicable. But we have much analytic work to do before we can fully and clearly state—much less solve—some of the problems which face us.

## NOTES

1. See Rex Martin and James W. Nickel, "A Bibliography on the Nature and Foundations of Rights 1947-1977," *Political Theory* (forthcoming).

2. See, for example, Aldo Leopold, *A Sand Country Almanac and Sketches Here and There* (New York: Oxford University Press, 1949); Christopher Stone, *Should Trees Have Standing?: Toward Legal Rights for Natural Objects* (Los Altos, Ca.: Kaufmann, 1974).

3. H. L. A. Hart, "Are There Any Natural Rights?," *Philosophical Review* 64 (1955): 175-91 argues that the natural right of men to be free is basic; Joel Feinberg, "Duties, Rights and Claims," *American Philosophical Quarterly* 3 (1966): 137-44; David Lyons "The Correlativity of Rights and Duties," *Nous* 4 (1970): 45-57.

4. H. J. McCloskey, "Rights," *Philosophical Quarterly* 15 (1965): 115-27, raises the question of whether art objects can have rights. A number of philosophers have recently argued for the rights of animals: Andrew Linzey, *Animal Rights* (Lon-

don: S. C. M. Press, 1976); Peter Singer, *Animal Liberation* (London: Jonathan Cape, 1976); on the other hand, see Joseph Margolis, "Animals Have No Rights and Are Not Equal to Humans," *Philosophic Exchange* 1 (1974): 119-23. See also M. and N. Golding, "Value Issues in Landmark Preservation," this volume.

5. Joel Feinberg, "The Rights of Animals and Unborn Generations," *Philosophy and Environmental Crisis,* ed. William T. Blackstone (Athens: University of Georgia Press, 1974), pp. 43-68, defends the opposite view.

6. See Peter A. French, ed., *Individual and Collective Responsibility: Massacre at My Lai* (Cambridge, Mass.: Schenkman 1972); Joel Feinberg, "Collective Responsibility," *Journal of Philosophy* 45 (1968): 674-87; W. H. Walsh, "Pride, Shame and Responsibility," *The Philosophical Quarterly* 20 (1970): 1-13; D. E. Cooper, "Collective Responsibility" *Philosophy* 43 (1968): 258-68.

# Technology Assessment, Human Good, and Freedom

## R. COBURN

TECHNOLOGICAL DEVELOPMENTS IN RECENT YEARS, AS EVERYONE IS aware, have given rise to a number of extraordinarily difficult policy issues. Some of the more obvious cases in point include: thermonuclear weapons, supersonic aircraft, nuclear reactors, kidney machines, space-exploration technology, and computers. Moreover, the literature on artificial intelligence, biomedical engineering, the fast breeder, and possible new weapons systems suggests that future developments may well issue in even more difficult social decision problems. These facts lie behind the growth of the new discipline called "technology assessment," which is concerned with increasing the likelihood of optimal policy decisions as regards technologies with potentially significant social and environmental impacts. More specifically, it embraces—anyhow when broadly defined[1]—three somewhat overlapping tasks: (1) determining the probable environmental and social impacts of the development and diffusion of given technologies, (2) evaluating the options available in the light of these probable impacts, and (3) defining the optimal process for selecting among the options open to us.

It takes little reflection to see that technology assessment so understood is an enterprise that involves many normative issues. Defining the optimal process for selecting among the technological options open to us involves, inter alia, deciding how important we regard democratic decision making as regards issues of major social importance, and in particular deciding what costs we are willing to bear in order to ensure that we come as close as possible to the (or some) democratic ideal vis-à-vis decisions concerning technological developments. Evaluating such options obviously requires decisions, for example, about the weights that should be given to such diverse matters as the preservation of highly developed sea. mammals, the community-disruptive effects of increased mobility of large segments of the society, the time-intensive values like friendship which increased leisure makes easier to cultivate, the absence of a need for armed policemen, and "the usually unconscious, but often intense, pleasure that the movement and vitality within a familiar street gives."[2] Then, too, there is the not insignificant matter of how we should handle the obvious fact that "a comprehensive theory of history is as illusory as the ideal of Laplace's determinism in physics, [that] we simply cannot possibly foresee all the consequences of adopting a particular innovation, or not adopting it, for that matter."[3] Indeed, even the process of determining the probable environmental and social impacts of the development and diffusion of given technologies cannot be carried out without the ineluctable intrusion of value judgments. For how can this determination be made independently of decisions, for example, concerning what is worth counting as a significant impact and when the process of tracing consequences, possible synergistic developments, etc., has been carried far enough given the costs in time and resources of further investigation?

The fact that technology assessment has normative aspects does not entail that the role reason can play in this discipline is limited to issues that concern straightforward matters of empirical fact. Indeed, it seems to me an open question at this stage in the history of thought whether there is *any* significant difference at all between the "factual" and the "normative" disciplines as regards the power of reason to generate intersubjective agreement. But however that may be, it is clear, I think, that many of the normative issues that the discipline of technology assessment engenders can be illumined if not resolved by careful reflection, and the present paper is intended to be a contribution of this kind. It will focus primarily on the second task distinguished above, namely, the task of evaluating policy options made available by technology, given a reasonable understanding of the important environmental and social impacts these various options involve. In the first part of the paper, I shall present some considerations designed to show that a certain family of approaches to the problem of how best to evaluate such options is unsatisfactory; in the second part, I shall sketch and defend an alternative approach which derives primarily from a thesis about the place of freedom—broadly conceived—in an ideal social order.

# I

Suppose you are entrusted with the power to decide whether or not a given society should develop a certain technological capability—for example, an effective, cheap, long-lasting, but reversible contraceptive pill for males, or a system for controlling the weather, or video telephones, or improved mood-control or memory-enhancing drugs. Suppose further that you have on your desk a well-funded, responsible, painstaking study of the probable environmental and social impacts that would result from development of the capability in question. How should you proceed in order to arrive at the best (wisest, most reasonable) decision?

One answer which might seem attractive at first blush is the following. You should try to estimate the costs and the benefits that attach to both of the options—the option to develop and the option *not* to develop the cabability in question—and then you should pick that option which maximizes net benefits or, if these are negative for both options, minimizes net costs. Without further elaboration, this answer is unclear in important respects, of course. But even in this sketchy form, it is easy to see certain of the attractions of the approach it involves relatively to several analogous ones. It is superior, for example, to the approach which requires that we pick from among the options open to us the one which makes everybody better off, for of course, as regards at least many (and perhaps the vast majority) of the decisions we shall ever face of the sort under consideration, there just is no option which satisfies this condition. It is also superior to the approach which requires that we choose the option which yields a "Pareto improvement" over the status quo ante, i.e., the option whose consequences will make at least one member of the society better off and nobody worse off, for the same reason. After all, technological developments always entail costs; these inevitably fall on somebody's (or some group's) shoulders, and unless the benefits are significant and quite evenly spread, it seems likely in many cases that the costs some will bear will not outweigh the benefits, if any, which accrue to them from the development in question. Moreover, it is plausible to assume that the option of not developing the technology in question will in at least many cases make some worse off than they were in the status quo ante or not better off. Furthermore, the approach mentioned seems on the face of it quite reasonable. How else, it might be asked, should we decide these issues if not by appeal to the costs and the benefits of going one way rather than another? And if these are the things we should be concerned about, then reason surely requires that we maximize our net gains—or lacking this possibility, at least minimize our losses. After all, an individual who does not make his/her choices in accordance with the maximization principle indicated would surely count as less than fully rational.[4] It is plausible, then, to think that a society that does not choose in accordance with such a principle is to be similarly characterized.

Further reflection on this answer to our question, however, brings out some serious, and I believe unsolvable, problems. To begin with, the questions immediately arise as to what is to count as a benefit and a cost and how benefits and costs so understood are to be measured. The answers provided by orthodox "cost-benefit analysis," as this technique has developed in recent economic theory, are these. First, what counts as a benefit is a development's (or state-of-affairs') answering to what someone prefers to its absence (*ceteris paribus*). And, *pari passu,* what counts as a cost is a development's (or state-of-affairs') answering to what someone prefers not to occur (or obtain). Secondly, benefits and costs so understood are to be measured by appeal to the "compensating variations" of the persons in the appropriate set, viz., the persons who will be affected one way or the other by the policy decisions in question, where the *compensating variation* of individual $i$ ($CV_i$) is defined as (a) "the maximum sum he will pay rather than go without" the technological development in question, if he prefers the development to take place, or (b) "the minimum sum he will accept to put up with" the development, if he prefers that it not take place.[5]

Supplemented in this way, the answer under consideration becomes somewhat clearer. Unfortunately, what it gains in clarity, it loses in plausibility. In the first place, it's not at all obvious how we are to find out what the appropriate CVs are for the relevant population. This difficulty, which is widely appreciated of course, arises because of the absence of a market which enables individuals to reveal their CVs by how much of a good they choose to buy and how much they will pay to avoid a "bad." And this absence is usually ineluctable because developments of the sort in question characteristically are "pure public goods," that is, goods which like national defense possess or come close to possessing the feature that if anybody gets any, everybody else gets the same amount whether he wants it or not. To be sure, one might try to get information about the CVs of the relevant population by means of questionnaires, for example.[6] But how adequate would these be? Not very, it seems to me. I simply have no idea what I would require to be paid in order to acquiesce in a development which would, for example, increase my chance of dying before the age of fifty by (say) 0.002 percent— assuming that I derive no benefits from the development and suffer no other costs. I suspect most people are in the same boat, and that a vast majority of technological choices carry impacts which involve similar imponderables.

There is, however, an even more serious difficulty with the answer under consideration when it is clarified along the traditional lines just indicated. It is no longer plausible when the answer is clarified this way to believe it rational to try to maximize net benefits (or minimize net costs). After all, it appears prima facie rational to maximize net benefits (or minimize net costs) only if the notions of benefits and costs are connected in a certain way with the notions of human well-being or welfare or happiness, that is, only if an increase in the benefits which accrue to an individual amounts to or brings about some enhancement of his well-being or welfare or happiness—other things equal, and an increase in the costs which an individual bears amounts to or brings about a diminution of his well-being or welfare or happiness—other things equal. But when benefits and costs are understood by reference to what individuals prefer and are measured by reference to their compensating variations, it is far from obvious that the connections mentioned obtain. For nothing is more evident than that people do frequently prefer states of affairs which do not increase their well-being. They marry the wrong people, vote for the wrong candidates, pursue the wrong careers, choose the wrong life styles, and so on *ad indefinitum*. Moreover, it is not just ignorance of what is in their own best interests which explains these unfortunate preference systems— though there is a vast amount of this. Sometimes people knowingly prefer states of affairs that do not serve their well-being. Dostoyevsky's "underground man" with his "love" for "chaos and destruction" is neither a figment of the imagination nor even a rarity; indeed, he is in us all.

There is, of course, another way of understanding the notions of costs and benefits which helps to overcome this last difficulty. This is to employ the idea of a "rational preference" in the place of the idea of a preference *tout court* in the explanation of what is to count as a cost and what is to count as a benefit, where a rational preference is explicated by reference, for example, to what an agent prefers after he has carefully reflected on what he really wants, has taken careful account of all the relevant information about his circumstances, and has taken care to avoid hasty and fallacious inferences.[7] The notion of a CV, used in answering the question of how to measure costs and benefits, will undergo modification in an obvious way on this version. We now appeal not to what an individual will pay or take, but what he *would* pay or take under certain conditions. These new CVs I shall call CV*s. The reason that understanding the approach to the decision problem under consideration in this way helps with the last difficulty mentioned is, of course, obvious. For the relation between what an individual *rationally* prefers and his degree of well-being is much closer intuitively than is the relation between what an individual prefers *tout court* and his degree of well-being. In other words, it is much more difficult on the face of it to argue that people frequently prefer states of affairs which do *not* increase their well-being even after they, for example, have carefully reflected about what they really desire, have taken careful account of all the relevant information about their circumstances, and have taken care to avoid hasty and fallacious inferences, than it is to argue that they frequently so prefer when they have not satisfied the conditions indicated. Indeed, even the point about our "love" for "chaos and destruction" can be handled. For it can be said with considerable plausibility, I think, that if an individual prefers a bit of chaos or destruction after satisfying the rationality-making conditions noted, then getting what he prefers does increase his well-being or happiness after all—at least on one fairly natural way of explicating the latter notions.[8]

But be this as it may, the approach under consideration can still be faulted even when clarified in this second and ostensibly more satisfactory way.

To begin with, the epistemological problem of finding out people's rational preferences (or their CV*s), which is essential on this approach to determining in a precise way the costs and benefits which attach to different options, is even more severe than is the problem of finding out their preferences *tout court* (or their CVs). For now we are even less likely to get adequate answers via the questionnaire route than before. If, for example, people are not clear about which of several sets of consequences they prefer, how much less clear will they be about which they would prefer if they were to have reflected with great care about their wants, the information at their disposal, and the inferences they would make in deciding their preference on the basis of their wants and the relevant facts concerning their situations. And is there any practicable alternative to the questionnaire method for handling this problem?

Besides these epistemological problems, there is also a problem about whose preferences are to be taken into account in determining the overall costs and benefits associated with the options to be decided. As the view was presented earlier, the preferences of the persons affected by the policy decision in question constitute the appropriate reference class. But so stated the view is ambiguous; for "the persons affected" might be limited to actual persons (those now in existence), or it might be taken to cover future persons as well (i.e., those who will exist in the future). Unfortunately, whichever explication of the view we opt for, troubles spring up. If we restrict the reference class to actual persons, the approach can be faulted for leaving out of account considerations which seem obviously to be relevant to policy decisions of the sort in question, namely, the costs and benefits which will respectively be suffered and enjoyed by those who come after us. Surely we do not want to follow a decision procedure which gives *no* weight to, for example, the sufferings our policies impose on our unborn children and grandchildren, not to mention their progeny (if any). Such a procedure would be grossly inhumane. (This is not, of course, to say that it would be wrong to follow this procedure provided the decision it yielded were accompanied by a universal decision on the part of the persons now in existence not to have any more children. It is only if there [in all likelihood] will be sufferers that we need to take their sufferings into account; the mere [logical or physical] possibility of there being persons around in the future who have to live with the consequences of our policies does not impose any requirements upon our decision making, so far as I can see.) On the other hand, if we widen the reference class to include future persons, we greatly exacerbate our epistemological difficulties. For then we have not only to find out the rational preferences (or CV*s) of the actual persons affected by the policies under consideration, but we have to find out the rational preferences (or CV*s) of persons not yet born who may be affected. And this is an even more difficult problem than that of finding out the rational preferences (or CV*s) of the living. For not only are future persons not around to query about their preferences, but we are unlikely to be in a good position to guess either, given that people's values are obviously conditioned by the nature of the societies in which they are born and live their lives, and possibly also by genetic factors which reflect (inter alia) statistical facts about the differential reproduction rates of their ancestors.

Closely related to this problem is the failure of the approach under consideration to give any weight to the preferences—or perhaps I should say "preferences"—of nonhumans. To be sure, if the reference class were widened to include all the nonhumans who might be adversely or beneficially affected by the policy decisions under consideration, there would be very serious epistemological problems involved in determining the costs and benefits their being affected involves. How serious a cost is it if my cat's life expectancy is reduced by six months or its chances of contracting cancer increased slightly owing to the proximity of a nuclear power plant to the house in which she lives? Still, it does seem wrong to operate with a decision procedure which gives *no* weight to the interests of nonhumans, independently of the way the goodness or badness of their lives affects the lives of human beings. After all, it is surely perfectly clear—at least to most normal human beings—that pouring gasoline on a cat and then lighting it just "For the hell (or fun) of it" is monstrous. It is surely no accident that it was Smerdyakov, and not Alyosha, who fed biscuits containing razor blades to stray dogs!

Still another difficulty with this approach is the fact that it fails to give appropriate—or indeed any—weight to distributional considerations. That is to say, a decision maker who was apprised of the probable environmental and social impacts of several policies regarding the development or diffusion of some technology, and who employed the approach under consideration in order to determine which of these policy options to select, would pay no attention whatever to the way in which the costs and benefits associated with the different policies in question get distributed among the members of the relevant reference class. Thus, for example, a policy—call it A—which placed all of the costs on the least well off in the society and secured all of the benefits for those who were most happily situated as regards income, wealth, influence, prestige, and all the comforts and amenities which go with such advantages would, on the approach under consideration, be preferable to an alternative policy—B, say—which equalized the burdens and benefits, not to mention one—C, say—which functioned to reduce the welfare of the most well off and increase the welfare of the least well off, provided the net benefits which attached to A exceeded, by however small an amount, the net benefits associated with B and C. But on the face of it, an approach which has these consequences is defective. We do think the distributional consequences of social policies are relevant to their proper evaluation because we do believe that not all of the possible rules for determining the ways in which the benefits and burdens of social life get distributed are equally legitimate. Here one need merely call to mind that there is such a thing as an unjust tax structure, that some political systems are more just than others, that "the rule of law" is a desirable complex of institutions and procedures, that we have a right to equality of opportunity, etc.

Finally, there is a difficulty with the approach under consideration which arises because of the fact that policy decisions as regards the development and diffusion of technologies, like personal decisions about important matters such as whom to marry and what career to follow, can have long-range and profound effects on the values and hence preference-structures of those affected by these decisions. That personal decisions have long-range and profound effects on our values is obvious. We all know, if we live "the examined life" in any degree at all, how the kinds of people we live with, the level of our income, where we make our homes, etc. affect how we use our time, money, energy, etc., and insofar the character of and priorities among our values. Only a little reflection is required to make it evident that policy decisions of the sort in question can have similar effects on vast numbers of people. Think, for example, about the way the diffusion throughout American society of the private automobile has affected residential patterns, the development of the urban environment, the quality of the air, the structure of the economy, the ability of foreign states to disrupt the economy by withholding, or increasing the price of, oil, etc. And then reflect upon the ways the general features of a society can shape the values of its members. Now the reason this fact raises a difficulty is simply that if certain policy decisions can have profound effects on the values of the members of a society, then it becomes extremely difficult for the decision maker to determine which policy maximizes net benefits. For in light of the consideration mentioned, to do that it would be necessary for him to be able to predict the kinds of changes in the preference structures of the members of the society which adoption of the different policies will bring about, and it is very difficult to see how he could even begin to make reliable judgments on matters such as this. Worse, even if he could make reasonable determinations of this kind, there is the problem of how he could use these estimates together with his information about what the members of the relevant reference class rationally prefer *now* to arrive at a view as to which policy maximizes net benefits. For how is one to gauge the costs, say, of policy P vis-à-vis individual *a* when what *a* rationally prefers now is different from what he will rationally prefer in five years?[9]

## II

It might be said that in attacking the approach—or family of approaches—discussed above, I have been flailing a dead horse. Alternatively, it might be said that I have been knocking down a straw man. I think that there is no doubt that at least many people have been strongly attracted to some variant or other of the cost-benefit approach I have been considering, and hence that this approach is not a straw man.[10] On the other hand, since most of the objections I have presented have appeared in one form or another elsewhere,[11] it is probably true that it is by now a dead horse. Still, flailing dead horses is sometimes not without value. It can serve to make perspicuous some of the ingredients a better approach has to incorporate. With the foregoing then as propaedeutic, I turn now to the task of outlining such a better approach. I should say at the outset, however, that the approach I sketch next is clearly not the only alternative to the family of approaches I have so far considered.[12] But it—or some variant of it—does seem to me to have the most promise of bringing together in an appropriate way all of the considerations which reflection upon our considered judgments concerning the right and the good suggests should play a role in an ideal decision procedure.

The cynosure of the approach to the policy choices at issue that I wish to commend is the idea of human freedom, together with a certain view about the circumstances and institutions which protect and promote freedom. The approach rests essentially upon three propositions. The first is the familiar idea that the ideal society is one which enables its members to live the best (happiest, most meaningful) lives they are capable of. The second is that something close to the theory of human good (or happiness) that Rawls develops in *A Theory of Justice* is correct. According to this view—very roughly—the best (or happiest) life for an individual is specified by the life plan he would choose for himself if he were fully apprised of his most important desires, had complete information about the facts relevant to such a choice, and made no errors in calculation or reasoning—given that his plan in addition satisfies certain general rationality conditions and given also that he is placed in circumstances which are (more or less) "favorable" ones for human flourishing.[13] The third notion upon which the present approach rests is that the ideal society satisfies correct principles of distributive justice and that these require, at a minimum (at least in affluent industrialized societies), that the advantages or "goods" which a society has at its disposal to distribute be distributed equally so far as possible unless there is sufficient ground for departures from strict equality. In other words, it rests upon the thesis that the burden of proof is borne by those who think unequal distributive shares are legitimate as regards such things as wealth, opportunities, and the basic liberties, rather than the other way round.

All three of these theses are, of course, controversial. And though I believe they can all be defended, there is not space for a full defense of any of them here. I shall, however, briefly indicate the kind of argument which, in my judgment, best supports the last two. As regards theories of human good of the Rawlsian sort, it seems to me that the best defense consists in (1) pointing out the implausibility of views that make human good independent of what human beings desire; and then (2) making clear the unattractiveness of theories which try to connect human well-being or happiness or good with the satisfaction of any system of desires, whether or not these desires have been subjected to rational criticism and altered in the light of such critical scrutiny; and finally (3) drawing attention to the variousness of human beings and hence the unlikelihood of there being a single plan of life or system of ends which adequately defines the good for all.

The best argument in support of the conditional egalitarian thesis mentioned, in my judgment, runs in outline as follows: (1) The advantages or disadvantages (natural and social) with which a person starts life reflect merely "the arbitrariness of fortune."[14] (2) A person's initial advantages or disadvantages play a significant role in determining many of the important features he displays in later life, such as degree of health and vigor, creativity and intelligence; amount and kinds of specialized knowledge and general level of culture; quality of ego ideals and capacity for delayed gratification; and so on—not to mention such obviously important features as access to persons of influence. (3) Moreover, a person's eventual place in a social system like the one which currently exists in America, and so the advantages available to him during the larger part of his mature life, depend to a significant extent upon facts about him of the kind indicated in the preceding premise. (4) Hence, a person's eventual place in a social system like ours reflects to a large extent "the arbitrariness of fortune." But this means, of course, that (5) the fact that certain people have available to them a vastly greater proportion than others of the advantages which get distributed in a society like ours also reflects to a large extent nothing more than "the arbitrariness of fortune." But (6) if this last proposition is true, then the inequalities in the distribution of advantages which characterize a society like ours require either to be eliminated or justified. (Why, after all, should the life prospects of some be vastly greater than those of others, if the basis for this difference is largely arbitrary?) Therefore, (7) the inequalities in the distribution of advantages characteristic of a social system like ours ought to be eliminated, unless sufficient reason can be found for their retention.

If these ideas are correct, then it is plausible to hold, I believe, that the ideal society is one which is organized in such a way as to enable its members to live the best (happiest, most meaningful) lives they are capable of, where the good life for an individual is spelled out along the lines just sketched; and furthermore it is so organized that its members are treated equally in this regard so far as possible, unless sufficient reason can be given for providing some with relevant advantages which others lack. How does this rough picture of the ideal society yield a conception of the best way of deciding policy issues concerning technological developments of the sort we have been examining?

The answer to this question becomes evident once we consider the kinds of institutions and social circumstances that tend to produce a society organized in the ways just noted. If we assume that it is at least generally true that each individual is in the best position to define the life plan that it would be best for him to follow—owing to his self-knowledge, his natural self-interest, and his (normally) privileged epistemic position with respect to his own particular circumstances—then the kinds of institutions and social conditions in question are, I submit, those that maximize individual freedom, subject to the conditional egalitarian constraint I have indicated. Why is this so?

There are four distinguishable, though overlapping, kinds of "social freedom." First, there is the kind of freedom which consists (roughly) in the absence of the direct interference by private persons or agents of government in the lives of individuals by means of physical injury or constraints, or threats of injury or constraint. I shall call this "negative freedom." Second, there is the kind of freedom which is essential for political democracy to flourish; it includes freedom of thought and expression, freedom of assembly, freedom to form political associations, freedom to add alternatives to the agenda for political decision, etc. I shall call this "political freedom." Third, there is the kind of freedom which prevails to the extent that the members of a society have many and various options as regards plans and styles of life, and possess the wherewithal to choose from among these options without the sacrifices involved being overwhelming. I shall call this "positive freedom."[15] And, fourth, there is the kind of freedom which consists (roughly) (a) in the ability of individuals to follow the path that, by their lights, reason supports, (b) in the absence of manipulation by others of either their desires or the information available to them, and (c) in the lack of "alienation," where alienation is understood here as a condition which obtains to the extent that an individual is unable to identify with (or evaluate favorably) his own system of values. I shall call this "autonomy."[16]

Now the reason that these kinds of freedom are of central importance if the members of a society are to have the best possible chance of achieving their true good is this. If the plausible assumption mentioned above is correct—that is, the assumption that (generally) each individual is in the best position to work out a life plan that is most adequate for himself—then to the extent that there are limits on these kinds of freedom there will be limits both on the extent to which individuals can draw up and follow life plans of their own choosing as well as limits on the extent to which their circumstances are "favorable" ones. And to the extent that these kinds of freedom prevail, the ability of individuals to draw up and follow life plans of their own choosing will be maximal and so will be the "favorableness" of their circumstances. That these things are so is clear upon reflection, I believe. Thus the connections between the extent to which the legal structure of the society imposes restrictions upon an individual's freedom of movement, employment, marital possibilities, or living arrangements, etc., and the ability of individuals in the society to follow life plans of their own choosing is obvious. How institutions which limit or ensure political freedom, positive freedom, and autonomy are related to individuals achieving their true good is equally clear though perhaps not quite so obvious. Thus political freedom, for example, tends to maximize the number of people who get the social policies they want. It is also plausibly argued to be an important contribution to the self-respect of the members of a society,[17] which in turn is of fundamental importance if goals and activities are to be pursued with vigor and zest.[18] Without positive freedom people (inter alia) lack the resources to live as they wish. And social structures which undermine autonomy ipso facto undermine people's ability to follow what seems to them the most reasonable life plan, to pursue their chosen goals with zest, and to draw up plans which are reasonable approximations to their ideal plans. Those which promote autonomy ipso facto enhance these abilities.

But now if freedom of these kinds is of central importance for reasons of the sort indicated, then a natural answer to the question concerning the ideal decision procedure when one is confronted with policy choices concerning technological developments of the sort we have been considering is that these choices should be made in such a way as to preserve or promote those conditions and institutions which tend to maximize negative freedom, political freedom, positive freedom and autonomy—subject of course to the egalitarian constraint imposed by the thesis asserting that advantages in general and hence freedoms in particular should be distributed equally among the members of a society so far as possible, unless adequate reason for an unequal distributive profile can be provided.

This answer is, as it stands, obviously quite vague and sketchy; and, in view of the arguments of part I of the paper, it is also obviously in need of qualification. It requires qualification in order to take account of those interests of both future generations and nonhumans which we feel intuitively ought to impose constraints upon our policy decisions. It is vague and sketchy because, as it stands, it provides no light as regards (inter alia) such matters as: (a) what trade-offs among the four kinds of freedom are acceptable; (b) what sorts of considerations justify departure from equalities in freedom; and (c) what specific conditions or institutional arrangements tend to maximize autonomy, positive freedom, etc. Moreover, when qualified in the ways required, it also needs to be developed so as to make clear (d) how the appropriate interests of nonhumans and future persons are to be weighed against those of persons now living. Should we, for example, rule out trades of negative and political freedom for increases in positive freedom under certain circumstances, as Rawls maintains? Ought we to impose a heavier justificatory burden on departures from equality as regards negative freedom than we do for positive freedom? What principle(s) should we adopt by way of defining limits on majority rule? Is it possible to maximize positive liberty, subject to the conditional egalitarian constraint, within a capitalist system? Should we opt for a principle as regards future generations that goes like this:

> No generation should pursue policies which seriously limit the freedom of later generations unless these policies also give rise to benefits that will accrue to these same later generations and that adequately compensate them for the costs in freedom they suffer,

or one that is less restrictive, like the following:

> No generation . . . they suffer [as above], except in cases where the failure to adopt such a policy will carry costs in freedom to the generation in question which clearly outweigh the fact that later generations are not adequately compensated for the costs this policy imposes upon them.

It is clearly desirable to have answers to questions like these. However, even in their absence, the approach I have outlined is by no means vacuous, and it appears to possess a number of clear advantages over the cost-benefit family of approaches described and criticized earlier.

Among the more obvious advantages are the following. First, it is not plagued with the kinds of epistemological problems which beset cost-benefit approaches, problems, that is, about how to discover what the preferences (or CVs), or rational preferences (or CV*s), of the members of the affected population(s) are. Second, it is not open to the criticism that it is wrongly indifferent to distributional considerations. And third, it is not faced with the problems that arise with cost-benefit approaches owing to the fact that major policy decisions of the kind in question can have long-range effects on the preference schedules or value systems of the members of a society.

That the approach I have sketched is not vacuous, even in its relatively undeveloped state, becomes evident when one reflects on some of the more specific implications it carries. Among these are, I submit, the following. (1) It will count strongly in favor of a policy option on this approach that it will probably reduce population growth—at least in circumstances like those that obtain at present in the United States and in most of the rest of the world. This is obvious when one reflects upon the ways burgeoning populations, for example, restrict opportunities; increase the amount of inter- and intra-societal friction and hence both the need for government interference in our lives and the danger of war; and tend to exacerbate pollution and resource problems, with consequent threats to security, health, and the freedom of future generations. (2) It will count strongly against a policy option that it will probably lead to greatly increased needs for government surveillance and repression of political radicals owing, for example, to the great danger to society of successful terrorist acts once the technology in question has been developed and deployed. The reason for this, of course, is largely the incompatibility between significant surveillance and repressive actions on the part of government and the proper functioning of a vital political democracy. (3) It will count strongly in favor of a policy option that it will probably lead to significantly increased leisure for large segments of the affected population, since obviously without leisure, the capacity to develop and follow a life plan of our own choosing cannot but be severely limited. (4) It will count strongly against a policy option that it will probably lead to an increased capacity on the part of government officials to restrict privacy, that is, the ability of individuals to control the extent to which others can gain access to certain kinds of information about them. This is because of the many ways in which "the right to privacy" protects and enhances our freedom.[19] (5) It will count strongly in favor of a policy option that it will increase the availability of low-cost energy, increase life expectancy, prevent or delay the onset of senility, or open up new possibilities for prenatal diagnosis of inherited disorders or intrauterine treatment of fetal disease or defect. (6) It will count strongly against a policy option that it paves the way for increasingly efficient methods of controlling or influencing thought, desire, or behavior in ways that make knowledge of or escape from such control or influence on the part of the persons affected difficult or impossible. (N.B. To count strongly for or against a policy option is not to count *decisively* for or against that option.)

Of course, the above are not the only policy implications of the approach in question. It also carries implications for policy options that would or might (i) involve the rapid depletion of certain crucial nonrenewable resources, (ii) preclude the redevelopment of industrial civilization after a catastrophe destroys it, (iii) put severe pressures on the global ecology, (iv) make reversing ourselves impossible if the technological development in question turned out to have untoward consequences, (v) carry consequences that would show up only when it's too late to do anything about them should they be very unfortunate or disastrous, (vi) destabilize the nuclear balance, (vii) lead to developments which depend for their safety upon long periods of social stability and a regular supply of highly-trained personnel. However, the implications mentioned make it especially clear how the focus on freedom which characterizes the approach in question significantly distinguishes it from all of the cost-benefit approaches described earlier, and also how this focus could play an important role in altering the perceptions and judgments of those decision makers who, for good or ill, hold the shape of the future in their hands.

## NOTES

1. Cf. Harvey Brooks, "Technology Assessment as a Process," *International Social Science Journal* 25 (1973): 250–51. See also Harvey Brooks and Raymond Bowers, "The Assessment of Technology," *Scientific American* 222 (1970); *Technology: Processes of Assessment and Choice,* Report of the National Academy of Sciences, Committee of Science and Astronautics, U.S. House of Representatives (1969); Joseph F. Coates, "Some Methods and Techniques for Comprehensive Impact Assessment," *Technological Forecasting and Social Change* 6 (1974); and Mark Berg, Kan Chen, and George Zissis, "A Value-Oriented Policy Generation Methodology for Technology Assessment," *Technological Forecasting and Social Change* 8 (1976).

2. Stuart Hampshire, "Thinking About Social Costs," *The New York Times,* March 24, 1976, op. ed. page.

3. Joshua Lederberg, "The Freedoms and the Control of Science: Notes from the Ivory Tower," *Southern California Law Review* 45 (1972): 605.

4. At any rate, this one familiar use of "rational" according to which such a view has some plausibility.

5. See, for example, Ezra Mishan, *Cost-Benefit Analysis* (New York: Praeger, 1971), p. 159 and pp. 126ff.

6. Cf. ibid., pp. 177f.

7. Cf. David Gauthier, "Reason and Maximization," *Canadian Journal of Philosophy,* 4 (1975); Richard Brandt, "The Concept of Welfare," in *The Structure of Economic Science,* ed. S. R. Krupp (Englewood Cliffs, N.J.: Prentice-Hall, 1966); and John Rawls, *A Theory of Justice* (Cambridge, Mass.: Harvard University Press, 1971), sections 63 and 64.

8. Cf. Rawls, *Theory of Justice,* section 83.

9. Cf. J. H. Dales, *Pollution, Property and Prices* (Toronto: University of Toronto Press, 1968), pp. 36 ff.; and Laurence H. Tribe, "Technology Assessment and the Fourth Discontinuity: The Limits of Instrumental Rationality," *Southern California Law Review* 46 (1973), especially sections II and V.

10. See, for example, the references in Laurence Tribe, "Policy Science: Analysis or Ideology?," *Philosophy and Public Affairs* 2 (1972).

11. See, for example, Ezra Mishan, *Cost-Benefit Analysis;* Laurence Tribe, "Technology Assessment"; Bernard Williams, "A Critique of Utilitarianism," in J. J. C. Smart and Bernard Williams, *Utilitarianism: For and Against* (Cambridge: Cambridge University Press, 1973); and also Alasdair MacIntyre, "Utilitarianism and Cost-Benefit Analysis: An Essay on the Relevance of Moral Philosophy to Bureaucratic Theory," in K. Sayre, ed., *Values in the Electric Power Industry* (Notre Dame, In.: University of Notre Dame Press, 1977).

12. The great divide in moral and political theory is between utilitarian and other kinds of "teleological" theory on the one hand and so-called "deontological" theories on the other. The approaches just criticized are of the former kind. Among the teleological alternatives are certain views which Rawls places under the heading "Perfectionism" (see *A Theory of Justice,* section 50). Although the approach I sketch belongs to the deontological tradition, most alternatives of this sort arise from conceptions of basic human rights or needs that differ from the conception implicit in the view I present.

13. See Rawls, *A Theory of Justice,* pp. 92–93, sections 63–64, and passim.

14. Ibid., p. 74.

15. I owe this formulation to J. Lawrence Crocker. (I follow his use of the label "positive freedom" too.) In an unpublished monograph Crocker elaborates this notion of freedom at length.

16. This account of autonomy differs from the analysis of, for example, Gerald Dworkin in "Autonomy and Behavioral Control," *The Hastings Center Report* 6 (1976). However, I have borrowed from his discussion.

17. Cf. Rawls, *A Theory of Justice,* section 82.

18. Cf. ibid., section 67. "Self-respect," Rawls writes, "includes a person's sense of his own value, his secure conviction that his conception of his good, his plan of life, is worth carrying out. And second, self-respect implies a confidence in one's ability, so far as it is within one's power, to fulfill one's intentions." He continues thus by way of spelling out its role in a person's achieving his real good. "When we feel that our plans are of little value, we cannot pursue them with pleasure or take delight in their execution. Nor plagued by failure and self-doubt can we continue in our endeavors. . . . Without it nothing may seem worth doing, or if some things have value for us, we lack the will to strive for them. All desires and activity become empty and vain, and we sink into apathy and cynicism" (p. 440).

19. See, for example, Charles Fried, *An Anatomy of Values* (Cambridge, Mass.: Harvard, 1970), ch. 9; J. Rachels, "Why Privacy is Important," *Philosophy and Public Affairs,* 4 (1975); and H. Gross, "Privacy and Autonomy," in J. Feinberg and H. Gross, eds., *Philosophy of Law* (Encino and Belmont, Calif.: Dickenson Publishing Co., 1975).

# Corporate Modernity and Moral Judgment: Are They Mutually Exclusive?

## A. MacINTYRE

THE LITERATURE ON THE THEORY OF ORGANIZATIONS IS BY NOW MASSIVE in quantity—and yet we are as far from a credible unified body of theory as we are anywhere in the social sciences. Charles Perrow in his excellent account of the varieties of organizational theory[1] make it clear just how many unresolved issues there are. What I want to suggest is that perhaps the variety and the incoherence within the theoretical literature reflect the variety and the incoherence within the life of organizations. I am not making the tritely familiar point that there are many types of organization; I am rather suggesting that within any one large formal organization not only variety, but incoherence is to be found—that corporate structures fragment consciousness and more especially moral consciousness.

If this were true it would have important implications not only for our evaluation of recent literature on the theory of organizations but also for our evaluation of recent writing on moral philosophy. For moral philosophers all too often write as though our moral discourse was a unity, as though there were a set of expressions which comprise *the* language of morals. This is of course a convenient and labor-saving assumption. It rescues the philosopher from any tasks of empirical enquiry; he or she need not ask precisely *whose* moral discourse is being studied at any given moment. But suppose that this assumption is false; suppose that uses of moral language not only are intimately connected with specific social backgrounds, but that they can only be made fully intelligible in terms of these backgrounds. This is the supposition I now want to explore, using as an example the social structures of the modern corporation. I do not of course want to suggest that contemporary society consists of nothing but corporate structures. It is in fact a curious amalgam of different and heterogeneous elements, drawn from almost every century in our past. When therefore I speak of corporate modernity, I am attending to only one element in that disordered whole—but an undeniably important one.

122

# I

Individuals in modern corporate organizations who are sensitive to the demands made upon them by the organization which employs them often discover that incompatible and contradictory demands are being made. Every organization implicitly, and to varying degrees explicitly, recognizes a set of virtues and vices, dispositions which those in authority seek to inculcate or eradicate. Unfortunately the very same quality is often presented in one guise as a virtue, in another as a vice. The same executive is characteristically required to be meticulous in adhering to routines, to a be good committeeman, to be responsive to certain pressures from superiors and peers, to place the achievements of the team above those of individual members of it *and* to show initiative, to break rules creatively, to form independent opinions and to act on his or her own. Expecially perhaps among upwardly mobile middle management, contemporaries in the organization are presented at one and the same time as those *with* whom he or she is expected to cooperate and *against* whom he or she is expected to compete. And at many different levels of management, there is a tension between the requirement that areas of responsibility are sharply delimited so that each individual knows what he or she has to do and so that individual performance can be precisely evaluated, and the requirement that individuals look to the larger and longer-term consequences of what they are doing so that the organization is not the victim of that type of blindness and irresponsibility which arises from too complete a demarcation of functions.

Someone may demur even at this early point: Incompatible qualities, yes; but ought we to speak of virtues and vices in this connection? There seems to me a strong case for saying that we ought. Modern corporations characteristically do not purchase managerial and executive skills and labor and time in the same way that they purchase raw materials or machine tools. This is obvious when the corporations are universities or hospitals; it is less often acknowledged but also true when the corporations are banks or power companies or manufacturers. That is, corporations often expect from their employees loyalty to certain ideals and standards, sometimes, although not always, the ideals and standards of a profession; and they often invite from their employees a kind of loyalty which presupposes that the corporation itself serves some distinct human good. Note that I say "often" and not "always." There are of course some corporations which embody everything that a crude, vulgarized Marxism imputes to the capitalist firm; but those are untypical, especially of the large domestic corporation. Much more characteristic is the large accounting firm in which professional skills and study on the one hand and the performance of visible public good works on the other—fund-raising for charity, acting as a trustee for hospitals or colleges—is as much part of the executive's responsibility as is the profitability of his activities. And the pursuit of profitability is not contrasted with—it is rather assimilated to—these other areas of responsibility. The modern corporation is characteristically informed by an image of itself as seeking some public good, some aspect of the good for man, to put the matter in Aristotelian terms. Hence the qualities which it seeks to inculcate it presents as virtues; they are those qualities the cultivation of which will realize at least some aspects of the good.

Thus the modern corporation presents itself as a moral being; it is because of this that businessmen are as sensitive as they are to moral criticism. It is because of their blindness to this, their willingness to see *only* profit seeking and cynicism, that the radical critics of business usually fail to understand the kind of human authority which the corporation exerts. Yet it is perhaps partly because of its moral pretensions rather than because of its economic power that the modern corporation is so dangerous. For part of what I want to argue is that the modern corporation is an agency which by its moralizing splinters morality into dissociated parts; and the contradictions in its teaching about the virtues have a good deal to do with this. Those contradictions are not accidental or marginal circumstances. They are, I shall now suggest, central to the character of modern formal organizations.

All large, long-term organizations experience a tension between a pressure to routinize as many activities as possible, to order every process by a set of standard procedures, and the need to cope with the unexpected and the unpredictable by varying degrees of improvisation. The former pressure is closely connected with the requirement that the organization be conceived in terms of roles and not of persons. Any role, any position, will be filled from time to time by different persons. Each of those persons temporarily becomes the organization in one of its aspects as it confronts others; correspondence for example is conducted with this or that office of the organization and not—except accidentally—with individuals. Hence the formal character of bureaucratic correspondence; hence the importance of files. Each file has a history which outlives that of the individuals who contribute to it. From the observation of this impersonal character of bureaucratic processes springs the aspiration actually to mechanize such processes, as far as possible. Where one person can be substituted for any one out of a large number of other people, surely a computer can be substituted for a person.

It is notable that those senior bureaucratic executives who become champions of mechanization, of the substitution of computers for clerks, rarely advocate the mechanization of their own role, the substitution of computers for vice-presidents. That is because they are forced to recognize in their own case what they would like to ignore in the case of their subordinates, the other, unmechanizable side of the bureaucratic process. For the more routinized an institution becomes, the less capable it is of coping adequately with unpredictable contingencies, whether external or internal. The sources of such contingencies are manifold: Human error results in lost files or misplaced items; transactions are systematically given different and conflicting interpretations by those taking part in them; technical innovation disrupts social convention and habit; markets shrink or grow in unforeseeable ways; educational change subverts well-established beliefs. The list is indefinitely long.

Burns and Stalker have shown that the more control is decentralized, the more centers of decision making are multiplied, the more local autonomy is fostered, the better able a firm is to confront innovation and unpredictability. But the ability to tolerate such properties in an organization is always limited by the need of those in authority to control, to direct, to enforce upon, or to induce in their subordinates an acceptance of the standpoint of senior management. Hence we often find in the history of organizations an oscillation between the pressures toward routinization and the need for local autonomy. Correspondingly, we find shifts between types of management. But for many executives the result is an attempt at the impossible, at embodying in themselves the incompatible qualities of both kinds of what they take to be virtue. Moral incoherence becomes itself a kind of norm.

The outcome is the creation of more than one self. The agent has to fabricate distinct characters. From Aristotle and Theophrastus until quite recently, character was taken to be fixed and largely unchanging in an agent; types of character were limited and each agent's character was of a determinate type. But now in the modern corporate organization character has become more like a mask or a suit of clothing; an agent may have to possess more than one. So the difficulties, indeed the impossibilities, which would result from trying to embody a contradictory and incoherent set of virtues systematically are avoided; each character is allocated its own place and its own tasks in the corporate world. Nonetheless the corporation itself delimits the range of possibilities; what it takes to be the good provides a moral horizon.

## II

I break off the argument at this point in order to consider the implications for moral philosophy so far. Since we have found the language of virtues, vices, and the good an appropriate means for characterizing the moral stance of the corporate executive, a comparison with Aristotle is obviously a priority. Aristotle makes two central claims in the *Ethics*. One is that he is specifying the good, the *telos* for man as such, and that therefore the virtues and vices he lists are the virtues and vices of all human nature. The other is that the good for man can be achieved only in and through the community of the *polis*, of the peculiarly Greek and peculiarly sixth to fourth century B.C. city-state. The universal claims of the good and the virtues are linked to the claims of a form of social structure which seems to have required highly specific conditions for its coming into existence and for its relatively brief flourishing. This is sometimes treated as evidence of Aristotle's time- and place-bound vision. But perhaps Aristotle was right in seeing a close inter-dependence between virtues and social structure. Perhaps the practice of morality requires certain institutional arrangements and excludes others. Yet there is a crucial difference between Aristotle's claim about the relationship of the pursuit of the good and the structure of the *polis* and my claim about the relationship between modern corporate structures and a rival set of claims about the virtues. For Aristotle possesses a concept of essential human nature which provides him with a criterion for the good, independently of all social structures; and it is not just that Aristotle personally and privately claims the possession of such a concept and such a criterion. What he articulates is in outline, if not in detail, something that many Greeks would have recognized as part of their common intellectual stock.

In the modern corporate world, by contrast, no such shared concept of essential human nature is to be found; and this not just because of the histori-cal defeat of the classical view of human nature in the sixteenth and seven-teenth centuries. For in the present the lack of a shared concept of essential human nature is intimately connected with the nature of corporate existence. I have already suggested that the corporation often requires alternative versions of character. Let me now reinforce this suggestion by considering two other ways in which corporate existence splits and divides up the personality.

I have identified elsewhere[2] the dominant characteristics of argument *within* corporate situations. The executive is required to treat certain goals as given and, within certain very broad constraints, he or she is set to consider how he or she may most economically and efficiently use present resources to reach these goals. The means-ends structure of such executive reasoning reproduces, so I have argued, the structure of classical utilitarianism; and the framework of such executive reasoning is socially defined so that certain limits are placed upon what questions may and may not be raised about it. These limitations take the form of a definition of responsibility. In his capac-ity of corporate executive, the manager not only has no need to take account of, but *must* not take account of certain types of considerations which he might feel obliged to recognize were he acting as parent, as consumer, or as citizen.

Corporate existence, that is, presupposes a separation of spheres of existence, a moral distancing of each social role from each of the others. Consider the oddity that would be involved if the modes of argument appro-priate to corporate structures were transferred either to the family or to the polity. If transactions within the family were dominated by the utilitarian model, then the achievement of familial goals might well require characteristically and as a matter of course the sacrifice of this or that member of the family. Children or invalids might be declared redundant and paid off, older relatives declared obsolete and discontinued, and an annual dividend distributed to the stockholders. What makes this a bad joke is not of course that things analogous to these never happen. It is that the presupposition even of our contemporary family life is of a certain set of norms which require a mutual responsibility of each for each in the family independent of consequences. In the family, if these norms are valid, it cannot be true that everybody counts for one and nobody for more than one or that utility is to be invoked so that parental sacrifice is weighed against the prospects of the children in a realistically defined calculus. The notion of duty involved in familial relationship is in some respects at least Kantian. The fluctuations of inclination and sentiment are no measure of familial responsibility. Where someone—in the family or elsewhere—does his or her duty for the sake of duty, then inclination and sentiment do indeed direct themselves upon the objects of duty (a part of Kant's teaching not always recollected). But psychological attachment is to be sustained by responsibility and duty and not vice versa.

Thus when the executive shifts from the sphere of the family to that of the corporation he or she necessarily shifts moral perspective. Attitudes appropriate in the one context become radically inappropriate in the others, and as with the shift from the family to the corporation, so with that from the corporation to the polity. The image of governmental responsibility is the obverse of that of corporate. Just those aspects of his or her activity which the executive qua executive can and must ignore become part of that to which he can and must attend qua citizen, so there is a whole range of concerns which provide the subject-matter for debate within the polity; and the conceptualization of those concerns is of a very different kind from that which holds within either corporate or familial existence. But to identify the characteristics of the political realm, I must first note a general feature of the argument so far. I want to emphasize how, in characterizing the variety of conceptual structures which inform and define such existence, I have continuously been led to make reference to key points in the history of moral philosophy. I have suggested that crucial resemblances obtain between characteristic contemporary modes of thought and practice on the one hand and such moral philosophies as Aristotelianism, Kantianism, and Benthamism on the other. The differences are of course important too and I shall try to bring out the importance of some of them at a later stage. But I do want to insist on the importance of seeing contemporary social life as a theater with a set of adjoining stages upon which a number of very different moral philosophical dramas are being acted out, the actors being required to switch from stage to stage, from character to character, often with astonishing rapidity. But this metaphor breaks down when we look at the activities of the polity—of government and of the citizens.

For if we view in the moral perspectives of the separate spheres of existence the activities of the political order it at once becomes clear that precisely here is an area in which an acute conflict of values must occur. The claims of the corporation encounter the claims of the family; the claims of one part of corporate existence—management—encounter the claims of other parts—labor and consumption; the claims of the hospital, the university, and the church encounter those of the corporation and of the family. The scene appears to have been set for acute moral and indeed metaphysical argument and conflicts. Many of the founders of the modern state viewed government not as a place where moral and metaphysical argument went on, but as an institution where it had been or shortly would be resolved. So it was with Robespierre and the Jacobins; so in another way with Napoleon. So it was with James Mill and Bentham or with Macaulay and the Whigs of 1832. But of course the rulers of the modern liberal democratic state were never able to count on the kind of agreement at which Robespierre or Mill or Hegel had hoped to arrive; they were and are confronted instead with deep underlying moral conflicts which our society possesses no means of resolving. Yet irresolvable conflict and effective modern government cannot coexist. It is crucial therefore that liberal democratic government suppress within its sphere all ultimate moral and metaphysical questions, all philosophy. It must become, what it often nowadays boasts of being, pragmatic. All questions must be resolved into questions of immediate or relatively short-term interest; any question that cannot be so resolved must be excluded from the institutions of government, so far as possible. Hence morality insofar as it does intervene in government becomes either reduced to moral language without substance, to protective rhetoric, or to the expression of negative protest. Liberal democratic government always aspires to the condition which the end of ideology theorists took to have been realized in the society as a whole; such theorists might indeed be viewed by an uncharitable observer as attempting to portray society in the image of liberal democratic government, in order thereafter to justify such government by appealing to the conditions of society.

We add then to the multiplicity of spheres of existence yet another with its own moral, or in this case would-be non-moral, structures. We add to the multiplicity of roles and characters between which the self is parcelled out yet another type of role and character. Thus there is an important resemblance between life within the corporation and life outside it. In a world dominated by corporations, multiplicity and fragmentation of the moral self become dominant themes.

Rival moral philosophies have in the past been the expression of rival claims of total ways of life. When Hobbes encounters Aristotelianism, when utilitarianism seeks to overthrow a Burkean conservatism, when Hegelian and Kantian stances conflict as during the rise of the nineteenth-century German empire, it becomes clear that the truth of the claims made by the one system excludes the possibility of the truth of the other. In both theory and practice, the different conceptual schemes are mutually exclusive alternatives. But it is quite other with contemporary corporate existence. Many of us tend to behave in one sphere as quasi-Kantians, in another as imitation utilitarians, in yet another as Neo-Aristotelians, and in a fourth as pragmatically distanced from all philosophical claims. The exigencies of social existence disguise from us the fact that if utilitarianism is true, Kantianism is false, and that both are incompatible with Aristotelianism. It is not surprising that many philosophical observers of the present have seen as a central feature of morality the absence of any rational criteria for resolving evaluative disagreement. What they ascribe to morality as such is in fact only what modernity has made of morality; for many people now have to live a good deal of their lives at least *as if* there were no such criteria. Hence at one level a certain kind of moral eclecticism seems to reign; the principles of each view encounter the principles of all the others without there being any available means for deciding the contest rationally. But at another institutionalized level, that of established social and more particularly corporate roles, there is no contest. Each view has its own segregated sphere of application; no one point of view is allowed to invade the sphere of another. But just this will remain invisible to the philosopher if moral philosophy remains at the level of the analysis of moral language, as that has been understood by the key analytical thinkers in American or British universities. Such moral philosophy, by remaining at a level of linguistic fact which detaches the uses of language from any highly specific or particular institutional contexts, itself becomes ideological, a means of preserving intact a certain level of unconsciousness of our moral condition. Theories such as emotivism, prescriptivism, descriptivism, and the post-Wittgensteinian "form of life" moral theory all share this nonsociological, nonhistorical character.

## III

If I am right in suggesting that the moral structures of corporate modernity are distinctive in important ways, it is important to characterize this distinctiveness further. Consider what may have become of the self in the structures that I have described. Erving Goffman, in more than one context, has elaborated an account of the self according to which there is no self apart from the social roles which it temporarily inhabits. Or rather, even the word "inhabits" is misleading; the self is, when the roles are stripped away, nothing but "the peg on which something of collaborative manufacture will be hung for a time."[3] Beyond the separate roles, there is no "true self"; the notion of such a "true self" is a superstitious fiction.[4] Hence the relationship of individual to social role is not like that of an actor to his part in a play; *how* the individual plays his or her role is structured just as is his or her role playing and, when the individual is alone, it is not that all role playing is put aside, but that a different type of role playing takes place. It is important to see that Goffman is involved in two denials and not just one; for he not only repudiates that notion of a substantial self independent of all its roles but also the notion of a certain kind of continuity in the history of the self. In fact in his failure even to raise the question of continuity in any systematic way, we are perhaps given the clue as to why the true self has disappeared from Goffman's account and only the roles are left.

All Goffman's examples are brief and anecdotal: a social situation is presented, the characters are introduced, the episode occurs. The characters do not bring with them anything which derives from and is only intelligible in terms of past social situations, whether their own or those of the institutions and practices—families, local communities, churches, schools, games, sciences, crafts—which have formed their present selves. The social situation exists without a history either; it too is always a segment of the present, encountered independently of its past. Thus the partitioning of selves into their roles is another aspect of the same phenomenon as the division of both the self and its roles from the past. Goffman's account of society is thus not accidentally ahistorical; but it is for the moment less important to consider what his account thereby omits and distorts than what that account captures and illuminates.

For Goffman reproduces in his theory precisely that separation of roles and spheres which corporate organization produces in its practice; his portrait of what social existence always must be turns out to have as its true subject distinctively modern social existence in its bureaucratized forms. And what his account omits as nonexistent is precisely that in the human condition to which corporate organization refuses social recognition.

This conclusion will be surprising to readers overimpressed by the cynicism of Goffman's style. For he is certainly in no sense a direct or willing defender of that status quo whose character he so accurately depicts; his style exempts no facet of social life from mockery. But precisely because his cynicism and his mockery make no exemptions, because everything is equally devalued, the effect is to leave everything precisely as it is. And what more could those who aspire to be the defenders of corporate existence demand? Goffman's role in relation to modernity turns out to be surprisingly traditional; he is its court jester.

But now we must ask: Why does it matter to moral philosophy whether what Goffman asserts is true or false? We can bring out the relevance not only of his work, but of the whole of sociology to moral philosophy, by pointing out the answer. If what Goffman asserts is true and if we accord his assertions unrestricted generality, then *nobody ever makes moral judgments,* at least in any sense in which they have been customarily understood. For the traditional—in a very broad sense of "traditional"—notion of a moral judgment requires not only that moral judgments are expressed in certain lingustic forms, but also that the making of a moral judgment satisfy certain conditions. One is that an appeal is being made to a criterion which holds for man as such, and not merely for this or that kind of man. A moral judgment is one that is to hold equally for Frenchmen or Italians, for Athenians or Corinthians. Another condition is that a moral judgment in appealing to such a criterion shall provide a reason for action; and by a reason for action is intended a consideration that need not be, but in standard social conditions could be, effective in changing both attitudes and actions. Neither of these conditions would be satisfied if society were as Goffman described it: the norms actually obeyed by individuals would be role specific rather than hold for man as such; and moral judgments would be totally ineffective—merely part of the stage furniture—unless they merely reproduced what roles already demanded. Hence perhaps Goffman's cynicism; but this cynicism would lose its point in premodern cultures.

Thus in different cultures the same uses of apparently moral language could have a quite different import. It is perhaps a partial understanding of this that has led some contemporary writers to identify the moral self with that which is totally distinct from all social roles, thus inverting Goffman's thesis. What Goffman sees as mere fiction, such writers—Sartre is the most eminent example—see as the only conception of the self endowed with moral substance. Where Goffman liquidates the self into its roles, Sartre separates the self wholly from them. And in so doing Sartre makes his thought as symptomatic of modernity as is Goffman's.

For the counterpart to the theory and practice of corporate existence in the modern world is the theory and practice of rebellion against such existence. The one aspires to divide the self up into its role-governed functions; the other seeks to distinguish the authentic self from any of its identifications with role or function. But like Goffman, Sartre, the rebel, deprives action of any historical or narrative dimension. All narrative, all history on his view falsifies. This is one central contention of *La Nausée.* Its consequence—very different from the consequence of Goffman's enmity to history—is that the traditional set of the virtues is replaced by one single, central virtue: *authenticity.* Where Goffman provides no social space within which the traditional exercise of the virtues could be practiced, Sartre's account provides a space within which only one new virtue can be practiced. For authenticity consists precisely in the self making its words and deeds truly its own, whatever they are; virtue has nothing to do anymore with the content of action, but only with its relationship to the self.

The literary history of this development toward treating *authenticity* as a virtue has been written once and for all by Lionel Trilling;[5] but when it is written as social history, we are able to see authenticity as the response of the excluded self to the social order which seeks to partition it out between roles, a response as distorted as that to which it responds. Both complementary conceptions share in their exclusion of the possibility of the traditional moral judgment—the one because it leaves no room for the concept of *man as such;* the other because it leaves no room for the exercise of rational, impersonal criteria.

## IV

The morals for moral philosophy are becoming clear and the first is that—if it is to be understood as it has been by recent analytical philosophers— there is no such subject. The study of moral language in isolation from those social institutions in which it operates results in false abstraction. In order for moral judgments to be made at all certain social conditions have to be satisfied, conditions which are incompatible with the structures of corporate modernity. But to say no more than this is to be merely negative. What positively would have to be the case to provide the conditions for a society in which the concepts of *man as such* and of rational criteria could have a place?

To answer this question would require far more than a single paper. We can, however, say a little about what once did provide the concept of moral judgment with substantial application. Every society of course has invited individuals to inhabit roles with different requirements. But difference has not entailed the kind of separation, the kind of partitioning which is peculiar to corporate modernity. For in certain kinds of traditional precapitalist society, morality has its place within practices informed by the conception of society as having a total order which both integrates diverse roles and subordinate orders, such as the household and the family, and whose polity is nothing but that total order expressed in the relevant practical terms. Examples of such societies include a surprising variety of different institutional orders: ancient Greek city-states and modern Greek highland villages, medieval Christian and Arab kingdoms and Scottish Highland clans before 1600, the Sioux nation, the Bedouin of the Western desert, and the Irish of the Blasket islands. One needs only to recite their variety to recognize that modern corporate social existence and its predecessor, the society of free-market capitalism, have been the odd men out, the exceptions, the deviants among human societies.

Four types of concepts are useful in making the distinction between corporate modernity and the majority of the forms of human social existence. One is that of honor and insult. A man's honor is what is due to him and to his kin and household by reason of his or their place in the social order. To dishonor someone is to fail to acknowledge what is thus due. Hence the concept of an insult is a crucial one in all these societies and in many of them a certain kind of insult merits death. In corporate society only certain ghosts of the concept of honor and insult survive, and there is no clear shared conception of what the first consists in and the second deserves. This is because a man has become viewed in large part as a bundle of roles and each role has a place in its own order of social existence; whereas the concept of honor belongs with the concept of an overall human and social order, of a man who is always something more than his roles.

Just as the concept of honor has almost disappeared—we have, as Peter Berger[6] has pointed out, no legal or quasi-legal recourse in modern societies such as the United States, if we are insulted—so have the concepts of blasphemy and obscenity. The belief of the type of premodern society to which I am referring is that the human social order embodies and is a part of a divine, cosmic order. If I fail to acknowledge your place in that order, I dishonor you; if I fail to acknowledge the order itself, I insult God and indeed the whole community. Hence blasphemy is a deliberate challenge to the social order. Similarly obscenity is a challenge to the social ordering of sexuality. Note that neither blasphemy nor obscenity are punished in such societies because they are shocking or offensive. They are punished because they are symbolic transgressions of a cosmic order, which is why they are *also* shocking and offensive. It is only when belief in such an order is no longer shared—or when for that or for some other reason religious belief has been separated off from beliefs about society—that a tendency to shock or offend becomes a reason for punishing. Legislators and judges in modern society who will not acknowledge a cosmic order will recognize the existence of emotions, even although these emotions are irrational unless belief in a cosmic order is presupposed.

Third, we may note that we have a variety of established ways of making the entrance and the exit to various spheres of modern corporate social existence; but we have fewer and fewer public and shared ways of making the entrance and the exit of the individual from the social order as such—because corporate existence recognizes no social order as such. The public ceremonies of birth and death play very little part in our lives. Hertz[7] pointed out long ago that the funerary rituals of primitive peoples express the idea that death is an event that happens to the community and not just to individuals, that the community in such rituals is mourning the loss of part of itself and reconstituting itself in the process. In such a society it is a literal truth that "every man's death diminishes me." But now death has become an event of private life, and dying is treated not as a moment in the life of the social order, but as a disturbing occasion for the dying person and his or her relatives. Like blasphemy and obscenity, death is being psychologized.

Fourth, we ought to notice the situation of the aged. In an integrated social order, the old often occupy a formal position—the elders may sit in council *as* elders. The old may no longer be able to discharge the functions that they once did; but they acquire a new function simply by being old. They are a key part of the collective memory of that through which the past is inherited and transformed. Hence they are owed honor, the specific honor of being listened to. Modern societies not only have a tendency to discard the past; but in the separation of spheres of existence, they abolish the possibility of a collective memory. For each sphere of existence may have a history; but there is no longer a history of the unified social order, just because there is no unified social order in respect of which the old, for example, might have a function. There are cultures of course—Vietnamese, for example—in which not only the old, but the ancestors have a voice. We have, so far as we can, disenfranchised the dead and moved toward disenfranchising the old. Because the old are functionless, they do indeed become boring. Narratives that would once have been a contribution to the common recognition of identity in a society now become pointless anecdotes. Story telling becomes a peripheral social activity.

Thus in four ways the moral structure of the modern corporate world can be defined by negation—by the striking absence of honor, of blasphemy, of ceremonial death, and of the story-telling elders. From this point of view the modern world is a set of impoverished fragments. But that is not of course its self-image. Yet, does it have a coherent self-image? Either, with Goffman, it can find no place for a concept of the individual over and above social roles; or, with Sartre, it can find a place only for the individual conceived of as distinct from all social roles. Neither view can find a place for either the individual or the role as historical.

## V

This paper has had three central, interrelated themes. The first has concerned the inadequacy of moral philosophy as recently conceived. The second has had as its subject the contrast between the structures of morality in modern corporate society and certain of its predecessors. These have differed in three respects: first with regard to the degree of coherence in such structures; second, with respect to the items which appear in the list of virtues; third, and perhaps most strikingly, in the extent to which the conditions for actually making moral judgments are satisfied.

But there has also been a third theme arising from the other two. At various points I have remarked not only upon the contrasts between the social structures of modernity and those of its predecessors, but also upon the variety of issues which divide the modern world intellectually from its predecessors. For the modern world and its predecessors represent not merely rival social and cultural alternatives, but rival intellectual alternatives too. How we understand the history of the individual and of social groups, the relationship of individual to social identity, and the place of death in human life will determine where we stand or ought to stand in the conflicts which are still generated within modernity by the survivals of tradition. If the argument of this paper is in any way correct, this is *a,* and perhaps *the,* central issue confronting moral agents in our time. It is therefore crucial to pass verdict on this argument since if it is in any way correct it will also be true that the methods of recent moral philosophy render it incompetent even to identify this conflict, let alone to help judge which side we ought to take in it.

## NOTES

1. Charles Perrow, *Complex Organizations* (Chicago: Scott Foresman, 1971) passim.

2. "Utilitarianism and the Presuppositions of Cost-Benefit Analysis" in *Values in the Electric Power Industry,* ed. K. Sayre (Notre Dame, In.: University of Notre Dame Press, 1977).

3. Ervin Goffman, *The Presentation of Self in Everyday Life* (Garden City, N.Y.: Doubleday, 1959), p. 253.

4. *Encounters* (Indianapolis, In.: Bobbs-Merrill 1961), p. 152.

5. Lionel Trilling, *Sincerity and Authenticity* (Cambridge, Ma.: Harvard University Press, 1972).

6. Peter Berger, *The Homeless Mind* (New York: Random House, 1975).

7. Robert Hertz, *Death and the Right Hand,* tr. R. & C. Needham (Glencoe, Ill.: Free Press, 1960).

# PART THREE
# Applications to Substantive Issues

# Starvation and Human Rights

## ALAN GEWIRTH

DO PERSONS THREATENED WITH STARVATION HAVE A STRICT RIGHT TO BE given food by those who have it in abundance? This question is, of course, far from academic. But its analysis and development can throw light not only on one of the most pressing moral issues of our time but also on the ability of moral philosophy to deal with such issues. The reason why this ability is called into question is that the topic of rights and duties bearing on relief of starvation involves serious conflicts both of interests and of moral criteria. The capacity of a moral philosophy for clarifying and resolving such conflicts provides an important test of its adequacy.

## I

Although recent moral philosophers, following on the work of legal thinkers,[1] have done much to clarify the concept of a right, they have devoted considerably less attention to the criteria for having rights when these are moral ones. The conceptual and criterial questions are, of course, related, but still they are distinct. If, for example, we know that for one person A to have a strict right to something X is for A to be entitled to X and also for some other person or persons to have a strict duty to provide X for A as his due or to assist A's having X or at least to refrain from interfering with A's having X, this does not tell us when or why A is entitled to X and when or why the other person or persons have such a strict duty to A. Further conceptual considerations may of course be added to indicate the grounds or reasons for which A has the right or other persons have the correlative duty. But these considerations are then not only conceptual but also ultimately moral because, in addition to telling something about the meaning of a word or concept, they give or suggest justificatory answers to controverted moral problems.

We may distinguish at least two criterial questions about moral rights. First, there is the general question: How, if at all, can it be known that any persons have any such rights? Second, there is the more specific question:

Who has moral rights to what, and how, if at all, can this be known? Both questions ask for the ground or reason for having moral rights. Although moral rights, by definition, have moral grounds or criteria, there still remain the questions of whether moral reasons can justify anyone's having rights at all, what are those reasons, and what rights do they justify as belonging to which persons.

Recent moral philosophers have provided at least four different answers to these criterial questions. The intuitionist answer that humans' possession of certain unalienable rights is self-evident can be found at least from the Declaration of Independence to Nozick's peremptory assertion that "Individuals have rights, and there are things no person or group may do to them (without violating their rights)."[2] Like other intuitionist positions, this one is impotent in the face of conflicting intuitions. The institutionalist answer that rights arise from transactions grounded in formal or informal rules of institutions, such as promising,[3] incurs the difficulty that there may be morally wrong institutions, so an independent justification must still be given for the institutional or transactional rules which are held to ground the rights. A third answer is that persons have rights because they have interests.[4] This, however, indicates at most a necessary condition for having rights, since there would be an enormous and indeed unmanageable proliferation of rights if the having of any interest X were sufficient to generate a right to X. Even if "interests" are restricted to basic or primary interests or needs, the logical question still remains of how a normative conclusion about rights can be derived from factual premises about empirically ascertainable characteristics such as the having of interests. The fourth answer, that persons have rights because they have intrinsic worth or dignity or are ends in themselves or children of God, may be held simply to reduplicate the doctrine to be justified. Such characterizations are directly or ultimately normative, and if one is doubtful about whether persons have rights one will be equally doubtful about the characterizations which were invoked to justify it.

I shall now approach the problem of the criterion for having rights through their familiar connection with claims. Rights may, of course, be had even when they are not claimed, and claims are also not in general sufficient to establish or justify that their objects are rights. As against such an assertoric approach to the relation between claims and rights, I shall follow a dialectically necessary approach. Even if persons' having rights cannot be logically inferred in general from the fact that they make certain claims, it is possible and indeed logically necessary to infer from the fact that certain objects are proximate necessary conditions of human action that all rational agents logically must hold or claim, at least implicitly, that they have rights to such objects. Thus the criterion for having at least certain basic moral rights will be shown to depend on the consideration that all persons have certain needs relative to their being actual or prospective agents, namely, needs for the necessary conditions of action. At the same time, the logical problem of how rights can be inferred from facts will be avoided because the argument proceeds through the conceptual analysis of human action. By this analysis, from the necessary conditions of action a certain fact is inferred about rational agents that they logically must claim or at least accept that they have rights to these necessary conditions. Although what is thus directly inferred is a statement not about persons' rights but about their claiming to have them, this provides a sufficient criterion for rights because the claim must be made or accepted by all rational agents so that it holds universally within the context of action, which is the context within which all rights ultimately have application. The argument is dialectically necessary in that it proceeds from what all agents must claim or accept, on pain of contradiction. To see how this is so, we must briefly consider central aspects of action. Since I have presented the argument in some detail in various other places,[5] I shall here confine myself to outlining the main points.

All moral and other practical precepts, regardless of their varying specific contents, are concerned directly or indirectly with how persons ought to act. Insofar as actions are the possible objects of any such precepts, they are performed by purposive agents. As is shown by the endeavor which each agent contributes to achieving his purposes, he regards his purposes as good according to whatever criteria (not necessarily moral ones) are involved in his acting to fulfill them. Hence, the agent also a fortiori regards as necessary goods the proximate necessary conditions of his acting to achieve his purposes. These conditions, which pertain alike to all actual or prospective agents, are freedom and well-being, where freedom consists in controlling one's behavior by one's unforced choice while having knowledge of relevant circumstances, and well-being consists in having the other general abilities and conditions required for agency. The components of such well-being fall into a hierarchy of goods. Basic goods are the essential preconditions of action, such as life, physical integrity, and mental equilibrium. Nonsubtractive goods are the abilities and conditions required for maintaining undiminished one's level of purpose-fulfillment, while additive goods are the abilities and conditions required for increasing that level. Just as the basic goods are generically the same for all agents, so too are the nonsubtractive and additive goods. I shall call freedom and well-being the *generic features* of action, since they characterize all action, or at least all successful action, in the respect in which "action" has been delimited above.

Every rational agent logically must claim or accept, at least implicitly, that he has rights to freedom and well-being. If any agent were to deny that he has these rights, he would contradict himself. For in holding, as he rationally must, that freedom and well-being are necessary conditions of his agency, he holds that they are necessary goods; and because of his conative attachment to his purposes he holds that it is necessary that he have these goods in that he (prudentially) ought to have them. The meaning of this "ought" includes the idea of necessary restrictions on the interference of other persons with his having freedom and well-being. The agent holds that these restrictions are justified and are owed to him, from the standpoint of his own prudential purposes, because of their necessity for his engaging in action. If he were to deny that he has rights to freedom and well-being, then he would hold that it is permissible for other persons to interfere with his having these goods, so that it is all right that he not have them. This, however, would contradict his conviction that it is necessary that he have them because they are necessary goods without which he cannot be an agent. Hence, every agent must hold or claim, on pain of self-contradiction, that he has rights to freedom and well-being. I shall call them *generic rights,* because they are rights to the generic features of action. They are not yet moral rights but only prudential ones, since their ground is the agent's own pursuit of his purposes, whatever they may be. For the rights to be also moral ones, they must be shown to have a further ground in the agent's favorable consideration of the purposes or interests of other persons besides himself. Let us see why the agent must also take this further step.

Every agent must hold that he has the generic rights on the ground or for the sufficient reason that he is a prospective agent who has purposes he wants to fulfill. Suppose some agent A were to hold that he has these rights only for some more restrictive reason R. Since this would entail that in lacking R he would lack the generic rights, A would thereby contradict himself. For since, as was shown above, it is necessarily true of every agent that he holds implicitly that he has rights to freedom and well-being, A would be in the position of saying both that he has the generic rights and that, as lacking R, he does not have these rights. Thus, on pain of self-contradiction, every agent must accept the generalization that all prospective purposive agents have the generic rights, because, as we have seen, he must hold that being a prospective purposive agent is a sufficient condition or reason for having the generic rights. This generalization entails that the agent ought to refrain from interfering with the freedom and well-being of all other persons insofar as they are prospective purposive agents. Since to refrain from such interference is to act in such a way that one's actions are in accord with the generic rights of all other persons, every agent is logically committed, on pain of inconsistency, to accept the following precept: Act in accord with the generic rights of your recipients as well as of yourself. I shall call this the Principle of Generic Consistency (PGC), since it combines the formal consideration of consistency with the material consideration of the generic features and rights of agency.

To act in accord with someone's right to freedom is to refrain from coercing him; to act in accord with someone's right to well-being is to refrain from harming him. These rights, as thus upheld, are now moral ones because they are concerned to further the interests or goods of persons other than or in addition to the agent.

The above argument has provided the outline of a rational justification of the PGC, both for the formal reason that to deny or violate the principle is to contradict oneself and for the material reason that its content, comprising the generic features of action, necessarily imposes itself on every agent, as against the purposes, interests, inclinations, or ideals for which some agent may contingently act and whose requirements he may hence evade by shifting his desires or opinions. The PGC is the supreme principle of morality because its interpersonal requirements, derived from the generic features of action, cannot rationally be evaded by any agent. The main point, put succinctly, is that what for any agent are necessarily goods of action, namely, freedom and well-being, are equally goods to his recipients, and he logically must admit that they have as much right to these goods as he does, since the ground or reason for which he rationally claims them for himself also pertains to his recipients.

It follows from the argument to the PGC that the primary criterion for someone's having moral rights is that he is an actual or prospective agent having certain necessary needs relative to his agency. The argument has established this conclusion through what I have called a dialectically necessary method, in that it has proceeded from what logically must be upheld or admitted by every agent. Although the conclusion is thus relative to the requirements of agency, this relativity still enables the PGC and its ensuing criterion to be categorical. For since agency is the proximate general context of all morality and indeed of all practice, whatever is necessarily justified within the context of agency is also necessary for morality, and what must logically be accepted by every agent is necessarily justified within the context of agency. What has been established, then, is that simply by virtue of being actual or prospective agents who have certain needs of agency, persons have moral rights to freedom and well-being.

Since all humans are such agents, the generic rights to freedom and well-being are human rights. They are strict rights in that they entail correlative obligations on the part of persons other than the right-holder. But they are also primarily negative rights in that the primary obligation of these other persons is to refrain from interfering with the right-holder's freedom and well-being. There are, however, certain kinds of situations where, if some person A is inactive in the face of serious harm impending to another person B, A interferes with B's basic well-being. In such situations the PGC with its criterion of rights requires action rather than refraining from action because to refrain is to interfere with someone's basic well-being and hence constitutes a violation of his right to well-being.

I shall now apply these considerations of the PGC to the case of starvation. It is obvious that starvation is a basic harm, a deprivation of basic well-being. Since every person has a right to well-being, he has a right that other persons not interfere with his well-being, and other persons have the correlative duty not to interfere. Under what circumstances does this duty require positive action to prevent other persons from starving? I shall deal with this question, first, by considering certain conceptual matters; second, by applying the PGC to the problem of starvation within interpersonal morality; and third, by extending this application to international morality.

## II

If some person A lacks a component of basic well-being such as food, this does not of itself entail that he lacks an effective right to food. In general a person lacks an effective right to something X if and only if he has a right to X and this right of his is violated. Thus, although it is indeed a necessary condition of A's lacking an effective right to X that he in fact lacks X (where this lack is either occurrent or dispositional, as the case may be), this is not a sufficient condition, for he may not have a right to X. But even if A has a right to X and he in fact lacks X, it still does not follow that he lacks an effective right to X. As we have seen, that A has a right to X entails that all other persons ought to refrain from interfering with A's having X. Hence, for A to have an effective right to X entails that all other persons do in fact refrain from interfering with A's having X, where A has a right to X. Such interference constitutes a violation of A's right to have X. Consequently, although every prospective purposive agent has a right to basic well-being, if A, who is a prospective purposive agent, lacks some component of basic well-being such as food, this does not of itself entail that A lacks an effective right to food unless his lack of food is caused by the interference of some other person or persons.

Such interference may occur in different ways. Persons may quite involuntarily cause obstacles to be put in the way of A's having food, with the result that he lacks food. For example, from ignorance of methods of scientific farming, from lack of required fertilizer, or through other circumstances beyond their control, persons may bring about a crop failure, with the result that A starves. Such persons do not, however, violate A's right to have food, for this violation would be a failure to fulfill their duty to refrain from interfering with A's having food—the duty which is entailed by A's having a right to food. Insofar as "ought" implies "can," since the persons in question are assumed to be unable to refrain from interfering with A's having food, it follows that they do not have the duty to refrain from such interference. (I here use "duty" in the general sense in which it is equivalent to a practical "ought," not in the more restricted sense in which it signifies a task assigned by social rules to some role or status.) Similarly, if other persons do not have enough food to supply their own minimal needs, then they are unable to provide food for A so that they have no duty to do so. Here again A's right to have food is so far not violated.

It is also possible that A may himself be the cause of his lack of food. He may intentionally starve himself for a variety of reasons, including a desire to lose weight or to go on a hunger strike. Or he may be too lazy to take care of himself or to work and hence to supply his basic needs. In such cases A's lack of food does not show that other persons have interfered with his having food; hence, they have not violated his right to have food.

In order to determine, then, whether A's right to have food has been violated and by whom, we must exclude both the involuntary actions and nonactions of other persons and the voluntary actions of A himself. What remains is the voluntary actions of other persons. For these persons to have the duty of supplying A with food, so that their interfering with his having food constitutes a violation of his right, they must both be aware that he lacks food from causes beyond his control and be able to repair this lack. They must have sufficient resources to have a surplus from their own basic food needs so as to be able to transfer some to A. By virtue of this ability, it is within their control to determine by their own unforced choice whether or not A has food. If, under these circumstances, A lacks food and they withhold food from him, then they voluntarily interfere with his having food and hence inflict basic harm on him. Thereby they violate his right to have food.

The better to understand this argument, which is derived from the PGC, let us apply it to a particular case of interpersonal morality. Suppose Ames, a bachelor, has a very large amount of food while Bates, another bachelor who lives nearby, is starving to death. None of the voluntary factors mentioned above applies to Bates. Ames knows of Bates's plight but doesn't want to give away any of his food, despite Bates's appeals for help. Bates dies of starvation.

In depicting this situation I have intentionally provided only the most meagre details about Bates's involuntary starvation, omitting all reference to any other psychological, historical, or institutional contexts. In the situation as thus depicted, the PGC supplies the sufficient ground for Ames's duty to give food to Bates. The principle prescribes, as a matter of strict duty, that agents refrain from inflicting basic harms on their recipients where such infliction violates the recipients' rights to basic well-being. But since Ames, in failing to give food to Bates, inflicts a basic harm on him, Ames violates

Bates's right to food. Ames thereby violates a strict duty imposed by the PGC. Since to violate the PGC is to incur self-contradiction, Ames's violation is shown to lack the most basic kind of rational justification.

Certain questions must now be considered about this application of the PGC. The principle sets a requirement for every agent, that he act in accord with the generic rights of his recipients. Since, however, Ames is passive and inert in the face of Bates's starving, it may be objected that Ames is here not an agent and hence not subject to the PGC's requirement. In reply, we must note that for someone to be an agent he need not engage in gross physical movement; it is sufficient that he engages in voluntary and purposive behavior. Ames is here an agent because his inaction in the face of Bates's plight is something he unforcedly chooses for purposes of his own while knowing of Bates's urgent need for food. Bates, moreover, is here Ames's recipient, since Ames's intentional knowing inaction crucially affects Bates's effective possession of the right to basic well-being. If Ames had given food to Bates, Bates would not have died; since he did not give food to Bates, Bates died.

It may be further objected that even if Ames's inaction crucially affects Bates's basic well-being, it is not the cause of Bates's death, nor does Ames bear any responsibility for it. For only a "positive" event can cause another event to occur; the mere absence of an event, as in Ames's inaction, cannot be a cause. But since the PGC prohibits that an agent inflict basic harm on his recipient, that is, that he positively act to cause his recipient to suffer basic harm, such as by killing him, it follows that Ames has not violated the PGC.

The answer to this objection is that an event, and a fortiori a harmful event, may be caused by a person's inaction or other omission as well as by his positive action. A train wreck may be caused by a signalman's omitting to move a switch; a man's failure to reach a physician in time may cause him to die of appendicitis. In such cases, what is properly singled out as the cause of the event is the particular antecedent circumstance, an omission, which makes the difference from the normal course of events (where "normal" may have either a statistical or a normative interpretation) and which is such that, if it had not occurred, the event would not have occurred. Ames's omission, his voluntary and purposive failure to give food to Bates, is the cause of the latter's death because Ames is subject to a valid normative rule which he has violated, and which is such that, if he had obeyed it, Bates would not have died.

There is indeed a difference between the cases of the train wreck and of Bates's death from starvation. The signalman's failure to move the switch is not only a violation of a valid prescriptive rule to which he is subject; it is also a deviation from a regular pattern of operations and of accompanying expectations so that it makes the difference from what regularly occurs and is hence the cause of the unusual occurrence of the collision. In the case of Bates's death, on the other hand, there may not be an ongoing rule-regulated system of expectations to which Ames's inaction comes as an exception. Nevertheless, even if Ames and Bates live in a society in which, as a matter of empirical fact, persons are not expected to care for one another, Ames's inaction is still morally wrong and the cause of Bates's death. What makes it such a cause is that Ames, as a rational agent, is aware of and is subject to the moral requirements of the PGC. It is against the background of these requirements that Ames's intentional failure to give food to Bates counts as the cause of his death. This background is a normative moral one and not, as in the case of the signalman, an empirical one. It is indeed the case that Bates would have died even if Ames had not lived nearby or had known nothing of Bates's plight. But, given the actual circumstances of Ames's knowledge, proximity, and easy ability to fulfill the PGC's requirement, the PGC makes it appropriate and indeed mandatory to single out Ames's inaction as the cause of Bates's death. For the PGC, as the supreme principle of morality, provides the primary normative standard, deviation from which is the relevant description or consideration in accounting for such an event.

It may also be objected that there remains another important difference between the cases of the signalman and of Ames. The railroad rules require that the signalman positively do something, so that he is blameable for the omission. But the PGC requires rather that an agent *not* do something: that he refrain from causing basic harm. Since Ames does not do something when he fails to give food to Bates, he has not violated the PGC as the signalman has violated the railroad rules. It must be noted, however, that the PGC does impose on every agent the duty to respect his recipients' rights to well being as well as his own. Such respect includes that he not treat them as mere means to his own purpose-fulfillment with no positive consideration for their own well-being. In ignoring Bates's plight, Ames fails to respect Bates's right to well-being; he permits a process to continue which he knows to be drastically harmful to Bates and which he could have reversed without any comparable cost to himself. In thus failing to respect Bates's right to well-being, Ames violates the PGC's prohibition against inflicting basic harm.

This consideration also bears on the possible objection that if Ames is the cause of Bates's starving to death, then he is also the cause of many other events which he could have prevented, such as a nearby cat's chasing and killing a mouse, or a neighbor boy's lacking a cherished bicycle which Ames could have bought for him. This objection requires that we supply a differentiating ground to distinguish when someone's inaction is and is not a cause of events which he fails to prevent.

Such a ground is given by the PGC. Since the principle requires that each agent act in accord with the generic rights of his recipients insofar as the latter are prospective purposive agents, it does not apply to cats and mice, which lack the capacities of knowledge, reflective choice, and control required for agency. As for the case of the bicycle, the principle does not impose the strict duty of positive beneficence in the sense of providing particular additive goods for other persons. Thus the neighbor's boy does not have a strict right to the bicycle or to Ames's buying it for him. The PGC bears rather on the right to well-being; it requires that each agent respect the well-being of others, where well-being signifies having the abilities and conditions required for agency. Thus the PGC provides what is relevant to the causal description of events characterized by the inaction of prospective agents.

## III

This conclusion has an obvious bearing on one of the central sociopolitical problems of our age: the extreme contrast between the great affluence of some nations and the great poverty of others, where millions of persons in Asia and Africa are threatened or actually engulfed by famine. One way to deal with this problem is to note that the PGC, in addition to its direct applications to the actions of individual persons toward their individual recipients, also applies indirectly to such actions through the mediation of social rules or laws. In such indirect applications the PGC requires that laws have certain contents which are instrumental toward persons' treating one another with the mutual respect for rights directly required by the principle. Since the PGC requires the relief of starvation, it also requires that such relief be facilitated, where necessary, by appropriate legal measures to be undertaken by the political authorities.

This indirect application, however, deals with the relation of each state to its individual members, not with the relation of states to one another. How is this latter relation to be treated? Since states are not individual persons, there seems to be a gap between a principle of personal morality concerned with relations among individuals and the kind of morality which should govern international relations. This gap must be bridged if international morality is not to be left completely separated from a general rational moral principle and if the application of moral philosophy to complex social problems is to be given adequate rational guidance.

The relation of states to one another may be assimilated to the relation between individual persons when one nation, through the actions of its government, is able to affect the basic well-being of sizeable numbers of persons in the other nation. It is true that these actions lack certain elements of the voluntariness or freedom and purposiveness which are the generic features of individual actions: In constitutional regimes the behavior of government officials is controlled and directed not by their individual choices and purposes but rather by legal rules. Nevertheless, insofar as these rules result in turn from the advocacy of individuals and groups within the society, the rules and the ensuing actions or inactions may be assimilated to the voluntary and purposive behavior of individual agents. And just as individuals implicitly claim rights to freedom and well-being on the ground of their being prospective purposive agents, a similar implicit claim may be attributed to states insofar as freedom and well-being are required at least for the actions of their corporate representatives as well as for the population at large. The recipient states, in turn, may also be assimilated to the individual recipients of particular actions, for at least two reasons. The states consist of individual persons who are prospective purposive agents, and their basic well-being may be drastically affected by the action or inaction of other states. The actions of states toward one another are not, then, devoid of the personal cognitive and volitional controls which characterize the actions of individuals so that the causal and moral responsibility found among the latter may also be attributed to the conduct of societies and their relevant political officials. Thus the requirements of personal morality may be extended, with due qualifications, to the morality of the relations between states or nations.

From this it follows that, just as Ames had a strict duty to give food to Bates, so Nation A has a strict duty to give food to Nation B where Nation A has an overabundance of food while Nation B lacks sufficient food to feed its population so that sizeable numbers are threatened with starvation. Nation B has a correlative strict right to be given this food, for it is relevantly similar to Nation A in that regard in which the members of the latter implicitly claim for themselves rights to freedom and well-being. The members of Nation B, like those of Nation A, need food for survival and hence for agency, and they necessarily claim a right to food on this ground. To give this food is a moral duty for Nation A quite apart from considerations of self-interest. It may well be the case that underdeveloped nations will promote increasing international tension and unrest unless they are given relief from the pressures of underdevelopment and resulting insecurity, including the danger or actuality of famine. But even if such threatening tendencies can be kept securely in check, the moral duty is no less urgent.

This urgency is also unaffected by historical considerations, although these may affect the specific nature of Nation A's moral obligation to Nation B. If Nation A has had an exploitative relation to Nation B, coercively extracting copious goods from the latter and giving little in return, then Nation A may bear considerable responsibility for Nation B's underdevelopment, including its inability to ward off famine. In such a case, Nation A owes Nation B assistance, including food supplies, as a matter of compensatory justice. But even if the United States as well as other developed countries which are plausible exemplars of Nation A have not had such a relation to many underdeveloped countries (there is disagreement on this question),[6] this does not affect Nation A's strict moral duty to prevent starvation in Nation B, and the latter's strict moral right to be given food where it is unable to help itself.

At least two alternatives to this position may be upheld. One is that Nation B does not have a strict moral right to be given food; such giving by Nation A is only an act of charity or generosity and thus only a "loose" or "imperfect" duty, but not a strict duty of justice. The other alternative is that although Nation B may have a strict moral right to be given food, this is not a human right but only a more special or localized right.

The former alternative must be rejected because, as we have seen, every person, qua prospective purposive agent, must accept that all other persons as well as himself have strict rights to freedom and well-being which are the necessary conditions of agency. Since such a claim is logically ineluctable within the context of agency, no actual or prospective agent can deny or reject it except at the price of self-contradiction. The necessary conditions of agency include having sufficient food at least for subsistence, and persons' rights to such food are violated when it is withheld under circumstances like those discussed above. This applies to Nation A and Nation B viewed as composed of actual or prospective purposive agents.

The latter alternative turns on the precise meaning to be given to "human rights." The point of this consideration is that if the right to be rescued from starvation is not a human right, then to prove that the right exists requires showing something more than that the starving persons are human. One would have to show in addition that some promise has been given, or some contract arranged, or that some other specific transaction or undertaking has occurred which serves to ground the right.

Cranston has offered three tests for a moral right's being a "human" one.[7] The test of paramount importance is obviously met by the right to food for averting starvation. The test of practicability is met at least in the short run: Nation A is assumed to have an adequate surplus of food from which it can supply Nation B's immediate needs, although, as we shall see, problems of capability arise for the longer run.

The main difficulty is in the test of universality. According to Cranston, for a moral right to be a human one it must be a right of all men against all men: all men must have the strict duty of acting in accord with the right, and all men must have the strict right to be treated in the appropriate way. Thus all men must be both the agents and the recipients of the modes of action required by the right. This test is passed by the rights to life and to freedom of movement: Everyone has the duty to refrain from killing other persons and from interfering with their movements, and everyone has the right to have his life and his freedom of movement respected by other persons. But in the case of the right to be prevented from starving, only some persons have the right—those who are threatened by starvation—and only some persons have the duty—those who are able to prevent this starvation by giving food.

The answer to this objection need not concede that this right, like other economic and social rights, is universal, only a "weaker" sense, in that while all men have the right to be rescued from starvation, only some men have the correlative duty.[8] Within the limits of practicability, all men have the right and all have the duty. It is, indeed, logically impossible that each man be at the same time both the rescuer and the rescued, both the affluent provider and the starving pauper. In contrast, it is logically quite possible that each man at the same time both respect the lives of all other men and have his own life respected by all other men. Nevertheless, the right to be rescued from starvation is a strong human right in that both it and the correlative duty pertain to all men insofar as they are prospective purposive agents. That this is so is shown by the PGC, which is addressed to all agents and which requires that each agent respect the well-being of all his recipients as well as of himself. Where such respect requires positive action to rescue other persons from starvation, the requirement can, of course, be fulfilled only by some persons toward some other persons. But this does not alter the fact that all persons come under the protection and the requirements of the PGC both as agents and as recipients. Hence, all the generic rights upheld by the PGC have the universality required for being human rights.

When it is said that the right to be rescued from starvation and the correlative duty pertain to all men insofar as they are prospective purposive agents, this does not violate the condition that for human rights to be had, one need only be human, as against fulfilling some more restrictive description. As was indicated earlier, all normal humans are prospective purposive agents; the point of introducing this description is only to call attention to the aspect of being human which most directly generates the rights to freedom and well-being. The fact that some prospective purposive agent may not at some time be able to rescue others from starvation does not remove the fact that he has a duty to do so when he does have the ability. As we have seen, this duty stems, in the way indicated earlier, from the claim he necessarily makes or accepts that he has the generic rights by virtue of being a prospective purposive agent. The universality of a right, so far as concerns the duty it imposes, is not primarily a matter of everyone's actually fulfilling the duty, let alone his doing so at all times. Nor is it even a matter of everyone's always being able to fulfill the duty. It is rather a matter of everyone's always having the duty to act accordingly when the circumstances arise which require such action and when he then has the ability to do so, this ability including consideration of cost to himself.

Even though the circumstances and the ability are not always present, the duty (and hence the correlative right) is still universal because it pertains in principle to every prospective purposive agent. In this regard it differs from duties which pertain to persons not simply by virtue of being prospective purposive agents but only in some more restricted capacity, such as being teachers as against students, umpires as against batters, or judges as against defendants. The universality of human rights derives from their direct connection with the necessary conditions of action, as against the more restrictive objects with which nongeneric rights are connected. And since Nation A and Nation B are composed of prospective purposive agents, the latter's right to be given food by Nation A is a human right.


## IV

Thus far I have argued from a somewhat simplified model of the relation between Nation A and Nation B, where the human right of the latter to be given food by the former stems simply from what the PGC requires by virtue of the relation between impending starvation and abundant means of preventing it. We must now consider some factors which complicate the model and thereby bring it closer to reality. These factors consist in various diversities: between short-run and long-run problems, and between the conditions and values that may exist within both Nation B and Nation A. These diversities give rise to conflicts not only of interests but also of relevant moral criteria.

Although, as indicated above, to talk of "Nation A" and "Nation B" as distinct substantive entities analogous to Ames and Bates is in some respects justified, the analogy breaks down in a crucial respect. It is not nations that are fed but individual persons. Thus when it is said that "Nation B" is starving, this is an abbreviation for the statement that sizeable numbers of individuals in Nation B are starving. The salient point is that who gets food in Nation B is determined not only by the existence or availability of food supplies within Nation B but also by the distribution of wealth and other forms of power, including effective mechanisms for providing food. Thus in many of the underdeveloped nations those who are rich have abundant food while those who are poor have very little. This contrasts at least in degree if not in kind with the relation between rich and poor in developed nations but the difference of degree is often very great.[9]

In this regard, the relation of Nation A to Nation B is different from Ames's relation to Bates. Bates is not internally divided into rich and poor parts of himself (unless he may be described, with doubtful relevance, as being spiritually rich while corporeally poor). Thus the directness of Ames's relation of obligation to Bates is replaced by a more complex relation wherein

Nation A's obligation to Nation B consists not merely in sending food but in seeing to it that the food is effectively distributed to those poor persons who need it. If, however, the social and political structure of distributive justice, or rather injustice, in Nation B is one of the chief causes of the starvation or serious malnutrition of sizeable masses of its inhabitants, then it would seem that Nation A cannot fulfill its moral obligation without interfering with that structure. Such interference raises problems of a political nature; it may involve restrictions on the freedom of the political authorities in Nation B.[10] Thus Nation A may be faced with a conflict of moral obligations: between the obligation to prevent the starvation of masses of persons in Nation B and the obligation to respect the political freedom of individuals and officials in that state.

This conflict is aggravated when the problems of starvation are viewed in long-run terms. There is evidence that when famine is averted in such a state as Nation B, its population tends to increase, especially when concomitant improvements occur·in health care. This, however, aggravates the problem of distributing a limited food supply whose growth does not keep pace with the growth in population. Hence, the Malthusian warnings against population growth outstripping food supplies have been newly applied on an international scale in such assertions as that sending food to avert starvation in underdeveloped countries simply encourages further population growth and thereby leads to increased subsequent famines. It might seem, then, that Nation A's moral obligation to send food to the existing people of Nation B is also in conflict with a further moral obligation: to refrain from actions which lead to future famines in Nation B. If, moreover, the people of Nation B will not voluntarily desist from producing more children than can be supported by their available food supply—an assumption for which there is considerable evidence[11]—then it may seem that the conflict of moral obligations just noted inevitably extends to the point where Nation A's moral obligation to send food is in conflict with its moral obligation to refrain from interfering with the procreative freedom of persons in Nation B.

In addition to these conflicts, the moral duty to send food may also be held to clash with certain rights within Nation A itself. The acquisition and dispatching of food supplies will presumably be paid for by taxes levied proportionately on the citizens of Nation A. But it may be objected that to compel someone to contribute to such provision against his will is to violate his rights to freedom and property. It is to use him as a mere means for the benefit of other persons. The uniqueness and separateness of each individual, however, preclude making him a means to some greater social good.[12] Since the PGC requires that the agent act in accord with the generic rights of his recipients as well as of himself, it may seem that the principle itself is involved in internal conflict on this point, for if Nation A must act in accord with Nation B's right to basic well-being, then Nation A cannot also act in accord with its own right to freedom.

All four of the conflicts just indicated bear on the discordant tendencies of the rights to freedom and to well-being, both where these rights belong to the same party and where the agent's right to freedom clashes with his recipient's rights to well-being. Nation A's moral obligation to send food to Nation B stems from the PGC's requirement that the agent act in accord with his recipients' right to well-being, where such action requires at a minimum that the agent refrain from inflicting basic harm on others by letting them undergo a starvation which it is in his proximate capacity to prevent. This moral obligation with regard to Nation B's well-being conflicts with Nation A's moral obligation to act in accord with Nation B's rights to political and procreative freedom as well as with Nation A's own right to freedom. For present purposes, there need not be any separate consideration of Nation A's moral obligation to refrain from actions which may lead to future famines in Nation B. For since the actions in question are here viewed as contributing to unchecked population growth, the problems they raise may be assimilated to the moral obligation to respect the procreative freedom of persons in Nation B.

The first point to be noted about these conflicts of obligations is that the freedoms which form one of their respective poles are of different degrees of moral importance. What determines such degrees is shown by the PGC's derivation from the rights of agency. These rights fall into an order of priority in that one right is morally more mandatory than another insofar as the former is more necessary for agency. We saw above that every prospective agent must regard his freedom as a necessary good in that it is a necessary condition of his acting in pursuit of his purposes. But cases of such freedom may vary in several relevant ways. Most obviously, there is the distinction between long-range or dispositional freedom and short-range or occurrent freedom. If, for example, one is imprisoned, then one loses one's ability to perform a wide variety of actions which would otherwise be subject to one's unforced choice. If, on the other hand, a locked door prevents one's using it to enter a building, one's freedom is only momentarily interfered with if another adjacent unlocked door is available. In addition to this quantitative difference, there is also a qualitative distinction as to the kinds of actions one is free to perform. While many considerations are relevant here, actions may be distinguished according to their bearing on one's ability to perform many further actions, so that the freedom to eat when one is hungry is qualitatively different from the freedom to play some game about which one feels relatively indifferent.

I shall now briefly indicate how the PGC, through the consideration of such distinctions, helps to resolve the conflicts of obligations noted above. Let us begin with the conflict between Nation A's moral obligation to send food to

Nation B and Nation A's own right to freedom. The latter right stops where it serves to inflict serious harm on other persons by failing to prevent the severe loss of well-being entailed by starvation. The reason for this may be put in either of two interrelated ways. Nation A has no right to use its freedom in such fashion as to contribute to serious harm for Nation B. The rights of starving persons to be fed take precedence over the rights of other persons to make free use of all their property because the former rights are obviously more important for agency than the latter.

It may be objected that if individuals' rights to freedom and property may be invaded whenever this is needed to prevent harm to other persons, then there will be no limit to such invasion and hence in effect no rights. This slippery-slope contention fails, however, because in the present argument the harms in question are limited to interferences with basic goods. These are serious enough in their destructive effects on agency to require, as a matter of strict justice, such legally sanctioned intervention.

Persons are not treated as mere means when they are taxed in order to help persons who are starving or are otherwise in dire need of basic goods. As was indicated above in discussing the universality of the right to be saved from starvation, the principle underlying the taxation of the affluent to help the needy is concerned with protecting equally the rights of all persons, including the affluent. The PGC requires that all prospective purposive agents refrain from inflicting basic harm on one another. The fact that only some persons may actually be in a position to perform such infliction at a particular time, and hence do not then need to have their rights protected, does not alter the universality of the protection of rights. Such protection is not only occurrent but also dispositional and a matter of principle; it manifests an impartial concern for any and all persons whose basic rights may need protection. Hence, the PGC's requirement involves treating all persons as ends, not merely as means.

There is a further way of resolving the conflict between the freedom and the moral obligations of individuals within Nation A. The taxation whereby Nation A finances its food exports to Nation B derives from a commonly accepted decision procedure based on an electoral method which is itself an application of the PGC's generic rule of freedom. This application is a necessary-procedural one. Just as in its direct individual applications the PGC requires that each person be allowed to control his behavior by his own unforced choice without coercion by other persons, so in its indirect institutional applications where masses of persons are involved in structured interdependent relations, the PGC requires that there be a decision procedure resting on civil liberties wherein each person can uncoercedly participate in setting forth his views and in voting, with the decision going to some previously agreed majority or plurality. The procedure is itself on a higher level of authority than the decisions reached by its means, so that those decisions cannot rightly extend to abolishing the procedure itself or the freedom and well-being required for its operation. There may indeed be a conflict between the freedom of the procedure and the required outcome of averting starvation. This conflict is strongly mitigated, however, by the fact that the procedure is tied to the other rational components of the PGC, especially the duty to prevent basic harms.

The other conflicts of obligations mentioned above cannot be resolved as readily as can the conflicts within Nation A, for there may be no legal, institutional framework embracing Nations A and B which provides a decision procedure jointly accepted by them. It might be thought, in view of the immense seriousness of the threat to basic well-being, that draconian interventions are required, including compulsory sterilization and coercive replacement of uncooperative regimes. The use of such methods might, indeed, be justified on utilitarian grounds. These grounds are consequentialist: the end of maximizing well-being justifies the means. No special consideration needs to be given to freedom: it must at most take its place among the other "values" which are to be "weighed." Utilitarianism is at the opposite pole from libertarianism, for which freedom is the only value.

As against these extremes, the PGC requires that the freedom of one's recipients be maintained as long as possible, and that every possible effort be made to combine freedom with well-being. The use of coercive methods like those mentioned above would, indeed, be serious violations of the rights to freedom and to basic well-being in Nation B. In addition, it would open the door for other developed nations to impose enslavement and even genocide while proclaiming the same lofty motives. The absence of a commonly accepted civil-libertarian decision procedure makes such a slippery-slope argument more potentially applicable than when it is applied within Nation A. Realistic note must also be taken of further possible immoral abuses of power by Nation A itself.

The civil-libertarian decision procedure must, nevertheless, be used as fully as possible to resolve the other conflicts mentioned previously. It was noted above that there may be a conflict between Nation A's moral obligation to send food in order to prevent starvation in Nation B and Nation A's moral obligation to respect Nation B's political freedom, if the latter's sociopolitical structure is one of the chief obstacles to an equitable distribution of food supplies. The very sending of food, however, with the concomitant expression of deep concern by Nation A, may itself be held to constitute interference with Nation B's internal affairs. Such expression of concern is justified regardless of its impact on the sensitivities of governing officials in Nation B, because the right to basic well-being on the part of its inhabitants takes precedence over the officials' right to be spared embarrassment. Where the nutritional needs of poor persons in Nation B are ignored by its governing officials who derive their power from richer segments of the population, the offer of Nation A to send food must be accompanied by full use of methods to assure that the needy can make their voices heard so that their needs are met. So far as possible, civil-libertarian procedures must be encouraged within Nation B. The justification for this stems both from the intrinsic value of the civil liberties as human rights and from the contribution they can make, when equitably distributed, to the equitable distribution within Nation B of food and other components of basic well-being.

As against military intervention to guarantee that food supplies reach those who need them, the entire set of problems must be exhibited in a rational context which provides a common understanding of causes, rights, and duties. This common understanding must be pursued in ways which lead to mutual practical support of remedial measures. Other kinds of aid, such as fertilizer and money for land-purchase, must also be channeled so as to go to the poor and hence help toward the greater equalization of wealth and power, whose maldistribution causes a large segment of the problem of famine and malnutrition.

A similar approach must be taken to the conflict between Nation A's moral obligations to prevent starvation in Nation B and to respect its procreative freedom. Between the extremes of compulsory sterilization and completely unchecked population growth there are many different alternatives, some of which are more respectful of equal freedom than others. Procreative freedom ranks very high among human freedoms for many obvious reasons. But in countries like Nation B its use is often a response to conditions of extreme poverty, in that the having of many children is viewed as necessary to assure basic well-being and future economic security. It seems, then, that if there is to be any possibility of checking excessive population growth in Nation B by voluntary means, these economic causes must be ameliorated. Ways must be found so that couples' having more than two children is not, and is not viewed by them as, a necessary condition of their avoiding poverty and economic insecurity.

This is in part a bootstrap problem because excessive population growth exacerbates the very poverty which in turn promotes the excess. Nevertheless, measures like those indicated above can be of value. The more equitable distribution of fertilizer and machinery which help to avoid famine can also help to raise living standards. This must be accompanied by information about birth control, provision of contraceptives, and appropriate incentives to use them.

The consideration of the relief of starvation as a human right has suggested that it is closely connected with the civil liberties so highly prized in the Western constitutional democracies as human rights. There may, indeed, be political dictatorships which promote an equitable distribution of food and hence secure one human right at the expense of another. But, entirely apart from the problem of assuring that even in these countries uncontrolled political power will continue to work in this direction, in many underdeveloped countries dictatorship has the opposite effect, so that both kinds of human rights are violated. The relief of starvation is a political as well as a technical problem, and the moral guidance of both sorts of problem requires that the freedom of the recipients be protected equally with their well-being, and this for the sake of well-being itself.

## NOTES

1. See W. N. Hohfeld, *Fundamental Legal Conceptions* (New Haven: Yale University Press, 1919); John Salmond, *Jurisprudence,* 10th ed. (London: Sweet and Maxwell, 1947), pp. 229ff.

2. Robert Nozick, *Anarchy, State, and Utopia* (New York: Basic Books, 1974), p. ix.

3. Cf. H. L. A. Hart, "Are There Any Natural Rights?," *Philosophical Review* 64 (1955): 175ff.

4. Cf. H. J. McCloskey, "Rights," *Philosophical Quarterly* 15 (1965): 124. Elsewhere, McCloskey holds that persons have a prima facie right to the satisfaction of needs: "Human Needs, Rights and Political Values," *American Philosophical Quarterly* 13 (1976): 9-10.

5. See my "Categorial Consistency in Ethics," *Philosophical Quarterly* 17 (1967): 289-99; "Obligation: Political, Legal, Moral," in J. R. Pennock and J. W. Chapman, eds., Nomos no. 12, *Political and Legal Obligation* (New York: Lieber-Atherton, 1970), pp. 55-88; "The Normative Structure of Action," *Review of Metaphysics* 25 (1971): 238-61; "The Justification of Egalitarian Justice," *American Philosophical Quarterly* 8 (1971): 331-41; "Moral Rationality," Lindley Lecture, University of Kansas, 1972; "The 'Is-Ought' Problem Resolved," *Proceedings and Addresses of the American Philosophical Association* 47 (1974): 34-61. In my *Reason and Morality* (Chicago: University of Chicago Press, 1978) I present the whole argument more extensively.

6. See, on the one hand, Paul Baran, *The Political Economy of Growth* (New York: Monthly Review Press, 1957), esp. ch. 5; and on the other, P. T. Bauer, *Dissent on Development* (Cambridge, Mass.: Harvard University Press, 1976).

7. Maurice Cranston, *What Are Human Rights?* (London: Bodley Head, 1973), pp. 66ff. See also his contribution in D. D. Raphael, ed., *Political Theory and the Rights of Man* (London: Macmillan & Co., 1967), pp. 96ff.

8. Raphael in *Political Theory and the Rights of Man,* pp. 65ff., 112.

9. See Thomas T. Poleman, "World Food: A Perspective," *Science* 188 (1975): 515. (This whole issue of *Science* [9 May 1975] is devoted to important articles on the world food problem.) Cf. also Gunnar Myrdal, *Asian Drama: An Inquiry in the Poverty of Nations* (New York: Twentieth Fund, 1969), vol. 2, pp.

895-99, and S. Reutlinger and M. Selowsky, *Malnutrition and Poverty* (Baltimore: Johns Hopkins University Press, 1976).

10. Cf. Pierre R. Crosson, "Institutional Obstacles to Expansion of World Food Production," *Science* 188 (1975): 522, 523, and Harry Walters, "Difficult Issues Underlying Food Problems," ibid., 530.

11. See Kingsley Davis, "Population Policy: Will Current Programs Succeed?," *Science* 158 (1967): 730ff.

12. See Nozick, *Anarchy,* pp. 30-33, 170, 179n., 238.

# Technology and the Sanctity of Life

## KURT BAIER

### I

Few achievements of our civilization are as impressive as those of our inventors and engineers. Yet it is plain by now that technology has not brought all the benefits hoped for or even all those most confidently expected.

There are many reasons for this. Some lie in developments within technology itself. One especially troublesome aspect of the present situation is, of course, the difficulty and danger of keeping our technology going at the rate at which it is expanding or even at the level to which we have become so accustomed: The servant we have built and on whose services we have become abjectly dependent is rapidly gobbling up the reserves of fuel it takes to feed him, and is at the same time choking us with his poisonous wastes. About this aspect of the situation I shall have nothing to say. I shall assume that somehow new sources of energy will eventually be found, that the problem of pollution will be solved or at least sufficiently ameliorated, that the population pressures will be eased, and that consumption will be sufficiently reduced to allow human life to continue.

If these problems cannot be solved, there will in any case be no occasion to worry about those others with which I am concerned. However, even if they can be solved, there remains a second disconcerting aspect of the situation, namely, the disappointing yields of much of our technology. When we look at the services of this industrious new servant of mankind, they appear to have much less value than expected. The automobile has brought almost as many traffic problems as it has solved. The side effects of many miracle drugs seem to be almost as harmful as their main effects are beneficial. The increase in individual life span appears not to have made the extended lives any happier; the net effect appears to be mainly that "the fag end of life" is longer and harder to bear both for the old themselves and for their younger fellows. One could multiply the examples indefinitely.

Two general observations are in order. While technology was simply a servant-substitute, it did not seem to have these undesirable effects. All it did,

160

then, was to make the master's life easier, releasing him from humdrum chores so that he could devote himself to the truly worthwhile. But with technological advance came more ambitious technology, which enabled the possessor to do things no one was able to do before: to travel at great speed, to fly, to see through solid objects, to survive serious injuries and illnesses, to remain alive by artificial means, and to kill, destroy and lay waste on an ever more impressive scale. Armed with this lamp of Aladdin, the possessor can satisfy desires no human servants could satisfy for him. In this way the range of things a man can do is vastly expanded and his dependence on others seemingly reduced. However, this appearance of increased power is deceptive. It is not so much that there is a scarcity of the things wanted as that one person's doing what is necessary to satisfy his desire interferes with another's doing it also. One cannot drive from A to B when too many other people want to do the same. One cannot enjoy the beauties of nature and wilderness if too many travel agencies and tourist organizations "develop" these beauties. If one person has a gun, he is able to prevent others who don't have one from getting what he wants. If they, too, have guns, they are not merely no better off than before anyone had a gun. Actually, they are worse off because they now not merely have no "threat advantage," but are likely to suffer more serious injuries in the competitive struggle for what they want to have or do. Where one man's ability to satisfy a desire implies the absence of that ability in others or requires the power to prevent or deter these others from using their ability, there mass technology often makes things worse for everyone rather than better. It works not like providing a willing servant for everybody but more like pressing the same weapon into everybody's hands.

The second observation, based on the first, is that we cannot hope, simply by increasing our ability to satisfy our desires whatever they may be, to build satisfactory or happy lives independently of others. One (though, of course, only one) of the reasons for this is that a general increase of such ability mutually cancels out the individual gains hoped for. Where such an increase in everyone's ability to attain his ends is supposed to occur as a result of making advanced technology available on a large scale, there we must expect disappointment because of grave side effects which (somewhat as in the improvements in our weapons technology) not only do not increase our ability to attain a desired end (security) but constitute an enormous cost burden as well as threatening serious harm, through the side-effects of its use.

The melancholy lesson taught by the advance of technology is that there are rather narrow practical limits to increasing *both* individual power and freedom. We must therefore always consider what would happen if given general desires were generally satisfied in the way made possible by available technology. If that has rather serious side effects, which outweigh the gains, then such a desire should not be satisfied in this way by *everyone* and so (for reasons of fairness) not by *anyone* (except for special reasons, as when the police, but not everyone, are allowed to carry arms). It should, rather, be frustrated or even altogether eradicated. This may mean that we should be willing (as we already are in the case of drugs) to prohibit the introduction of new technology, perhaps even the retention of some already in use, where its employment on a large scale does have such undesirable consequences. We should be prepared to accept such prohibitions even though this is an interference with what we have regarded as, and what surely has been, an extremely valuable liberty. It does appear to be an inescapable corollary of the increase of individual power that its use must be more carefully supervised and regulated, if we want to be sure that ignorant or reckless or shortsightedly selfish use of such power by an individual or a class does not destroy the very foundation of human existence.[1]

## II

My topic in this paper concerns a somewhat different type of case. It is one in which, through advances in technology, it becomes possible, either for the first time or at any rate more easily, reliably, cheaply, or with fewer undesirable side-effects than before, to do things many always would have liked to be able to do but which our established morality forbids. Technological advance thus produces a situation in which something regarded as wrong, which was previously attainable at most to the privileged few, now becomes accessible to all. Such a change invites us to rethink the conventional prohibition on it, particularly if, as frequently happens, the easy accessibility proves an irresistible temptation to large numbers. The case I wish to discuss is that important cluster of convictions which we group together under the label of the sanctity of life. As might be expected, this ancient ideal is capable of a variety of interpretations, each forbidding and licensing rather different things. Since the stakes are high, it is worth making the effort to maneuver between the Scylla of adhering to misguided values and the Charybdis of jettisoning sound ones.

The first and oldest conception of the sanctity of life is one I shall call "the sacred-process interpretation." It is undoubtedly religious in origin, though it has for some time been secularized and now often means simply, meriting respect or serious consideration.[2] Although it has long been on the wane, it still has a profound and often unrecognized influence on our views of what ought and ought not to be done. If, as I believe, this view can now be seen to lack rational foundation, it is important to be clear where it still has a hold on us.

Early religious world views conceive of the world as a creation of the gods and of many things in it as manifestations or revelations of the divine and, therefore, as sacred. The chief attribute of the gods, their terrible power, is most characteristically manifested in the divine wrath. The sacred, a manifestation of the divine, is therefore conceived as something to which the proper response is fear, awe, submission, and respect. As a manifestation of the divine, the sacred is capable of revealing the divine will, to which men must submit and conform: "For religious man, the cosmos 'lives' and 'speaks.' "[3] Gods appear to men in trees, on mountain tops, in animals, and thus reveal their will. They may also give (more or less unambiguous) signs.[4] Another way in which men can conform to the will of the gods is by imitating cosmic behavior. They assiduously look for parallels between the life of the cosmos and the life of man, in order to sanctify the whole of life.[5] As a result of experiencing various aspects of life as imitations of the sacred cosmic processes, early religious men converted the principal physiological functions including the whole of the human life cycle into *sacraments,* thus transforming them into fixed sacred rituals not modifiable for profane ends. Practices such as castration, sterilization, and artificial birth control undertaken for secular purposes are therefore seen as profanations of what is sacred; as presumptuous and irreverent in the extreme, somewhat like Adam and Eve eating of the forbidden tree or Prometheus stealing fire from heaven.

History records the gradual secularization of all events in the world. The emerging scientific concept of nature represents the world around us as a cosmos free from the irruptions of the supernatural. With this exclusion of the sacred, nature ceases to be a guide to behavior. We can no longer find any significant homologies between the behavior of heaven and procreative life. Nor do we perceive the cycle of the seasons or the life cycle of animals and plants as a compelling model for our own lives.

The place of nature as a guide has increasingly been taken by human reason. With reason as our guide, we can now see in retrospect that the general attitude toward the human life cycle fostered by the early religions was well adapted to the conditions under which men then lived. For there is a serious danger of the extinction of the tribe, perhaps the whole race, where individual life expectation is short and infant mortality high and where survival and prosperity for all, but particularly support in old age, depend on having a large family. Under such conditions, it is imperative (if the tribe or race is to be preserved) that everyone do his bit towards keeping life's flame burning. Fertility worship is natural, going forth and multiplying a boon. But wasting one's seed for personal reasons (as did Onan) or interfering (by contraceptive techniques or abortion) with the natural events leading to reproduction is selfish, antisocial, and immoral.

Many forms of Christianity have inherited from the Old Testament the sacred-process version of the ideal of the sanctity of life, with its insistence on fertility. They have, however, added another, potentially opposed attitude, namely, guilt about sexual pleasure, as expressed by St. Paul and St. Augustine, and frequently revived.[6] The two attitudes are precariously united by the doctrine that sexual intercourse (and the pleasure even marriage cannot altogether take from it) is permissible only and in as far as it is used for procreation. The so-called sexual revolution has brought about a softening of the Christian denunciations of sexual pleasure, without however significantly changing its attitude toward fertility, or its opposition to separating sex from reproduction. Many Christians still perceive rational planning of family or population size as impious, sacrilegious, a form of "playing God." And even among non-Christians and atheists, one still finds the conviction that reproductive vigor is a virtue, childlessness selfish and a vice.

The seriousness of the dangers of overpopulation does, however, raise not merely the question of whether it is morally permissible for a couple to take the measures modern technology makes available to them to prevent conception *if they want to,* but the more serious one of the number of children it is desirable or permissible for them to have, and the even more frightening one of whether society may see to it that people do not exceed their permissible quota. The sacred-process interpretation of the sanctity of life is not, of course, the only factor which makes for excessive procreation. But it may be a sufficiently important one so that, once the unsoundness of that interpretation is recognized, governments may succeed in reducing the procreative fervor by laissez faire methods, that is, by economic incentives and moral appeals, without having to resort to the sterner measures which the Indian government recently felt it had to use.

## III

The second, "the sacred-individual interpretation," differs from the previous one on two important points. The first concerns that which is sacrosanct. It is no longer the whole of biological life[7] or even the whole of the human life cycle but only that phase of it which we regard as "the natural life span" of an individual human being. On this interpretation, what is sacrosanct is the human individual, not the genetic materials whose fusion (at any rate in sexual beings) is a precondition of the existence of such individuals. This ideal contrasts with that of some geneticists who treat with reverence not the human individual but the "gene pool."[8]

The second concerns what we mean when we think of it as sacrosanct. The core-idea now is no longer the sacred, as in the sacred-process interpretation, but the fundamentally different idea of a natural right to life. This is the secular moral doctrine that human individuals, in virtue solely of some property characteristic of humans, have a right to life. Their right to life is thus based on their characteristic nature, not on the type of society into which they are born or on the economic and other conditions in which that society finds itself.

The doctrine of the natural right to life, properly understood, appears sound to me. A right is itself a sort of good. "N has a right to A" means that it is or would be a good thing for there to be, or become recognized in a given society, and perhaps suitably enforced, a rule imposing on all other members of the society the requirement of noninterference with N's having A, or even the requirement that certain people secure A for him, if he wants it. That N has a right to A thus implies not merely that it is a good thing for him to have A, but also a good thing for there to be machinery securing that possession for him. The good a person has who has a right to A is not the same good as A, for he may have the right without having A, and vice versa. Nor is it the same as the availability to him of the machinery which secures A for him, for his right to A may be unrecognized. The good he has in having a right to A, whether recognized or unrecognized, moral or legal, is merely the (to him welcome) fact that it is or would be a good thing for there to be machinery to secure for him the possession of A. To say that the right is "natural" is to say that the ground of having the right is simply having the appropriate nature, and is not some special prior condition, such as a contract, some special performance entitling him to A, or some authority's conferment on him of the right to A.

The question is whether every human individual has such a natural right to life, in the sense, at least, of being allowed to live his natural life span. In other words, the question is whether it would actually be a good thing, if in any society whatsoever, every human individual were protected by his society's enforcement machinery, primarily of course its law, to live to the end of his natural life span. And when the question is posed in this way, the answer must surely be Yes. For surely everyone would have every reason to wish to be so protected, even though this necessarily involves everyone, including himself, being prohibited from doing many things which would shorten the natural life span of others. For (biological) life is, to most of us, an extremely important good. It is not merely that it is the condition of the realization of all other goods, but that being alive is itself treasured by most of us. And even though there are things worse than death and values greater than life itself, for most people most of the time life is more precious than anything else with which it happens to come into conflict. This would seem sufficient reason not only for *everyone* to want (himself) to be protected but to want it to be the case that everyone is protected against others taking, endangering, or shortening his life.

However, from the fact that life is a good so precious that we must acknowledge a natural right to life, it does not follow that one does not have a right to terminate one's own life. According to some philosophers, "some things to which human beings are entitled we often feel should not be the subject of options. Obvious examples are the right to life...."[9] These philosophers feel that "certain benefits and protections are such that all men ought to have them and that men in general cannot properly alienate or deprive themselves of these rights or deem themselves to have no rights."[10] Now, this point is well taken, if it refers only to *the protection* which having a right ought to confer. We rightly feel that no one should be able to give away or sell a right to certain important goods, such as life. But that still leaves them free to refuse or to give away, if they do not want it, *the good* secured to them, if they want it, by the right. There is all the difference between the undesirability of allowing the abolition, relinquishment, renunciation, or transfer *of a right* to something, and the relinquishment, renunciation, or transfer *of the something* to which one has a right. If rights were not, as Hart rightly claims, in this sense optional, then in those important cases in which one man's right to X is constituted by another man's duty to secure X to him, such a nonoptional right to X would necessarily amount to a duty to have X.[11] If my right to the firewood I have ordered from the supplier and paid for were not optional in this sense, I would have a duty to receive the firewood even if I no longer want it. And even though the right to life is not thus constituted by the correlative duty (not to kill, etc.), still the same optionality must hold.[12] Surely the natural right to life does not *entail* the natural duty to live, any more than the right to receive firewood entails the duty to receive it. It may be that we also have such a duty to live, but it cannot be extracted from the *inalienability* of the natural right to life. And once this is seen, it is also clear that there is no other good reason to think there is such a natural duty. One need only bear in mind that, at certain stages, our lives, far from being a good, can become a terrible burden to us. There surely are, at least in such cases, very strong reasons to think that there is a natural right to terminate one's life, to release others from the duty to keep one alive, and even from their duty not to terminate one's life.

I think it is primarily the residue of the sacred-process conception of the sanctity of life, which powerfully sways us in the other direction. When we no longer think it impious to interfere with the natural life cycle, no longer think that in doing so we are arrogating to ourselves divine prerogatives, we have no good reason left to object to the widespread conviction that there is a right to die as well as a right to life.

## IV

Two questions must now be examined. The first concerns that aspect of human nature in virtue of which human beings have the natural right to life.

The second concerns the exact points at which the individual human life and the right to life begin and end. Two rival views have dominated discussion. One holds that this property is human individuality, that the life of the human individual begins at conception and ends with biological death and that the natural right to life therefore begins at conception and ends in death. The other takes that property to be something which is characteristically, perhaps uniquely, human and which appears only some time after conception and may disappear before death, and that the natural right to life is not, therefore, coextensive with human individuality.[13]

Because of our enormously increased ability to prolong life by patching up the failing function of body and mind, attention has become focused on desirable limits to the prolongation of human life. An important new concept is the "quality of life," as this term is used in the context of "critical care medicine." There it means what may be called the internal quality of life, that is, the quality of *experienced* life. This is something which tends gradually to deteriorate in old age, as vigor, agility, mobility, perception, memory, and sharpness of mind decline. Although poor quality of life in this sense is quite compatible with a rich and fulfilling personal life, as is demonstrated by the case of Helen Keller, it does make a worthwhile life less likely, and a certain minimum seems indispensable. An example of a sudden and particularly striking deterioration in quality of life is the well known case of Karen Ann Quinlan who has been in a deep coma for more than a year and whose internal quality of life has been reduced to zero level. In such cases, the main reason for holding that all human beings have a right to (biological) life has gone: to such human beings biological life is no longer a good. This is so, not just because they are unconscious, but because they are irreversibly so. To the temporarily unconscious person biological life can be said to be still a good, since he will again have a personal life when he regains consciousness. For this reason, even though we cannot commiserate with a person who has been killed in his sleep—he'll never know what hit him—we can say that in being robbed of biological life, he has been robbed of a good because having biological life is a condition of experiencing anything as a good (or evil), including one's qualitative life.[14]

At the starting point of individual human life we find, of course, an inverse development. Individual human life undoubtedly begins at conception. We cannot even entertain the hypothesis that a given individual should have been conceived at a different time from the actual one: what makes him the individual he is, would seem to be the fact that he was conceived at that moment and in that environment as the union of the very reproductive materials that formed the conceptus. This is probably the main consideration which leads people to insist that the sanctity of life in this interpretation (that is, the individual's natural right to life), protects *him* from the moment of conception. But this is a mistake. From the fact that the (biological) life *of the human individual* begins at conception, it does not follow that the right to life covers a human individual from that point on, any more than the fact that a human individual's life ends at (biological) death, entails that the right to life covers the individual until that moment. It all depends on what is the ground or rationale of that right. If the ground were the possession of human individuality, then it would indeed begin at conception and end with biological death (however defined exactly). But it is hard to see the moral relevance of this supposed ground. On the other hand, if the ground is that his qualitative (and therefore his biological) life is a good to an individual, then the right may well end earlier than biological death and begin later than conception, since at these stages the human individual may have no qualitative life and so nothing may be a good (or evil) to him.[15]

## V

On the third, the sacred-essence interpretation of the sanctity of life, what is sacrosanct is "the essential nature of a man", whether of an individual or of the species. Any tinkering with that nature would therefore be sacrilegious and wrong. Until not long ago, the more spectacular types of interference occurred only in science fiction. But recently biomedical and technological advances appear to have made possible modifications of the basic biological design of man which look, at least at first sight, as if they did constitute just such violations of man's nature. The most spectacular of these discoveries are those in genetics and brain manipulation. I shall not say anything about genetic engineering but confine myself to brain manipulation which includes neurosurgery, electrical stimulation by the implantation of electrodes in various parts of the brain, and chemical stimulation by various drugs. So far the bulk of experiments has been performed on animals, but in the absence of contrary evidence it is not unreasonable to assume that similar results could be achieved in human beings.[16]

What is peculiar to these new techniques is not that they are cases of behavior modification. Such deliberate modifications of someone's responses to the environment, with or without his explicit consent have always occurred: when doctors treated patients; when educators increased a student's skills; when religious conversion or the administration of drugs brought about a personality change; or when a person through the manipulation of information available to him (propaganda), through inducements, threats of various kinds of deprivation, or actual torture, was made to do something he would not otherwise have done. In all such cases, one person exercised deliberate control over another's behavior. The various professions involved, physicians, educators, the media, even religious missionaries, have evolved their own professional ethics which cope more or less effectively with the conflicts of interests which arise in these relationships. But the problems that have arisen with these new techniques go beyond these standard conflicts of concern.[17]

Consider the description of the technique given by Perry London:

> Animals and men can be oriented toward each other with emotions ranging from stark terror or morbidity to passionate affection and sexual desire. Docility, fearful withdrawal, and panicked efforts at escape can be made to alternate with fury and ferocity of such degree that its subject can as readily destroy himself by exhaustion from his consuming rage as he can the object of it, whom he attacks, heedless of both danger and opportunity. Eating, drinking, sleeping, moving of bowels or limbs or organs of sensation, gracefully or in spastic comedy, can all be managed on electrical demand by puppeteers whose flawless strings are pulled from miles away by the unseen call of radio and whose puppets, made of flesh and blood, look ''like electronic toys'', so little self-direction do they seem to have.[18]

The explosive social implications of such ways of brain manipulation clearly emerge from an example by José M. R. Delgado who studied an entire colony of rhesus monkeys. In such a colony, one monkey soon emerges as the boss, who has territorial privileges, has first choice of the females and the food, and maintains his ruling position by various gestures, grimaces, and postures, as well as actual attacks. One such monkey, called Ali, had an electrode placed in his brain and his caudate nucleus stimulated for five seconds once a minute for an hour. During that time he dropped his domineering behavior and the other monkeys lost their fear. But ten minutes after the stimulation was discontinued he returned to his old behavior and to dominance. When a lever was attached to the cave wall and pressed, it triggered stimulation in Ali, and his behavior become peaceful. A female monkey, Elsa, discovered that Ali's aggressiveness could be inhibited by pressing the lever, and so Elsa pressed it whenever Ali attacked her, thus significantly reducing Ali's dominant position.[19]

We must distinguish two different ways in which brain manipulation may produce behavior. One (stimulation in the lateral portions of the hypothalamus and the limbic system) produces some rewarding or penalizing ''subjective experiences'' thereby inducing the subject to act so as to secure or avoid these experiences. A rat, for instance, can learn to press a lever connected by cable to an electrode implanted in its lateral hypothalamus. ''Some of these animals 'self-stimulated' by pressing the lever more than 100 times every minute and they maintained this pace hour after hour.''[20] Here the question is how dominant these experiences would prove to be in human beings. Would they prove ''irresistible''? This sort of brain stimulation would correspond to getting a person hooked on cigarettes or heroin, or to subjecting him to torture or the threat of torture.[21]

A second type of stimulation (if it is possible) would, however, introduce a quite novel kind of interference. It would "directly" produce the behavior wanted by the controller without involving the subject's intelligent self-direction. R. L. Pinneo implanted a large number of electrodes (more than 60, with plans to use 240) in strategic positions in a monkey's brain and, with a suitable computer program, produced behavioral responses which (since the control center of voluntary movement in the cortex had been destroyed) were independent of the monkey's will. The behavior produced was quite complex, for example, reaching out to a dish in front of him, picking up a piece of food, and bringing it rapidly and smoothly to his mouth. Other computer programs produced other equally complex forms of behavior.[22]

If such stimulation could be produced in men, it would violate the sanctity of life in the sacred-essence interpretation. This type of interference combines the worst features of all types. A person is made to do what (perhaps) he does not really want to do, and without even having to be deceived by clever propaganda into believing something that would incline him to do it. And he does it without his will having to be bent, as in torture or the threat of torture. And it is something he is doing himself, not some movement which his body, or a part of it, is made to do by physical force, as when he is dragged away in handcuffs. The subject thus is not merely the controller's duped, frightened, or overpowered *servant,* but really his *puppet.* The controller has found, and is using those "strings of action" which normally only the agent himself can pull. The objection to this is, of course, that the agent's own rational control center has been bypassed and so man's essential nature, behavior control through his own reason, destroyed. This would really amount to a destruction in an individual of a core element of the species-nature of man.

Of course, we are (still?) a long way from producing human behavior in this way. Even if one day we acquire this power, the dangers of its coming to be used will not be serious until such brain stimulation can be achieved without the insertion of electrodes, perhaps by some external and possibly unnoticeable technique. This would seem to be still in the realm of science fiction. But the attempt to assess the risks of this sort of treatment have brought to light an important point: What is objectionable is not so much this form of interference as such but that it should be imposed in certain conditions, without the consent of the agent and for someone else's end. If a person is made to do things at the pleasure of another through the elimination of his own voluntary control center, then this is morally objectionable; it really is a violation of the sacred-essence interpretation of the sanctity of life. But if his voluntary control center was already blocked say, by a stroke, or if in certain brain lesions, tumors, etc., that rational control center was already bypassed and so some of his movements are no longer "under his rational control," and if the control button is in the agent's own hands, not in someone else's (as, in the case of Ali, it was in the hands of Else), then such an arrangement, such a production of behavior, is not morally objectionable. For then, with the aid of this new technology, the agent has been given an increased measure of self-control, greater (mechanical) will power, greater behavioral rationality. He can no longer walk, but he can still press the button of the computer program for walking whenever he wants to. He can no longer control his outbursts of anger, but he can still press the relevant "self-control" button.

## VI

To summarize briefly: I distinguished three social problems arising out of the use of technology on a large scale. The first is the problem of keeping the technology going on the current or a larger scale without destroying human and other forms of life with its toxic wastes. Only improved technology can solve this problem. I have not tried to examine the difficult question of how to determine the likelihood of the arrival of such improved technology at some crucial future date or what should be done if such improved technology is unlikely to be forthcoming before serious and irreversible damage is done to our environment.

The second problem consists in the mutual interference and frustration caused by the use of some technology on a large scale. The solution to this problem lies in judicious (fair) restrictions on the use of such technology. Again I did not examine the really important question of what to do if the fair accrual of benefits from the use of such technology requires the imposition of very stringent restrictions on its use.

Instead, I examined a case of the third type of problem which is raised by technology enabling its user to attain ends the attainment of which, though frequently desired, is considered wrong by the prevalent morality. This problem is an essentially ethical one: Can the benefits gained by the attainment of these ends with the help of the new technology morally justify the pursuit of these ends despite their prohibition by the currently accepted morality?

The case I examined concerned the use of medical technology, both old and new, relating to the prolongation of life, to contraception and to brain manipulation. The moral convictions with which certain uses of such technology conflict are often grouped together under the label of the sanctity of life. I distinguished three different interpretations of that ideal, the sacred-process, the sacred-individual, and the sacred-essence interpretations. Concerning the first interpretation, I argued that it now lacks rational

172        TECHNOLOGY AND THE SANCTITY OF LIFE

support, partly because its original religious foundation no longer coheres
with well-supported (scientific) beliefs about the nature of the world and
partly because the once prevailing circumstances, danger to the race from
insufficient numbers, which did give strong rational support to enthusiasm for
fertility, now no longer prevail.

Concerning the second interpretation, I argued that while the view that
normal adult humans have a natural right to life is perfectly sound and while it
is true that the biological life of the individual begins at conception and ends at
(biological) death, it does not follow from this and indeed is not plausible that
individuality is the ground for ascribing the right to life to normal adult
humans. It follows that the right to life may begin later and end earlier than the
individual's biological life.

The upshot of the discussion of these two interpretations was that while
the sacred-process interpretation lends support to the opposition to euthanasia,
birth control, and sterilization, it is without rational support; whereas the
sacred-individual interpretation, which is important and sound, does not lend
such support and only seems to do so to those who are swayed by an unac-
knowledged acceptance of the sacred-process interpretation.

In the final section, I argued that the sacred-essence interpretation is
sound and protects one of our rightly treasured possessions, the normal adult
individual's rational control of his own behavior. I also argued that the use of
new technologies for brain manipulation may but need not come into conflict
with the norms based on the third interpretation. I argued that the use of such
technology is a violation of these norms if its purpose is the control of the
behavior of others, but that it is not such a violation if it is used to enable those
people whose rational control of their own behavior had already been
weakened or impaired, to improve or regain such control.


NOTES

1. On this point I reluctantly find myself in agreement with much of what is
said by Robert L. Heilbroner in his alarming book, *An Inquiry into the Human
Prospect* (New York: W. W. Norton and Co., 1975).
2. See e.g., Glanville Williams, *The Sanctity of Life and the Criminal Law* (New
York: Alfred Knopf, 1972), esp. pp. ix–xi. Also, Rudolf Otto, *The Idea of the Holy*
(London: Geoffrey Cumberledge, 1952); and Mircea Eliade, *The Sacred and the
Profane* (New York: Harper Torchbooks, 1961).
3. Eliade, *Sacred and Profane*, p. 165.
4. "According to the legend, the *marabout* who founded El-Hamel at the end
of the sixteenth century stopped to spend the night near a spring and planted his stick in
the ground. The next morning, when he went for it to resume his journey, he found that

it had taken root and that buds had sprouted on it. He considered this a sign of God's will and settled in that place." Rene Basset, *Revue des Traditions Populaires* 22 (1907): 287. Quoted by Eliade, *Sacred and Profane*, p. 27.

5. "Woman is assimilated to the soil, seed to the *semen virile,* and agricultural work to conjugal union. 'This woman has become like living soil: sow seed in her, ye men!' says the *Atharva Veda* (XIV, 2, 14). 'Your women are as fields for you', says the *Koran,* (II, 225). A sterile queen laments, 'I am like a field where nothing grows!'. On the contrary, in a twelfth-century hymn, the Virgin Mary is glorified as 'ground not to be plowed, which brought forth fruit' *(terra non arabilis quae fructum parturiit)*" Eliade, *Sacred and Profane,* p. 166.

6. The most recent denunciations of sexual pleasure can be found in P. T. Geach's book, *The Virtues* (Cambridge: Cambridge University Press, 1977). The following quotation, though quite representative is only, so to speak, the tip of the volcano: "There is clearly an intimate connexion between sexuality as it now is . . . and original sin . . . man's generative powers and appetites are of necessity specially corrupted; for they are the very means by which the original corrupt appetite perpetuates itself. Christians hold that for this enormous evil God provided a remedy at once, not waiting till the Incarnation: the great good of marriage . . . complete healing there cannot be in this world; for the offspring of the best marriage will be born in Original Sin . . . ; but for all that children are the blessing and the crown of marriage. . . . Apart from the good of marriage that redeems it, sex is poison" (pp. 146–47).

7. By "biological life" I mean (roughly) living things, that is, things capable of metabolism, growth, responsiveness to the environment, and reproduction, or whatever it is in virtue of the possession of which things are alive. It is perhaps worth adding that the sacred process interpretation is a combination of two more general sentiments. One is an extended "fellow-feeling" for all (biological) life, a brotherhood of living things. The other is a kind of cosmic piety, a policy of handsoff whatever there is in the universe. Such piety may extend beyond even the realm of biological life and include such things as lakes, mountains, rocks, or rivers. For a particularly striking version of such a view, see e.g., Roderick Nash, "Environmental Ethics" in *Environmental Spectrum: Social and Economic Views on the Quality of Life* (New York: D. van Nostrand, 1974), pp. 142–50.

8. Thus, Howard L. Hamilton writes, in the entry on embryonic development in *The Harper Encyclopedia of Science:* "The embryologist knows the answer to the old riddle about which came first, the chicken or the egg: he knows that the egg is all-important because within it is embedded all surviving heredity from the past and from it will come all future life. The body is simply a temporary house which has undergone much remodelling over the millennia."

9. Geoffrey Marshall, "Rights, Options, and Entitlements," *Oxford Essays in Jurisprudence,* 2d series, p. 238.

10. Ibid., p. 239.

11. "Bentham on Legal Rights," *Oxford Essays in Jurisprudence,* p. 196.

12. I have briefly discussed the distinction between these two types of correlativity of rights and obligations in my paper, "Ethical Egoism and Interpersonal Compatibility," *Philosophical Studies* 24 (1973): 360–62.

13. On one view, a presupposition of having the right to life is the ability to lead a certain sort of life, namely, one which can have a certain sort of quality. Only sentient creatures can have or lead such a life. Plants, the lower animals, and even people in a coma lack such a life. There are two aspects of such a life which may be

called the "quality of life". In the case of a conceptus or a person in a coma, the "internal" quality of life is altogether lacking. In the case of the aged, it tends to deteriorate as their various faculties and powers decline. We can also speak of the "external" quality of life, namely, those environmental conditions on which the excellence of a given life depends. I shall not say anything about the external quality of life here, since my views may be found in my paper "Towards a Definition of 'Quality of Life,'" *Environmental Spectrum*.

14. Although being robbed of a good in this way is different from the standard cases in that it also deprives one of the ability to learn of and feel the loss, this only shows that one can be robbed without knowing it. Whether he knows it or not, a person who has his biological life taken away from him, also has his qualitative life, and so normally what would be his greatest good taken from him, if such deprivation were not at the same time also the destruction of him.

15. Cf., the interesting discussions of these issues in the paper by Michael Tooley already referred to, and in Mary Anne Warren's "On the Moral and Legal Status of Abortion," *The Monist* 57, no. 1 (Jan. 1973).

16. For a survey of experiments, see José M. R. Delgado, *Physical Control of the Mind* (New York: Harper & Row, 1969). Also Eliot S. Valenstein, *Brain Control* (John Wiley & Sons, 1973).

17. For a discussion, see Vernon H. Mark, "Brain Surgery in Aggressive Epileptics," *The Hastings Center Report*, 3, no. 1 (February 1973). See also *The Hastings Center Report*, Special Supplement (May 1973).

18. Serious doubt about that has been raised e.g., by Eliot S. Valenstein in his book, *Brain Control* to which I have already referred above.

19. Perry London, *Behavior Control* (New York: Harper & Row, 1969), p. 137.

20. José M. R. Delgado, *Physical Control of the Mind*, pp. 164–66.

21. Valenstein, *Brain Control*, p. 37.

22. These descriptions are taken from Valenstein, ibid., pp. 75–80.

# Why Preserve Landmarks?
# A Preliminary Inquiry

## M. P. and N. H. GOLDING*

AMONG THE ENVIRONMENTAL CONCERNS WHICH CURRENTLY ARE RECEIVING philosophical attention, man-made elements of the environment have not had a prominent place except in a negative way: there is a tendency to view man and his works as enemies of nature. While this tendency is perhaps more extreme in popular than in philosophical discussions, the perspective it represents can have a distorting effect on treatment of the environmental issues. To this perspective, the subject of landmark preservation may help in providing the needed corrective; for man's works are also part of our environment and some of these works—here specifically, historical landmarks—may also merit the same sort of care and consideration that environmentalists would have us accord to the natural and animal realms. Landmark preservation, in fact, has been compared to the preservation of animal species. Thus, Professor John J. Costonis writes: "Urban landmarks merit recognition as an imperiled species alongside the ocelot and the snow leopard."[1] Though Costonis does not develop the point, he implies that at least some of the reasons that may be given for preserving the ocelot apply to landmarks as well. Costonis has also written an article under the title "Do Buildings Have Rights?"—a title which derives from an environmentalist rhetoric that countenances ascribing rights to trees and other natural objects.[2]

In this paper we shall propose a rationale for landmark preservation. The reason for seeking such a rationale is basically the same as the case of natural preservation. A building, a site, or a neighborhood—no matter how beautiful and historically significant—is a resource for which other uses might be found. An old building may be viewed as standing in the way of "progress," and its destruction will follow as a matter of course unless it can be shown to merit landmark status. But why preserve landmarks? (Why preserve

*Naomi H. Golding wishes to thank the National Endowment for the Arts for an award of a fellowship to investigate the problem of landmark preservation.

the ocelot?) This question motivates our inquiry. We should note here, as we note again later on, that our rationale for landmark preservation does not settle the matter of which buildings or sites should be preserved. Nor does it imply that it is necessarily wrong to destroy a building that might otherwise merit preservation as a landmark. A society has many legitimate interests aside from the preservation of landmarks, which interests may, in a specific case, be weightier than the preservationist interest.

The structure of our paper is as follows. In order to give some precision to the topic, we begin with a discussion of the meaning of "landmark preservation." This is followed by an investigation of the suggested similarity between landmark preservation and the preservation of animal species and the natural environment. Here we shall find it necessary to examine the soundness of some sample environmentalist arguments on their own terms as well as to consider the possibility of extending them to the issue of landmarks. We then turn to the possibility of justifying landmark preservation on analogy to the preservation of art objects. After criticizing these approaches to the problem, we offer a positive one of our own in regard to landmark preservation but stake no claim to originality for it. We emphasize its preliminary character because its details are not fully developed. No pretense is made that any of the above subjects is treated with finality.

Clarification of the meaning of "landmark preservation" is the necessary starting-point of our discussion. Let us consider each of its constituent terms separately, taking "preservation" first. "Preservation," it turns out, is not an easy term to define within the context of our problem, for a reason that will emerge shortly. Since this term is often used interchangeably with "conservation" (e.g., "wildlife conservation," "wildlife preservation"), it will be helpful to contrast the two terms in one respect, even if this should appear somewhat arbitrary. "Conservation," as we employ it, refers to the saving of some resource or object for future consumption by the present generation or a later generation. An example of this is fuel conservation, in which fuel is saved for use—using it up—later on. In this sense one might speak of conserving the ocelot so that our grand-children can use ocelot pelts to make fur coats. Many of the early conservationists were great hunters, and they wanted to conserve wildlife in order to ensure a supply of game, among other things.

Admittedly, there are cases of conservation that are not directly covered by this sense of the term (e.g., conservation of a species of wildlife in order to protect the eco-system of a forest area), but the meaning just designated is the one we need in order to make our contrast between "preservation" and "conservation." For in contrast to conservation, preservation is the saving of a resource or object (1) with no later use for it in mind, or (2) if a use is intended, it is a use that does not involve "using it up," that is, a non-consumption use. Thus, the ocelot might be preserved simply to keep the species in existence or in order to enjoy its presence. Similarly a forest area might be preserved simply to keep it in existence or in order to enjoy its presence.

Landmark preservation involves saving an object (e.g., a building, a neighborhood—the term "object" is employed broadly here) from destruction or significant alteration and from any consumption use. When an object is designated a landmark it may be necessary to restore it to a state or condition (usually its original condition) such that it properly can serve as a landmark;[3] if it is already in that condition, further alteration of it may be forbidden. In line with the notion of preservation in the previous paragraph, landmark preservation is the saving of a certain type of object in order to keep it in existence or in order to enjoy its presence. The problem of this paper is whether arguments can be found for landmark preservation on the basis of one or the other of these aims.

More, however, needs to be said about the second of these aims. For if a landmark should be preserved in order to enjoy its presence, it would seem that this is a rather special kind of enjoyment, distinguishable, for example, from recreational enjoyment. Or to employ the terminology of "use," the use that is intended is a special kind of use. This special kind of use or enjoyment is difficult to describe, however, which is why "preservation" is not easy to define fully as far as landmarks are concerned. Perhaps we can approximate what it is by turning to the meaning of "landmark."

The dictionary, always a good place to begin, defines "landmark" as (1) an object (e.g., stone or tree) that marks the boundary of land; (2*a*) a conspicuous object that marks a locality; (2*b*) a structure used as a point of orientation in locating other structures; (3) an event or development that marks a turning point or stage (e.g., a novel that is a landmark in modern literature); and (4) a structure (e.g., a building) of unusual historical and aesthetic interest; especially one that is officially designated and set aside for preservation.[4] Two features of this definition deserve our notice. First, the definition allows as landmarks both events and things, and regarding things it allows as landmarks both natural and man-made objects (i.e., artifacts). Second, the last part of the definition seems to conjoin as criteria for a man-made object to be a landmark that it should be both of historical and aesthetic interest.

The inclusion of events as landmarks may be ignored for our purposes, and it is the last part of the definition which seems most relevant to our problem. This part excludes natural objects from consideration, so that if it is maintained for some natural object that it should be saved from destruction or alteration, the case would have to be made on the usual conservationist or preservationist grounds. Still, we think that there may be at least a few instances of natural objects for whose preservation one could argue on the special ground of landmark preservation. This will be discussed shortly. Another point to be considered is the role of aesthetic interest in landmark preservation.

City planners and architects, as one might expect, have written a good deal on the subject of landmarks. The conception of landmarks that may be gleaned from Kevin Lynch's influential book, *The Image of the City* (1960), is the following: A landmark is a visible element which helps people visualize their surroundings, define their spatial relationship to their environment, and (or?) conceive of that environment as one having a cohesive pattern. This conception is noteworthy in that landmarks are viewed more or less along the lines of the first and second parts of the dictionary definition, that is, in the way a stone or tree marks a boundary of land, and so on. As such, it is too narrowly conceived for our problem, but there is a core of meaning that is significant for it. Since Lynch is concerned with the "imageability" of a city and the psychic import of landmarks, his core conception of a landmark is that it endows one with a sense of orientation. If we add to this the view of many writers that architecture is concerned with man's use of space as an elaboration of culture (Edward T. Hall, *The Hidden Dimension*, 1966) or as an expression of social values and cultural patterns (Robert Gutman, *People and Buildings*, 1972), we can expand Lynch's position to be saying that a landmark enables people to achieve a sense of historical or cultural orientation to their environment. We prefer to put this somewhat differently, however. We regard a landmark as an object that enables one to achieve an orientation to one's historical or cultural environment. It is this formulation which brings out the special character of landmarks as part of current environmental concerns.

With the possible exception of Kevin Lynch, urban designers and architects quite naturally focus upon man-made landmarks (especially buildings, neighborhoods and districts), for urban design and architecture are now viewed as dealing with a physical artifact that represents a social interaction.[5] (The historic preservation movement is said to have begun in the United States with the acquisition of the Hansbrouck House, George Washington's headquarters in Newburgh, New York, in 1850.) But under certain conditions a natural object can also be a landmark. Instances of this are the Civil War battlefields of Chicamauga, Gettysburg, and Shiloh. The point of course is that a natural object can be *invested* with historical or cultural significance.

Perhaps the most unusual case is the New York City Landmarks Preservation Commission's designation of a tree that grows in Brooklyn as a landmark.[6] This tree, a *Magnolia grandiflora*, a species that rarely flourishes so far North, was planted in 1885 or thereabout, and was lovingly attended by a resident of the neighborhood for many years. The commission found that this tree "has a special character, special historical and aesthetic interest and value as part of the development, heritage and cultural characteristics of New York City.'' The language of the finding may seem a bit effusive, and perhaps it was necessitated by the legal charge under which the commission operates and has authority. In any case, the tree was not preserved merely as a tree, but as a tree that has historical and social significance, that is, because of a particular relationship it has to human beings. Though cases of this type will probably be exceptions to the rule, the scope of our problem can now be extended to natural objects, but in a respect that is essentially different from the usual environmentalist concerns. Our problem is what the grounds are for preserving elements of the historically and culturally significant environment, be they artifacts or natural objects.

We now can say a bit more about the special kind of use or enjoyment provided by landmarks, which use or enjoyment was earlier stated to be one of the possible aims of landmark preservation. This may be amplified to refer to the special kind of use or enjoyment derived from the experiencing of historically and culturally significant objects. Though it must be granted that this amplification is not very perspicuous, it also must be acknowledged that this sort of experience is difficult to analyze. Since it appears to be a near relative to aesthetic experience, it is hardly surprising that the last part of the dictionary definition of ''landmark'' should conjoin unusual historical and aesthetic interest as criteria for the designation of landmarks. This conjunction in fact suggests one of the arguments that can be given for landmark preservation, and we shall examine this argument shortly.

First let us note that some of the legislation on landmarks, as well as the dictionary, includes mention of an aesthetic element. A lawyer, the late Albert J. Bard, is credited with introducing the word ''aesthetic'' into the laws of the state of New York, in his amendment to the General City Law, adopted in 1956. ''The word *aesthetic* had, until the Bard Law was enacted, been carefully avoided in proper legislative circles.''[7] The Bard Law is the enabling legislation for the designation of landmarks and historic districts in the state. We already saw that the New York City Landmarks Preservation Commission used the term when it designated the magnolia tree as a landmark, although it is far from clear that aesthetic considerations were determinative. In federal legislation, the National Historic Preservation Act of 1966 authorizes the secretary of the interior to establish programs for the preservation of ''properties that are significant in American history, architecture, archeology and culture,'' and the National Park Service of the Department of the Interior has formulated criteria of eligibility for being listed on the National Register of Historic Places. (Before 1966, federal legislation gave limited protection to some historic sites.) These criteria include such qualities as ''integrity of location, design, setting, materials, workmanship, feeling and association'' in properties that are connected with significant historic events or persons; that embody distinctive characteristics of a type, period, or method of construction; that represent the work of a master; that possess high artistic values; or that are valuable sources of historic or prehistoric information.[8]

The question raised by this legislation is the relationship between the historical-cultural criteria for designation as a landmark or historic place and the aesthetic criteria. Are these two types of criteria independent? This is not the place to open the Pandora's box of the meaning of "aesthetic." Perhaps it is enough to say that certain of the aesthetic qualities of an object cannot be understood as such except in relation to an historical or cultural context (e.g., qualities that "represent the work of a master") and certain aesthetic feelings seem to be almost inseparable from feelings of historic and cultural association. Therefore, the designation of something as a landmark on aesthetic considerations will usually be tantamount to so designating it on historical-cultural considerations, and vice versa.

The question still remains, however, with respect to so-called intrinsic qualities of aesthetic excellence—the intrinsic beauty of a building, for instance. It seems plausible to hold that the aesthetic feeling derived from the experience or contemplation of such intrinsic qualities is unique and has no necessary relation to historical and cultural associations, just as these intrinsic qualities, by definition, have no necessary relation to an object's historical or cultural qualities. One may wonder, therefore, why sites of "high artistic value" should be eligible for inclusion on the National Register of Historic Places. If the Congress wished to preserve beautiful things, why did it not include beautiful paintings and statues under the terms of the National Historic Preservation Act? Perhaps there is no simple answer, but it is unlikely that Congress ever gave thought to the matter and deliberately decided to exclude paintings and statues. A more plausible explanation, if such there be, is that in view of the purpose of the act (namely, the preservation of significant American "properties"—sites) and the authority thereby delegated to the secretary of the interior, the Department of the Interior included "high artistic value" as one of a set of multiple but overlapping criteria for designation as an historic place. These criteria, it may be assumed, do not eliminate the need to find an historical-cultural basis for designation in a specific case. Yet they are important, for it is plain that not everything of historical or cultural interest can be preserved.

These remarks suggest an important distinction. It is necessary to distinguish between the rationale (the justification, ground) for landmark preservation in general—Why preserve landmarks at all?—and the criteria to be employed for selecting the objects to preserve.[9] We shall not consider how the reasons for landmark preservation affect the criteria for landmark designation.[10] Let us turn, instead, to the issue of justification. We earlier concluded that landmark preservation is the saving of an historically or culturally significant object in order to keep it in existence or to have it for use or enjoyment, in our special sense. What can be said in favor of these two aims? We shall consider each in turn. First, keeping landmarks in existence.

Two types of defense seem relevant to this aim. (1) It can be claimed that landmarks should be preserved on analogy with the preservation of natural things and animal species, insofar as natural objects should be preserved merely to keep them in existence; trees and ocelots, for example, have rights and presumably also a ''right to live''; so also landmarks. (2) It can be claimed that landmarks should be preserved on analogy with the preservation of art objects, insofar as art objects should be preserved merely to keep them in existence; Michelangelo's *Pietà,* for instance, has intrinsic value and it would be wrong to destroy it; so also landmarks. The common feature of these defenses is that no reference is made to the human usefulness of these things. But they are different kinds of arguments, and can be examined separately (though arguments for the preservation of natural objects sometimes appeal to the alleged inviolability of art objects).

Do natural things and animal species have rights? And if they do, do landmarks also have rights? The question of the rights of natural things is widely debated today and there is a large literature on it. We can look at only a few sample arguments in summary form.

It is commonly acknowledged that man's dealings with nature ought to be subject to various restrictions. Aside from conservationist and quality-of-life considerations (which invoke the human benefits that can be derived from subjecting ourselves to certain limits), this is most easily seen in connection with animals. It is wrong, for example, to torture an animal. And this is wrong not because, as some nineteenth-century writers thought, men derive a morally base pleasure from it, but because of the harm done to the animal. But does this imply that an animal has a right not to be tortured or can have any other rights?

According to Professor Joel Feinberg, the basic criterion for determining whether it makes sense to ascribe rights to some entity is the ''interest principle.''[11] Only the sorts of things that can or do have interests are things that can or do have rights. A right holder must be capable of being represented and be capable of being a beneficiary in his own person. Possession of these capabilities is impossible unless the entity in question has interests and is thus capable of being benefited or harmed. Interests, Feinberg says, are compounded out of desires and aims, both of which presuppose something like belief or cognitive awareness. One may question whether any animals have desires and aims in this sense, but Feinberg holds that many of the higher animals at least have conative urges and rudimentary purposes. So, in general, it makes sense to ascribe rights to them.[12] This conclusion, however, applies only to individual animals and not to species, for a species cannot be said to have interests.

Assuming this argument to be sound, how do landmarks fare? To use Costonis's words, Do buildings have rights? Clearly not, if one takes Feinberg's position. For landmarks do not satisfy the "interest principle." Any talk of "benefiting" or "harming" a landmark (for example, a historic building), while found in common speech, is purely figurative and does not conform to the terms of his argument, a point on which Feinberg is quite explicit. It might be noted that some writers would reject Feinberg's position on the rights of animals on the grounds that only *choosing* beings (persons) can have rights. This seems to be the position of H. L. A. Hart.[13] Hart maintains that the ascription of rights to animals attenuates the concept of a right and causes it to lose the specific function it plays in moral discourse. The fact that someone has a duty to benefit some individual does not entail that the latter has a right in relation to the former. The latter is a right holder in such a situation only if he can require the performance of the beneficial act or waive its performance, as he chooses, but this an animal cannot do. So an animal cannot be a right holder. Now, to a degree, Feinberg deals with this objection to his view, for he holds that a right holder must be capable of being represented, for example, by a guardian appointed for this purpose; and since an animal can be represented, the guardian can make the choice. It is not certain, however, that this reply is satisfactory. While a guardian *can* make the choice, it is far from clear that a "guardian" who chooses to waive the performance of a beneficial act should be conceived of as representing the animal's interests. Feinberg's position perhaps can be maintained if we draw a distinction made by one of the writers of this paper, namely, a distinction between welfare rights (which entitle one to receive goods, benefits) and option rights (roughly, sovereignty over oneself or others which is exercisable at one's option).[14] *If* animals have rights, it is welfare rights that they have. But this does not help the case of landmark preservation, because we should agree that the sense of "welfare" required by this position applies to buildings only in a figurative sense.

We are not convinced that animals do have rights. The fact that it is not right to torture an animal does not imply that an animal has a right not to be tortured. (The implication equivocates on the term "right.") Perhaps successful arguments for ascribing rights to animals can be found, but as long as they follow Feinberg's lines—as appears to us to be the case with other plausible arguments in the literature—the prospects of a rationale for landmark preservation are not enhanced. We shall conclude this discussion by noting that, although Feinberg maintains that animals can have rights, he denies that we should ascribe to them a "right to life" on the human model. It would seem that if he were to countenance ascribing rights to buildings, he would deny that they have a right to be preserved in existence as such. He does admit that there is a duty to protect threatened species, not as duties to the species, but as duties to future human generations. We shall see, later, that a similar argument can be constructed for landmark preservation, though it is parasitic on our general rationale.

So much for animals. What about trees and other nonanimal natural things? If these can have rights, perhaps landmarks can have them too. The ascription of rights to trees and other natural objects has been argued for by Professor Christopher D. Stone (contrary to the position of Feinberg, who holds that animals have rights but plants can not).[15] Stone enters the big thicket of environmental controversy, and his view has received the endorsement of Justice William O. Douglas in his dissenting opinion in *Sierra Club* v. *Morton.*[16] In a footnote (note 26) Stone suggests that his position on rights can be extended to nonnatural objects of cultural and historical significance.

Stone's argument, it should immediately be said, is focused on legal rights, and to present it in detail would require an exposition of the legal doctrines he is concerned with, particularly the complicated doctrine of "standing." We can present only the nub of his argument here. The essence of Stone's conclusion is encapsulated by Justice Douglas in noting that *Mineral King* v. *Morton* would have been a more proper label for the case than *Sierra Club* v. *Morton.* The problem in the case was the standing of the Sierra Club to challenge the Forest Service's grant of development rights for the Mineral King Valley. Stone wants to argue that a "friend" (e.g., the Sierra Club) of a natural object should be able to apply to a court to establish guardianship *in behalf of the object* (similarly to Feinberg's view on representation of animal's interests). This is one of the consequences Stone sees as resulting from recognizing legal rights for natural objects. Stone begins his argument by analyzing what it means to be a holder of a legal right. This includes the idea that the holder can institute legal actions at his (or its) behest. Although Stone slides over the matter as to how a tree could ever institute a legal action at its own behest, and thus seems to violate his own analysis, he maintains that natural objects should have standing in their own right (with their legal work being done for them by guardians).

Putting the legal technicalities aside Stone's argument is quite simple. The history of law shows the ever-widening extension of rights to what previously were regarded as "things," thereby according them the status of "persons" in the law. Rights accordingly have been extended to children, Jews, women, blacks, the insane, and aliens; even corporations are legal persons; ships have been held guilty of piracy; a pig has been hung for murder. It requires no great jurisprudential leap to accord legal rights to "forests, oceans, rivers and other so-called 'natural objects' in the environment.'' And, we might add, if trees can have legal rights, so can landmarks.

Stone's argument is not convincing. The personage of ships and pigs is no more than a *curiosa* of the law. And it is highly debatable that the personage of corporations should be taken literally: the rights and duties of corporate persons can be analyzed as rights and duties (suitably restricted) of individual humans or groups. The extension of rights in the other cases is, of course, the extension of rights to natural, moral *persons* previously regarded as things. (Admittedly, the personhood of fetuses and the comatose could be, and has been, argued both ways.) Missing in Stone's argument, in fact, is the claim that trees are natural, moral persons and should therefore be accorded legal rights. Or if the claim is there, no basis for it is supplied. Such a basis, presumably, would have to counter Feinberg's arguments against the rights of plants, etc. Stone's argument, however, might be construed as a *policy* argument for extending legal rights to natural objects, though not moral rights. But if this is the case, Costonis gives the correct reply to it: Stone's analysis ''does not deal adequately with the far more important question whether there are any *economic* reasons for according or refusing to accord these rights. . . . It is impossible to resolve the policy issue that lies at the heart of Stone's thesis, namely, whether environmental resources *ought* to have rights superior to those that American constitutional and economic practice have traditionally accorded to the 'owners' of these resources.''[17] Of course, if Stone's argument is a moral rather than a policy argument and is based on the natural, moral personhood of trees, the economic reasons against according them legal rights would have a lesser weight.

Before proceeding it will be useful to stress one of our motives for spending so much time on the matter of the rights of thornbushes and red snappers, *et al.* There are, of course, conservationist reasons for acknowledging limitations on our dealings with the environment, and preservationist reasons that make reference to human use and enjoyment too. But, as John Passmore indicates, such considerations are regarded as inadequate by the more uncompromising preservationists. They see a need for a transformation of man's attitude to nature, and they call for a new morality, a new religion, to promote it.[18] This new environmental ethic speaks of our ''obligations to the land'' and our ''debt to nature.''[19] This ethic maintains that it is intrinsically wrong to ''harm'' nature, and one way to explicate this claim is in terms of the possession of rights by animals and other natural things—for rights are to be taken seriously.

It is precisely here that our doubts begin. Rights are to be taken seriously, but the extension of rights beyond persons to trees and ocelots results in more than just an attenuation of the concept but also in a cheapening of the coinage of moral discourse. We realize that such an assertion opens us to the charge of "speciesism" or "human chauvinism." But the opposing side is guilty of anthropomorphism. If everything has rights, rights cannot be taken seriously. (How, at any rate, does one resolve the conflict of rights between the woodpecker and the pine-tree beetle?, one wonders.) The case of landmark preservation, then, is not helped by appealing to the rights of animals and other natural objects, even if these things have rights. We maintain, and here we agree with Feinberg, that it makes no sense to ascribe rights to buildings. Nothing that we have said, however, implies that we do not think it wrong to torture an animal, wantonly ruin a forest, or vandalize a landmark or other property.

We shall consider one further ground for landmark preservation before offering our own positive approach. It will be recalled that we are still concerned with whether a defense can be found for preservation that does not make reference to human use or enjoyment. The claim, now, is that landmarks should be preserved on analogy with the preservation of art objects, insofar as art objects should be preserved merely to keep them in existence; Michelangelo's *Pietà*, for instance, has intrinsic value and it would be wrong to destroy or vandalize it; so also landmarks. This defense has a good deal of initial plausibility. Our discussion of it will be brief, and we shall see it as a bridge to a different type of rationale for preservation.

The idea that it is wrong to destroy or vandalize art objects is more often assumed than argued, for it seems self-evident. (Even people with a minimal appreciation of art were outraged by a madman's attack on the *Pietà* a few years ago.) Yet an argument can be offered, and its outlines are plain. The concepts that it presupposes are difficult to explicate, however. Succinctly stated the argument is this: vandalization of an art object lowers its intrinsic value, and hence is wrong; destruction of an art object lowers the sum of value in the universe, and hence is wrong. (Whether someone can have a legal right to destroy an art object is not at issue.) The difficult concepts of course are intrinsic value, sum of value in the universe, and even the very concept of an art object. It would be out of place to enter into a discussion on these concepts here. It perhaps is only necessary to assume that we all have a rudimentary understanding of what it is to lower the aesthetic quality of an object. Let us pass quickly to the question of the relevance of this defense to landmark preservation.

The main issue to be confronted is whether landmarks have intrinsic value, that is, intrinsic value *as* landmarks. (Some landmarks are also beautiful, and have value as works of art.) It is plain, if such a question makes any sense at all, that the answer must be negative. For the intrinsic value of an object is the value it possesses independently of any relations it has to objects external to it. But the value of something as a landmark is dependent on external relations (e.g., that George Washington had his headquarters in the Hansbrouck House). This defense of landmark preservation, therefore, does not succeed.

These remarks are not meant to deny that there are significant similarities betwen landmarks and art objects. First of all, both possess an "integrity." In the case of art objects the act of vandalism destroys or impairs this integrity and so alters the object as to produce an offensive effect on one's aesthetic sensibility. The aesthetic value of the object is thereby diminished. So too for those historically and culturally significant objects that we designate as landmarks. They have an integrity whose impairment diminishes their capacity to be landmarks. There is a big difference between a landmark (a house George Washington slept in) and a memorial (a plaque on a ruin which states that George Washington slept in a house that once existed on the site). Certain alterations in a landmark, impairments of its integrity, diminish it *as* a landmark (and may also lessen any intrinsic aesthetic value it might have); major alterations can reduce it to a memorial.

Granted that more needs to be said about the notion of integrity, what can we conclude from this similarity between art objects and landmarks? Perhaps little more than this: once something has been designated as a landmark, and maybe even if it is designable as a landmark, it should not be impaired in such a way as to undermine its serving this function. This consideration, however, does not supply a general rationale for landmark preservation, though it may be helpful for determining the limits of alteration.

A second similarity between art objects and landmarks suggests another line of argument for preservation. Both art objects and landmarks can embody or represent standards of excellence, ideals, and values. In virtue of its embodiment of values, one may feel a certain respect for an art object that approaches the reverence one has for a sacred object. Art objects that have this character, it plausibly can be maintained, should be preserved. But landmarks may have this character, too. Aside from any strictly aesthetic values they may have, the values landmarks represent or symbolize are usually cultural or patriotic in nature, and landmarks may engender respect that borders on reverence. Therefore such landmarks should also be preserved.

It is not really necessary for us to examine the cogency of this argument, except to point out that with it we have crossed the bridge to a second kind of defense of landmark preservation, a rationale for landmark preservation which relies on the human uses of landmarks. We shall present only the outlines of this type of justification of landmark preservation, since this essay is a preliminary inquiry into the subject.

It is needless to stress the obvious: There is nothing original in claiming that a landmark enables one to achieve an orientation to one's historical and cultural environment.[20] Like the trees and the ocelots which concern the environmentalist, and also like art objects, landmarks are part of the physical environment. As such, the question of landmark preservation is an issue of environmental concern. But because landmarks have meaning as landmarks only in relation to human history and culture, the type of justification must be of a sort different from the kinds of justification for preservation of animals and other natural objects which we considered. The attempt to derive a rationale for landmark preservation by analogy to the preservation of natural things, as we tried to show, fails. Nothing is achieved for landmark preservation by appealing to the alleged rights of snow leopards and forests. So also for the attempt to derive a justification by analogy to art objects, although in it we found some suggestive lines of thought. Landmark preservation can be defended only on the grounds of the human uses of landmarks.

In a sense the issue of landmark preservation is closer to that of the conservation of natural resources than it is to that of natural preservation. The difference, however, resides in the fact that the special kind of use or enjoyment that is involved is a nonconsumptive use. Admittedly, the *practical* problems in landmark preservation are virtually identical to those that obtain in regard to the conservation and preservation of the natural environment. We do not fault Costonis, whom we cited in our opening paragraph, when he pointed to the similarity between the ocelot and the disappearing urban landmark. The problem of the conflict between individual freedom and the need for environmental safeguards, and the problem of the conflict between private property rights and the need for environmental safeguards, arise in both areas. Moreover, as Costonis says, there seems to be an unfavorable government attitude toward landmarks, especially urban landmarks; in the pursuit of "progress" through urban renewal and highway construction, landmarks have been uprooted much in the way that trees have. Real estate economics in downtown areas have also been a factor; and constitutional and property law in the United States tend to favor the private owner in clashes over the preservation of individual landmarks.[21] The gut issue in the preservation of landmarks is, as Costonis states, *who should pay*.[22] This is a central problem in environmental conservation and preservation too.

A great deal remains to be said about the special use and enjoyment of landmarks and about achieving an orientation to one's historical and cultural environment. We should readily concede that our rationale for landmark preservation is incomplete without further elaboration of these notions. We shall close with a few remarks on a subject which bears upon the shape of such an elaboration.

Landmarks obviously have an educational use, a use in promoting the orientation of which we have been speaking. The term "education" is employed here in both its narrow and broad constructions. Landmarks convey facts, but they also convey ideals and values. We noted above that landmarks may be used to convey a patriotic message. But this should not be their only educational use. Nor should landmarks be confined to the representation of cultural progress. Auschwitz and Buchenwald are memorials to their victims, but they also symbolize features of our history and culture. The moral message they convey is chilling, but we need to hear it. So do our descendents. Landmark preservation thus raises an issue which is also present in environmental conservation and preservation, the issue of obligations to future generations.[23] Do we have a duty to preserve landmarks in fulfillment of an obligation to future generations, just as we may have a duty to conserve natural resources on this ground? This question is not to be answered easily and quickly, for it turns on the relationship that one generation should have to the next (and beyond) in historical and cultural terms.

This question has a point of contact with the idea of the quality of life, which has played so important a role in environmentalist rhetoric. Here, perhaps, the term "enjoyment" comes into its own. Insofar as landmarks may be beautiful things (not all of them are), the enjoyment that is involved is not much different from the enjoyment of nature that environmentalists have stressed. Yet there is an aspect to the quality of life to which landmarks can contribute which needs to be emphasized on its own. Environmentalists have romanticized a great deal about nature.[24] While they have done a service by reminding us that man is part of nature, their message needs to be complemented and, we think, corrected in an important way. Men have a human history and culture. They are one with the birds, and the bees, and the flowers; but they are also apart from them. Landmarks, which are elements of the humanly created environment, can serve an important function in teaching future generations about what it is to live a human life and to have a human nature. In this respect landmarks can enhance the quality of life in their own special way. If we owe anything to future generations, we owe it to them to conserve and preserve elements of a human environment. In fulfillment of this obligation, therefore, landmark preservation would seem to have a significant place.

## NOTES

1. "The Chicago Plan: Incentive Zoning and the Preservation of Urban Landmarks," *Harvard Law Review* 85 (1972): 574.

2. *Student Lawyer* (December 1975): 13-17. Costonis does not explicitly answer the question his title poses (though an affirmative response is implied), nor does he consider the philosophical issues. His article is a capsule exposition of the transfer of development rights proposal (Chicago Plan) for the preservation of urban land-

marks. The title of this article is evidently inspired by Christopher Stone's *Should Trees Have Standing?—Toward Legal Rights for Natural Objects* (Los Altos, Calif.: William Kaufman, 1974), which first appeared as an article in the *Southern California Law Review* in 1972. Environmentalist rhetoric is hoisted by its own petard in a recent advertisement for a convertible sportscar which is depicted sitting amongst a group of disappearing animal species: "The convertible, alas, is fast becoming extinct.... Save an endangered species. Buy one."

3. Compare, however, John Ruskin's statement in *The Seven Lamps of Architecture:* "Neither by the public, nor by those who have the care of public monuments, is the true meaning of the word *restoration* understood. It means the most total destruction which a building can suffer: a destruction out of which no remnants can be gathered: a destruction accompanied with false description of the thing destroyed. Do not let us deceive ourselves in this important matter; it is *impossible,* as impossible to raise the dead, to restore anything that has ever been great or beautiful in architecture.... Do not let us talk then of restoration. The thing is a Lie from beginning to end." *The Genius of John Ruskin* (New York: Braziller, 1963), pp. 134–35.

4. This definition, somewhat abbreviated, is taken from the *Webster New Collegiate Dictionary;* other dictionaries are largely in accord with it.

5. See John Zeisel,˙ *Sociology and Architectural Design,* Social Science Frontiers no. 6 (New York: Russell Sage Foundation, 1975).

6. Landmarks Preservation Commission, May 20, 1970, no. 1 (LP-0641).

7. Harmon H. Goldstone, "Aesthetics in Historic Districts," *Law and Contemporary Problems* 36 (Summer 1971): 379. This issue of the journal is devoted to historic preservation and contains discussions of federal, state, and municipal legislation and practice.

8. See Oscar S. Gray, "The Response of Federal Legislation to Historic Preservation," *Law and Contemporary Problems* 36: 314–28.

9. This distinction is analogous to the more famous one made by H. L. A. Hart regarding the justification of punishment: (1) Why punish at all? What justifies having the institution of punishment? (2) Who should be punished? See Hart, "Prolegomenon to the Principles of Punishment," *Punishment and Responsibility* (London: Oxford University Press, 1968), pp. 1–27.

10. Although we believe that the reasons for preservation do affect the criteria for designation, we would concede that in practice the criteria may have arbitrary aspects. In New York City (which has already designated nearly 500 sites), for instance, a building must be at least 30 years old to qualify. This is one reason why the recent request to designate the Seagram Building as a landmark is unusual, since it is too young. The other reason is that the request comes from the owner.

11. "The Rights of Animals and Unborn Generations," in William T. Blackstone (ed.), *Philosophy and Environmental Crisis* (Athens, Ga.: University of Georgia Press, 1974), pp. 43–68. It is not entirely clear to us what Feinberg's argument for the "interest principle" is.

12. Another writer who countenances ascribing rights to animals is Leonard Nelson, *System of Ethics* (New Haven: Yale University Press, 1956). Against this view, see John Passmore, *Man's Responsibility for Nature* (New York: Charles Scribner's Sons, 1974), esp. pp. 115f.

13. "Are There Any Natural Rights?," *Philosophical Review* 64 (1955): 175–191.

14. M. P. Golding, "Towards a Theory of Human Rights," *The Monist* 52 (1968): 521–49, esp. pp. 540–48.

15. See above, note 2.

16. 405 U.S. 727, 742 (1972).

17. *Space Adrift: Saving Urban Landmarks through the Chicago Plan* (Urbana, Ill.: Univ. of Illinois Press, 1974), p. 169. Italics in original.

18. John Passmore, *Responsibility for Nature*, p. 110.

19. The classic text is Aldo Leopold's "The Land Ethic" in *A Sand County Almanac* (New York: Oxford University Press, 1949); see also, Leopold, "The Conservation Ethic," *Journal of Forestry* 31 (1933): 634–43.

20. This is acknowledged in landmarks legislation. The preamble to the 1966 Historic Preservation Act, for example, contains the statement that "Congress finds and declares ... that the historical and cultural foundations of the Nation should be preserved as a living part of our community life and development in order to give a sense of orientation to the American people."

21. See Costonis, *Space Adrift*, p. 4.

22. *Ibid.*, p. 170. For a concise critique of Costonis's Chicago Plan, see Robert Friedlander, "Do Buildings Have Standing?," *Student Lawyer* (Sept., 1976): 6–7. An illustration of the question, Who should pay?, is the designation of Grand Central Station in New York City as a landmark. Because the owners are not allowed to develop this property as they wish, they suffer an economic loss. Should they pay for this, in effect, or should the public, who presumably benefits from the landmark?

23. See M. P. Golding, "Obligations to Future Generations," *The Monist* 56 (1972): 85–99. For an application of this concept to the problem of population control (with mainly a negative conclusion), see Martin P. Golding and Naomi Golding, "Ethical and Value Issues in Population Limitation and Distribution in the United States," *Vanderbilt Law Review* 24 (1971): 495–523, esp. pp. 497–99.

24. See Passmore, *Man's Responsibility*, ch. 5, *passim*.

# Not for Humans Only:
# The Place of Nonhumans in
# Environmental Issues

## P. SINGER

WHEN WE HUMANS CHANGE THE ENVIRONMENT IN WHICH WE LIVE, WE often harm ourselves. If we discharge cadmium into a bay and eat shellfish from that bay, we become ill and may die. When our industries and automobiles pour noxious fumes into the atmosphere, we find a displeasing smell in the air, the long-term results of which may be every bit as deadly as cadmium poisoning. The harm that humans do the environment, however, does not rebound solely, or even chiefly, on humans. It is nonhumans who bear the most direct burden of human interference with nature.

By "nonhumans" I mean to refer to all living things other than human beings, though for reasons to be given later, it is with nonhuman animals, rather than plants, that I am chiefly concerned. It is also important, in the context of environmental issues, to note that living things may be regarded either collectively or as individuals. In debates about the environment the most important way of regarding living things collectively has been to regard them as species. Thus, when environmentalists worry about the future of the blue whale, they usually are thinking of the blue whale as a species, rather than of individual blue whales. But this is not, of course, the only way in which one can think of blue whales, or other animals, and one of the topics I shall discuss is whether we should be concerned about what we are doing to the environment primarily insofar as it threatens entire species of nonhumans, or primarily insofar as it affects individual nonhuman animals.

The general question, then, is how the effects of our actions on the environment of nonhuman beings should figure in our deliberations about what we ought to do. There is an unlimited variety of contexts in which this issue could arise. To take just one: Suppose that it is considered necessary to build a new power station, and there are two sites, A and B, under consideration. In most respects the sites are equally suitable, but building the power station on site A would be more expensive because the greater depth of shifting soil at that site will require deeper foundations; on the other hand to build on site B will destroy a favored breeding ground for thousands of wildfowl. Should the presence of the wildfowl enter into the decision as to where to build? And if so, in what manner should it enter, and how heavily should it weigh?

In a case like this the effects of our actions on nonhuman animals could be taken into account in two quite different ways: directly, giving the lives and welfare of nonhuman animals an intrinsic significance which must count in any moral calculation; or indirectly, so that the effects of our actions on nonhumans are morally significant only if they have consequences for humans.

It is the latter view which has been predominant in the Western tradition. Aristotle was among the founders of this tradition. He regarded nature as a hierarchy, in which the function of the less rational and hence less perfect beings was to serve the more rational and more perfect. So, he wrote:

> Plants exist for the sake of animals, and brute beasts for the sake of man—domestic animals for his use and food, wild ones (or at any rate most of them) for food and other accessories of life, such as clothing and various tools.
>     Since nature makes nothing purposeless or in vain, it is undeniably true that she has made all animals for the sake of man.[1]

If one major strain of Western thought came from Greece, the other dominant influence was that of Christianity. The early Christian writers were no more ready than Aristotle to give moral weight to the lives of non-human animals. When St. Paul, in interpreting the old Mosaic law against putting a muzzle on the ox that treads out the corn, asked: "Doth God care for oxen?" it is clear that he was asking a rhetorical question, to which the answer was "No"; the law must have somehow been meant "altogether for our sakes".[2] Augustine agreed, using as evidence for the view that there are no common rights between humans and lesser living things, the incidents in the Gospels when Jesus sent devils into a herd of swine, causing them to hurl themselves into the sea, and with a curse withered a fig tree on which he had found no fruit.[3]

It was Thomas Aquinas, blending Aristotle and the Christian writings, who put most clearly the view that any consideration of the lives or welfare of animals must be because of the indirect consequences of such consideration for humans. Echoing Aristotle, he maintained that plants exist for the sake of animals, and animals for the sake of man. Sins can only be against God, one's human neighbors, or against oneself. Even charity does not extend to "irrational creatures,'' for, among other things, they are not included in ''the fellowship of everlasting happiness.'' We can love animals only ''if we regard them as the good things that we desire for others,'' that is, ''to God's honor and man's use.'' Yet if this was the correct view, as Aquinas thought, there was one problem that needed explaining: Why does the Old Testament have a few scattered injunctions against cruelty to animals, such as ''The just man regardeth the life of his beast, but the bowels of the wicked are cruel?'' Aquinas did not overlook such passages, but he did deny that their intention was to spare animals pain. Instead, he wrote, ''it is evident that if a man practices a pitiable affection for animals, he is all the more disposed to take pity on his fellow-men.'' So, for Aquinas, the only sound reason for avoiding cruelty to animals was that it could lead to cruelty to humans.[4]

The influence of Aquinas has been strong in the Roman Catholic church. Not even that oft-quoted exception to the standard Christian view of nature, Francis of Assisi, really broke away from the orthodox theology of his co-religionists. Despite his legendary kindness to animals, Francis could still write: ''every creature proclaims: 'God made me for your sake, O man!' ''[5] As late as the nineteenth century, Pope Pius IX gave evidence of the continuing hold of the views of Paul, Augustine, and Aquinas by refusing to allow a society for the prevention of cruelty to animals to be established in Rome because to do so would imply that humans have duties toward animals.[6]

It is not, however, only among Roman Catholics that a view like that of Aquinas has found adherents. Calvin, for instance, had no doubt that all of nature was created specifically for its usefulness to man;[7] and in the late eighteenth century, Immanuel Kant, in lecturing on ethics, considered the question of our duties to animals, and told his students: ''So far as animals are concerned, we have no direct duties. Animals are not self-conscious and are there merely as a means to an end. That end is man.'' And Kant then repeated the line that cruelty to animals is to be avoided because it leads to cruelty to humans.[8]

The view that the effects of our actions on other animals has no direct moral significance is not as likely to be openly advocated today as it was in the past; yet it is likely to be accepted implicitly and acted upon. When planners perform cost-benefit studies on new projects, the costs and benefits are costs and benefits for human beings only. This does not mean that the impact of the power station or highway on wildlife is ignored altogether, but it is included only indirectly. That a new reservoir would drown a valley teeming with wildlife is taken into account only under some such heading as the value of the facilities for recreation that the valley affords. In calculating this value, the cost-benefit study will be neutral between forms of recreation like hunting and shooting and those like bird watching and bush walking—in fact hunting and shooting are likely to contribute more to the benefit side of the calculations because larger sums of money are spent on them, and they therefore benefit manufacturers and retailers of firearms as well as the hunters and shooters themselves. The suffering experienced by the animals whose habitat is flooded is not reckoned into the costs of the operation; nor is the recreational value obtained by the hunters and shooters offset by the cost to the animals that their recreation involves.

Despite its venerable origins, the view that the effects of our actions on nonhuman animals have no intrinsic moral significance can be shown to be arbitrary and morally indefensible. If a being suffers, the fact that it is not a member of our own species cannot be a moral reason for failing to take its suffering into account. This becomes obvious if we consider the analogous attempt by white slaveowners to deny consideration to the interests of blacks. These white racists limited their moral concern to their own race, so the suffering of a black did not have the same moral significance as the suffering of a white. We now recognize that in doing so they were making an arbitrary distinction, and that the existence of suffering, rather than the race of the sufferer, is what is really morally significant. The point remains true if "species" is substituted for "race." The logic of racism and the logic of the position we have been discussing, which I have elsewhere referred to as "speciesism," are indistinguishable; and if we reject the former then consistency demands that we reject the latter too.[9]

It should be clearly understood that the rejection of speciesism does not imply that the different species are in fact equal in respect of such characteristics as intelligence, physical strength, ability to communicate, capacity to suffer, ability to damage the environment, or anything else. After all, the moral principle of human equality cannot be taken as implying that all humans are equal in these respects either—if it did, we would have to give up the idea of human equality. That one being is more intelligent than another does not entitle him to enslave, exploit, or disregard the interests of the less intelligent being. The moral basis of equality among humans is not equality in fact, but the principle of equal consideration of interests, and it is this principle that, in consistency, must be extended to any nonhumans who have interests.

There may be some doubt about whether any nonhuman beings have interests. This doubt may arise because of uncertainty about what it is to have an interest, or because of uncertainty about the nature of some nonhuman beings. So far as the concept of "interest" is the cause of doubt, I take the view that only a being with subjective experiences, such as the experience of pleasure or the experience of pain, can have interests in the full sense of the term; and that any being with such experiences does have at least one interest, namely, the interest in experiencing pleasure and avoiding pain. Thus consciousness, or the capacity for subjective experience, is both a necessary and a sufficient condition for having an interest. While there may be a loose sense of the term in which we can say that it is in the interests of a tree to be watered, this attenuated sense of the term is not the sense covered by the principle of equal consideration of interests. All we mean when we say that it is in the interests of a tree to be watered is that the tree needs water if it is to continue to live and grow normally; if we regard this as evidence that the tree has interests, we might almost as well say that it is in the interests of a car to be lubricated regularly because the car needs lubrication if it is to run properly. In neither case can we really mean (unless we impute consciousness to trees or cars) that the tree or car has any preference about the matter.

The remaining doubt about whether nonhuman beings have interests is, then, a doubt about whether nonhuman beings have subjective experiences like the experience of pain. I have argued elsewhere that the commonsense view that birds and mammals feel pain is well founded;[10] but more serious doubts arise as we move down the evolutionary scale. Vertebrate animals have nervous systems broadly similar to our own and behave in ways that resemble our own pain behavior when subjected to stimuli that we would find painful; so the inference that vertebrates are capable of feeling pain is a reasonable one, though not as strong as it is if limited to mammals and birds. When we go beyond vertebrates to insects, crustaceans, mollusks and so on, the existence of subjective states becomes more dubious, and with very simple organisms it is difficult to believe that they could be conscious. As for plants, though there have been sensational claims that plants are not only conscious, but even psychic, there is no hard evidence that supports even the more modest claim.[11]

The boundary of beings who may be taken as having interests is therefore not an abrupt boundary, but a broad range in which the assumption that the being has interests shifts from being so strong as to be virtually certain to being so weak as to be highly improbable. The principle of equal consideration of interests must be applied with this in mind, so that where there is a clash between a virtually certain interest and a highly doubtful one, it is the virtually certain interest that ought to prevail.

In this manner our moral concern ought to extend to all beings who have interests. Unlike race or species, this boundary does not arbitrarily exclude any being; indeed it can truly be said that it excludes nothing at all, not even "the most contemptible clod of earth" from equal consideration of interests—for full consideration of no interests still results in no weight being given to whatever was considered, just as multiplying zero by a million still results in zero.[12]

Giving equal consideration to the interests of two different beings does not mean treating them alike or holding their lives to be of equal value. We may recognize that the interests of one being are greater than those of another, and equal consideration will then lead us to sacrifice the being with lesser interests, if one or the other must be sacrificed. For instance, if for some reason a choice has to be made between saving the life of a normal human being and that of a dog, we might well decide to save the human because he, with his greater awareness of what is going to happen, will suffer more before he dies; we may also take into account the likelihood that it is the family and friends of the human who will suffer more; and finally, it would be the human who had the greater potential for future happiness. This decision would be in accordance with the principle of equal consideration of interests, for the interests of the dog get the same consideration as those of the human, and the loss to the dog is not discounted because the dog is not a member of our species. The outcome is as it is because the balance of interests favors the human. In a different situation—say, if the human were grossly mentally defective and without family or anyone else who would grieve for it—the balance of interests might favor the nonhuman.[13]

The more positive side of the principle of equal consideration is this: where interests are equal, they must be given equal weight. So where human and nonhuman animals share an interest—as in the case of the interest in avoiding physical pain—we must give as much weight to violations of the interest of the nonhumans as we do to similar violations of the human's interest. This does not mean, of course, that it is as bad to hit a horse with a stick as it is to hit a human being, for the same blow would cause less pain to the animal with the tougher skin. The principle holds between similar amounts of felt pain, and what this is will vary from case to case.

It may be objected that we cannot tell exactly how much pain another animal is suffering, and that therefore the principle is impossible to apply. While I do not deny the difficulty and even, so far as precise measurement is concerned, the impossibility of comparing the subjective experiences of members of different species, I do not think that the problem is different in kind from the problem of comparing the subjective experiences of two members of our own species. Yet this is something we do all the time, for instance when we judge that a wealthy person will suffer less by being taxed at a higher rate than a poor person will gain from the welfare benefits paid for by the tax; or when we decide to take our two children to the beach instead of to a fair, because although the older one would prefer the fair, the younger one has a stronger preference the other way. These comparisons may be very rough, but since there is nothing better, we must use them; it would be irrational to refuse to do so simply because they are rough. Moreover, rough as they are, there are many situations in which we can be reasonably sure which way the balance of interests lies. While a difference of species may make comparisons rougher still, the basic problem is the same, and the comparisons are still often good enough to use, in the absence of anything more precise.

The principle of equal consideration of interests and the indefensibility of limiting this principle to members of our own species means that we cannot deny, as Aquinas and Kant denied, that we have direct duties to members of other species. It may be asked whether this means that members of other species have rights against us. This is an issue on which there has been a certain amount of dispute,[14] but it is, I believe, more a dispute about words than about substantive issues. In one sense of "right," we may say that it follows immediately from the fact that animals come within the scope of the principle of equal consideration of interests that they have at least one right, namely, the right to equal consideration. This is, admittedly, an odd kind of right—it is really a necessary foundation for having rights, rather than a right in itself. But some other rights could be derived from it without difficulty: the right not to have gratuitous pain inflicted would be one such right. There is, however, another sense of "right," according to which rights exist only among those who are part of a community, all members of whom have rights and in turn are capable of respecting the rights of others. On this view, rights are essentially contractual, and hence cannot exist unless both parties are capable of honoring the contract.[15] It would follow that most, if not all, nonhuman animals have no rights. It should be noted, though, that this is a narrower notion of rights than that commonly used in America today; for it follows from this notion of rights that not only nonhuman animals, but also human infants and young children, as well as mentally defective humans, have no rights. Those who put forward this view of rights do not believe that we may do what we like with young or mentally defective humans or nonhuman animals; rather they would say that moral rights are only one kind of constraint on our conduct, and not necessarily the most important. They might, for instance, take account of utilitarian considerations which would apply to all beings capable of pleasure or pain. Thus actions which proponents of the former, broader view of rights may condemn as violations of the rights of animals could also be condemned by those who hold the narrower view, though they would not classify such actions as infringing rights. Seen in this light the question of whether animals have rights becomes less important than it might otherwise appear, for what matters is how we think animals ought to be treated, and not how we employ the concept of a right. Those who deny animals rights will not be likely to refuse to consider their interests, as long as they are reminded that the denial of rights to nonhuman animals does no more than place animals in the same moral category as human infants. Hence I doubt if the claim that animals have rights is worth the effort required in its defense; it is a claim which invites replies which, whatever their philosophical merits, serve as a distraction from the central practical question.

We can now draw at least one conclusion as to how the existence of nonhuman living things should enter into our deliberations about actions affecting the environment: Where our actions are likely to make animals suffer, that suffering must count in our deliberations, and it should count equally with a like amount of suffering by human beings, insofar as rough comparisons can be made.

The difficulty of making the required comparison will mean that the application of this conclusion is controversial in many cases, but there will be some situations in which it is clear enough. Take, for instance, the wholesale poisoning of animals that is euphemistically known as "pest control." The authorities who conduct these campaigns give no consideration to the suffering they inflict on the "pests," and invariably use the method of slaughter they believe to be cheapest and most effective. The result is that hundreds of millions of rabbits have died agonizing deaths from the artificially introduced disease, myxomatosis, or from poisons like "ten-eighty"; coyotes and other wild dogs have died painfully from cyanide poisoning; and all manner of wild animals have endured days of thirst, hunger, and fear with a mangled limb caught in a leg-hold trap.[16] Granting, for the sake of argument, the necessity for pest control—though this has rightly been questioned—the fact remains that no serious attempts have been made to introduce alternative means of control and thereby reduce the incalculable amount of suffering caused by present methods. It would not, presumably, be beyond modern science to produce a substance which, when eaten by rabbits or coyotes, produced sterility instead of a drawn-out death. Such methods might be more expensive, but can anyone doubt that if a similar amount of human suffering were at stake, the expense would be borne?

Another clear instance in which the principle of equal consideration of interests would indicate methods different from those presently used is in the timber industry. There are two basic methods of obtaining timber from forests. One is to cut only selected mature or dead trees, leaving the forest substantially intact. The other, known as clear-cutting, involves chopping down everything that grows in a given area, and then reseeding. Obviously when a large area is clear-cut, wild animals find their whole living area destroyed in a few days, whereas selected felling makes a relatively minor disturbance. But clear-cutting is cheaper, and timber companies therefore use this method and will continue to do so unless forced to do otherwise.[17]

This initial conclusion about how the effects of our actions on nonhuman animals should be taken into account is the only one which follows directly from the argument that I have given against the view that only actions affecting our own species have intrinsic moral significance. There are, however, other suggestions which I shall make more tentatively which are at least consistent with the preceding argument, although much more discussion would be needed to establish them.

The first of these suggestions is that while the suffering of human and nonhuman animals should, as I have said, count equally, the killing of nonhuman animals is in itself not as significant as the killing of normal human beings. Some of the reasons for this have already been discussed—the probable greater grief of the family and friends of the human, and the human's greater potential. To this can be added the fact that other animals will not be made to fear for their own lives, as humans would, by the knowledge that others of their species have been killed. There is also the fact that normal humans are beings with foresight and plans for the future, and to cut these plans off in midstream seems a greater wrong than that which is done in killing a being without the capacity for reflection on the future.

All these reasons will seem to some not to touch the heart of the matter, which is the killing itself and not the circumstances surrounding it; and it is for this reason that I have put forward this view as a suggestion rather than a firm conclusion. For it might be held that the taking of life is intrinsically wrong—and equally wrong whatever the characteristics of the life that was taken. This, perhaps, was the view that Schweitzer held and which has become famous under his memorable if less than crystal-clear phrase, "reverence for life." If this view could be supported, then of course we would have to hold that the killing of nonhuman animals, however painless, is as serious as the killing of humans. Yet I find Schweitzer's position difficult to justify. What is it that is so valuable in the life of, say, a fly, which presumably does not itself have any awareness of the value of its own life, and the death of which will not be a source of regret to any member of its own species or of any other species?

It might be said—and this is a possible interpretation of Schweitzer's remark that there is the same "will-to-live" in all other forms of life as in myself—that while I may see my own life as all-important to me, so is the life of any living thing all-important to it, and hence I cannot justifiably claim greater importance for my own life. If I do, the claim will be true only from my own point of view. But this argument is weak in two respects. First, the idea of a being's life being important *for that being* depends, I think, on the assumption that the being is conscious, and perhaps even on the stronger assumption that the being is aware that it is alive and that its life is something that it could lose. This would exclude many forms of life from the scope of the argument, particularly if on reflection we decide that it is the stronger assumption that the argument requires. Second, the argument appears to rest on the implicit claim that if two things are each all-important for two independent beings, it is impossible to make a comparison which would show that in some objective or at least intersubjective sense that thing is more important for one than for the other. There is, however, no theoretical difficulty in a comparison of this kind, great as the practical difficulties may be. In theory, all I have to do is imagine myself living simultaneously the lives of both myself and the other being, experiencing whatever the two beings experience. I then ask myself which life I would choose to cease living if I could continue to live only one of the two lives. Since I would be making this decision from a position that is impartial between the two lives, we may conclude that the life I would choose to continue living is objectively or at least intersubjectively of greater value than the life I would choose to give up.[18] If one of the living beings in this thought experiment had *no* conscious experiences, then when imagining myself living the life of this being I would be imagining myself as having no experiences at all. It is hardly necessary to add that it would be no great sacrifice to cease living such a life. This suggests that, just as nonconscious beings have no interests, so nonconscious life lacks intrinsic value.

For Schweitzer, life itself is sacred, not even consciousness being necessary. So the truly ethical man, he says, will not tear a leaf from a tree or break off a flower unnecessarily.[19] Not surprisingly, given the breadth of its coverage, it is impossible for the ethic of reverence for life to be absolute in its prohibitions. We must take plant life, at least, if we are to eat and live. Schweitzer therefore accepts the taking of one form of life to preserve another form of life. Indeed, Schweitzer's whole life as a doctor in Africa makes no sense except on the assumption that the lives of the human beings he was saving are more valuable than the lives of the germs and parasites he was destroying in their bodies, not to mention the plants and probably animals that those humans would kill and eat after Schweitzer had cured them.[20] So I suggest that the idea that all life has equal value, or is equally sacred, lacks a plausible theoretical basis and was not, in practice, adhered to even by the man whose name is most often linked with it.

I shall conclude this discussion of the comparative seriousness of killing human and nonhuman animals by admitting that I have been unable to say anything about *how much* less seriously we should regard the killing of a nonhuman. I do not feel that the death of an animal like a pig or dog is a completely trivial matter, even if it should be painless for the animal concerned and unnoticed by any other members of the species; on the other hand I am quite unable to quantify the issue so as to say that a certain number of porcine or canine deaths adds up to one human death, and in the absence of any such method of comparison, my feeling that the deaths of these animals must count for something lacks both proper justification and practical significance. Perhaps, though, this will not leave practical decision making about the environment in as bad a way as it might seem to. For when an environmental decision threatens the lives of animals and birds, it almost always does so in a way that causes suffering to them or to their mates, parents, offspring, or pack-members. Often, the type of death inflicted will itself be a slow and painful one, caused, for instance, by the steady build-up of a noxious chemical. Even when death itself is quick and painless, in many species of birds and mammals it leaves behind survivors whose lives may be disrupted. Birds often mate for life, in some species separating after the young have been reared but meeting again, apparently recognizing each other as individuals, when the breeding season comes round again. There are many species in which a bird who has lost its mate will not mate again. The behavior of mammals who have lost their young also suggests sorrow and distress, and infant mammals left without a mother will usually starve miserably. In other social species the death of one member of a group can cause considerable disturbance, especially if the dead animal is a group leader. Now since, as we have already seen, the suffering of nonhuman animals must count equally with the like suffering of human beings, the upshot of these facts is that quite independently of the intrinsic value we place on the lives of nonhuman animals any morally defensible decision affecting the environment should take care to minimize the loss of animal life, particularly among birds and mammals.

To this point we have been discussing the place of individual nonhuman animals in environmental issues, and we have seen that an impartial consideration of their interests provides sufficient reason to show that present human attitudes and practices involving environmental issues are morally unjustifiable. Although this conclusion is, I think, obvious enough to anyone who thinks about the issue along the lines just discussed, there is one aspect of it that is in sharp contrast to an underlying assumption of much environmental debate, an assumption accepted even by many who consider themselves for animals and against the arrogant "human chauvinism" that sees all of nature as a resource to be harvested or a pit for the disposal of wastes. This assumption is that concern for nonhuman animals is appropriate when a whole species is endangered, but not when the threat is only to individual animals. It is in accordance with this assumption that the National Wildlife Federation has sought and obtained a court injunction preventing the U.S. Department of Transportation from building an interstate highway interchange in an area frequented by the extremely rare Mississippi sandhill crane, while the same organization openly supports what it calls "the hunter-sportsman who, during legal hunting seasons, crops surplus wildlife."[21] Similarly the National Audubon Society has fought to preserve rare birds and other animals but opposed moves to stop the annual slaughter of 40,000 seals on the Pribilof Islands of Alaska on the grounds that this "harvest" could be sustained indefinitely, and the protests were thus "without foundation from a conservation and biological viewpoint."[22] Other "environmentalist" organizations which either actively support or refuse to oppose hunting include the Sierra Club, the Wilderness Society, and the World Wildlife Fund.[23]

Since we have already seen that animals' interests in avoiding suffering are to be given equal weight to our own, and since it is sufficiently obvious that hunting makes animals suffer—for one thing, no hunter kills instantly every time—I shall not discuss the ethics of hunting, though I cannot resist inviting the reader to think about the assumptions behind the use of such images as the "cropping" of "surplus wildlife" or the "harvesting" of seals. The remaining ethical issue that needs to be discussed is whether it is still worse to hunt or otherwise to kill animals of endangered species than it is to kill those of species that are plentiful. In other words, suppose that groups like the National Wildlife Federation were to see the error of their prohunting views, and swing round to opposition to hunting. Would they nevertheless be justified in putting greater efforts into stopping the shooting of the Mississippi sandhill crane than into stopping duck-shooting? If so, why?

Some reasons for an affirmative answer are not hard to find. For instance, if we allow species to become extinct, we shall deprive ourselves and our descendents of the pleasures of observing all of the variety of species that we can observe today. Anyone who has ever regretted not being able to see a great auk must have some sympathy with this view. Then again, we never know what ecological role a given species plays, or may play under some unpredictable change of circumstances. Books on ecology are full of stories about how farmers/the health department/the army/the Forestry Commission decided to get rid of a particular rodent/bird/fish/insect because it was a bit of a nuisance, only to find that that particular animal was the chief restraint on the rate of increase of some much nastier and less easily eradicated pest. Even if a species has already been reduced to the point where its total extinction could not have much "environmental impact" in the sense of triggering off other changes, it is always possible that in the future conditions will change, the species will prove better adapted to the new conditions than its rivals, and will flourish, playing an important part in the new ecological balance in its area to the advantage of humans living there. Yet another reason for seeking to preserve species is that, as is often said, the removal of a species depletes the "gene pool" and thus reduces the possibility of "improving" existing domestic or otherwise useful animals by cross-breeding with related wild animals. We do not know what qualities we may want domestic animals to have in the future. It may be that existing breeds lack resistance to a build-up of toxic chemicals or to a new disease that may break out in some remote place and sweep across our planet; but by interbreeding domestic animals with rare wild varieties, we might be able to confer greater resistance on the former, or greater usefulness to humans on the latter.

These reasons for preserving animals of endangered species have something in common: They are all concerned with benefits or dangers for humans. To regard these as the only reasons for preserving species is to take a position similar to that of Aquinas and Kant, who, as we saw earlier, thought cruelty to animals wrong only because it might indirectly harm human beings. We dismissed that argument on the grounds that if human suffering is intrinsically bad, then it is arbitrary to maintain that animal suffering is of no intrinsic significance. Can we similarly dismiss the view that species should be preserved only because of the benefits of preservation to humans? It might seem that we should, but it is not easy to justify doing so. While individual animals have interests, and no morally defensible line can be drawn between human interests and the interests of nonhuman animals, species as such are not conscious entities and so do not have interests above and beyond the interests of the individual animals that are members of the species. These individual interests are certainly potent reasons against killing rare animals, but they are no more potent in the case of rare animals than in the case of common animals. The rarity of the blue whale does not cause it to suffer any more (nor any less) when harpooned than the more common sperm whale. On what basis, then, other than the indirect benefits to humans, can we justifiably give preference to the preserving of animals of endangered species rather than animals of species that are not in any danger?

One obvious answer, on the basis of the foregoing, is that we ought to give preference to preserving animals of endangered species if so doing will have indirect benefits for nonhuman animals. This may sometimes be the case, for if the extinction of a species can lead to far-reaching ecological damage, this is likely to be bad for nonhuman animals as well as for humans. Yet this answer to our question, while extending the grounds for preserving species beyond the narrow limits of human benefits, still provides no basis for attributing intrinsic value to preservation. To find such a basis we need an answer to the following modified version of the question asked above: On what basis, other than the indirect benefits to humans or other animals, can we justifiably give preference to the preserving of animals of endangered species rather than animals of species that are not in danger?

To this question I can find no satisfactory answer. The most promising suggestion, perhaps, is that the destruction of a whole species is the destruction of something akin to a great work of art; that the tiger, or any other of the "immensely complex and inimitable items produced in nature" has its own, noninstrumental value, just as a great painting or cathedral has value apart from the pleasure and inspiration it brings to human beings.[24] On this view, to exterminate a species is to commit an act of vandalism, like setting about Michelangelo's *Pietà* with a hammer; while allowing an endangered species to die out without taking steps to save it is like allowing Angkor Wat to fall into ruins and be obliterated by the jungle.

My difficulty with this argument is a difficulty with the allegedly less controversial case on which the analogy is built. If the analogy is to succeed in persuading us that there may be intrinsic value quite independently of any benefits for sentient beings in the existence of a species, we must believe that there is this kind of intrinsic value in the existence of works of art; but how can it be shown that the *Pietà* has value independently of the appreciation of those who have seen or will see it? If, as philosophers are fond of asking, I were the last sentient being on earth, would it matter if, in a moment of boredom, I entertained myself by making a bonfire of all the paintings in the Louvre? My own view is that it would not matter—provided, of course, I really could exclude the possibility that, as I stood around the dying embers, a flying saucer would not land and disgorge a load of tourists from Alpha Centauri who had come all the way solely in order to see the Mona Lisa. But there are those who take the opposite view, and I would agree that *if* works of art have intrinsic value, then it is plausible to suppose that species have too.

I conclude, then, that unless or until better grounds are advanced, the only reasons for being more concerned about the interests of animals from endangered species than about other animals are those which relate the preservation of species to benefits for humans and other animals. The significance of these reasons will vary from case to case, depending on such factors as just how different the endangered species really is from other nonendangered species. For instance, if it takes an expert ornithologist to tell a Mississippi sandhill crane from other, more common cranes (and I have no knowledge of whether this is so), then the argument for preservation based on the pleasures of observing a variety of species cannot carry much weight in this case, for this pleasure would be available only to a few people. Similarly, the value of retaining species that perhaps will one day be usefully crossbred with domestic species will not apply to species that have no connection with any domestic animal; and the importance we place on this reason for preserving species will also depend on the importance we place on domestic animals. If, as I have argued elsewhere, it is generally both inefficient and inhumane to raise animals for food, we are not going to be greatly moved by the thought of "improving" our livestock.[25] Finally, although the argument that the greater the variety of species, the better the chances of a smooth adjustment to environmental changes, is usually a powerful one, it has little application to endangered species that differ only marginally and in ecologically insignificant ways—like minor differences in the markings of birds—from related, nonendangered species.

This conclusion may seem unfavorable to the efforts of environmental groups to preserve endangered species. I would not wish it to be taken in that way. Often the indirect reasons for preservation will make an overwhelming case for preservation; and in any case we must remember that what we have been discussing is not whether to defend animals against those who would kill them and deprive them of their habitat but whether to give preference to defending animals of endangered species. Defending endangered species is, after all, defending individual animals too. If we are more likely to stop the cruel form of commercial hunting known as whaling by pointing out that blue whales may become extinct than by pointing out that blue whales are sentient creatures with lives of their own to lead, then by all means let us point out that blue whales may become extinct. If, however, the commercial whalers should limit their slaughter to what they call the "maximum sustainable yield" and so cease to be a threat to blue whales as a species, let us not forget that they remain a threat to thousands of individual blue whales. My aim throughout this essay has been to increase the importance we give to individual animals when discussing environmental issues, and not to decrease the importance we presently place on defending animals which are members of endangered species.

## NOTES

1. *Politics,* 1256b.

2. 1 *Corinthians* 9: 9-10.

3. St. Augustine, *The Catholic and Manichean Ways of Life,* tr. D. A. Gallagher and I. J. Gallagher (Boston: Catholic University Press, 1966), p. 102.

4. See the *Summa Theologica,* I, II, Q 72, art. 4; II, I, Q102 art. 6; II, II, Q25 art. 3; II, II, Q64 art. 1; II, II, Q159 art. 2; and the *Summa Contra Gentiles* III, II, 112.

5. *St. Francis of Assisi, His Life and Writings as Recorded by His Contemporaries,* tr. L. Sherley-Price (London, 1959); see also John Passmore, *Man's Responsibility for Nature* (New York: Charles Scribner's Sons, 1974), p. 112.

6. E. S. Turner, *All Heaven in a Rage* (London: Michael Joseph, 1964), p. 163.

7. See the *Institutes of Religion,* tr. F. C. Battles (London, 1961), Bk. 1, chs. 14, 22; vol. 1, p. 182 and elsewhere. I owe this reference to Passmore, *Responsibility for Nature,* p. 13.

8. *Lectures on Ethics,* tr. L. Infield (New York: Harper & Row, 1963) pp. 239-40.

9. For a fuller statement of this argument, see my *Animal Liberation* (New York: A New York Review Book, 1975), especially ch. 1.

10. Ibid.

11. See, for instance, the comments by Arthur Galston in *Natural History* 83, no. 3 (March 1974): 18, on the "evidence" cited in such books as *The Secret Life of Plants.*

12. The idea that we would logically have to consider "the most contemptible clod of earth" as having rights was suggested by Thomas Taylor, the Cambridge Neo-Platonist, in a pamphlet he published anonymously, entitled *A Vindication of the Rights of Brutes* (London, 1792) which appears to be a satirical refutation of the attribution of rights to women by Mary Wollstonecroft in her *Vindication of the Rights of Women* (London, 1792). Logically, Taylor was no doubt correct, but he neglected to specify just what interests such contemptible clods of earth have.

13. Singer, *Animal Liberation,* pp. 20-23.

14. See the selection of articles on this question in part IV of *Animal Rights and Human Obligations,* ed. Tom Regan and Peter Singer (Englewood Cliffs, N.J.: Prentice-Hall, 1976).

15. A clear statement of this view is to be found in H. L. A. Hart, "Are There Any Natural Rights?" *The Philosophical Review* 64 (1955).

16. See J. Olsen, *Slaughter the Animals, Poison the Earth* (New York: Simon and Schuster, 1971), especially pp. 153–64.

17. See R. and V. Routley, *The Fight for the Forests* (Canberra: Australian National University Press, 1974), for a thoroughly documented indictment of clear-cutting in Australia; and for a recent report of the controversy about clear-cutting in America, see *Time,* May 17, 1976.

18. This way of putting the question derives from C. I. Lewis, *An Analysis of Knowledge and Valuation* (La Salle, Il.: Open Court, 1946), p. 547, via the work of R. M. Hare, especially *Freedom and Reason* (Oxford: Oxford University Press, 1963) and "Ethical Theory and Utilitarianism," in *Contemporary British Philosophy,* 4th series, ed. H. D. Lewis (London: Allen and Unwin, 1976).

19. *Civilization and Ethics,* tr. John Naish, reprinted in *Animal Rights and Human Obligations,* p. 134. (Nor, says Schweitzer in the same sentence,will the truly ethical man shatter an ice crystal that sparkles in the sun—but he offers no explanation of how this prohibition is derived from the ethic of reverence for life. The example may suggest that for Schweitzer killing is wrong because it is unnecessary destruction, a kind of vandalism. For discussion of this view when applied to whole species of animals, as it more commonly is, see p. 203.)

20. There is, I suppose, an alternative rationale for Schweitzer's medical activities: that while all life is of equal value, we owe loyalty to our own species and have a duty to save their lives over the lives of members of other species when there is a conflict. But I can find nothing in Schweitzer's writings to suggest that he would take so blatantly a speciesist line, and much to suggest that he would not.

21. For the attempt to obtain a court injunction, see *The Wall Street Journal* January 9, 1976, and for the statement in support of hunting, Lewis Regenstein, *The Politics of Extinction* (New York: Macmillan, 1975), p. 32.

22. Victor Scheffer, *A Voice for Wildlife* (New York: Charles Scribner's Sons, 1974), p. 64, quoting "Protest, Priorities and the Alaska Fur Seal," *Audubon* 72 (1970): 114–15.

23. Regenstein, *Politics of Extinction,* p. 33. There are, of course, some who argue for the preservation of species precisely because otherwise there will be no animals left to hunt; for a brief discussion see Passmore, *Responsibility for Nature,* p. 103.

24. Val Routley, "Critical Notice of *Man's Responsibility for Nature,*" *Australasian Journal of Philosophy* 53 no. 2 (1975): 175. Routley uses this argument more as an ad hominem against Passmore (who accepts that works of art can have intrinsic value) than as the basis for her own view. For further discussion of this view, see Passmore, *Responsibility for Nature,* p. 103; and Stanley Benn, "Personal Freedom and Environmental Ethics: The Moral Inequality of Species," paper presented to the World Congress on Philosophy of Law and Social Philosophy, St. Louis, Mo., August 1975, especially p. 21.

25. Singer, *Animal Liberation,* esp. chs. 3 and 4.

# Contributors

KURT BAIER is professor of philosophy at the University of Pittsburgh.

ROBERT COBURN is professor of philosophy at the University of Washington.

RICHARD T. DE GEORGE is University Professor of Philosophy at the University of Kansas.

WILLIAM K. FRANKENA is the Roy Wood Sellars Professor of Philosophy (emeritus) at the University of Michigan.

ALAN GEWIRTH is the Edward Carson Waller Distinguished Service Professor of Philosophy at the University of Chicago.

JONATHAN GLOVER is a fellow of New College at the University of Oxford.

MARTIN GOLDING is professor of philosophy at Duke University.

NAOMI GOLDING is associated with the psychophysics laboratory at Columbia University and the Department of Community Health Services at Duke University Medical Center.

KENNETH E. GOODPASTER is assistant professor of philosophy at the University of Notre Dame.

R. M. HARE is White's Professor of Moral Philosophy and a fellow of Corpus Christi College at the University of Oxford.

ALASDAIR MACINTYRE is University Professor of Philosophy and Political Science at Boston University.

RICHARD ROUTLEY is senior fellow in philosophy at the Australian National University in Canberra.

VAL ROUTLEY is active in conservation affairs and frequently co-authors philosophical papers with Richard Routley.

KENNETH M. SAYRE is professor of philosophy and Director of the Philosophic Institute at the University of Notre Dame.

PETER SINGER is professor of philosophy at Monash University in Clayton, Victoria, Australia.

# Index